THRESHOLDS

75 STORIES OF HOW CHANGING YOUR PERSPECTIVE CAN CHANGE YOUR LIFE

SIMON CROWE
ROBIN VON SCHWARZ

Please join our Thresholds community at
thresholdstories.com or facebook.com/75Stories.
Thank you.

CONTENTS

DEDICATION

THIS BOOK is dedicated to Rafael Bejarano, who was known to many of the people who contributed stories to this book. Rafael was tragically killed in Egypt in 2015. He was 41 years old.

To everyone who knew Rafael, he was a beautiful and rare man. He embodied love, compassion, and a desire to bring people together unlike anyone I had ever met. He was funny and irreverent, yet a deeply powerful healer. Rafael was a shaman who always carried a bag of objects and curios to share with people. He was also a world-class musician, forever flanked by his 5-foot, richly-decorated didgeridoo, which he used to bless and heal people.

Anyone who knew Rafa had stories to tell of his exploits. He generated good energy, curiosity, and connection everywhere he went, and was a master at bringing people from different backgrounds together. Born in Mexico and having trained with the Huichol people, he had a passion for sharing the traditional practices of indigenous communities and building collaboration between indigenous people worldwide.

I could share many personal stories of how Rafael positively affected the lives of others. One tiny anecdote which speaks to the kind of man he was comes from a scene I witnessed in Liberia, west Africa. Our group was climbing aboard a minibus, ready for a journey back to the city. We were tired and the mood was somber. We were delayed a little because Rafael wanted to buy some pieces from some local guys who were selling wood carvings at the side of the road. Eventually, he climbed into the vehicle and I happened to notice, through the window, that one of the boys was wearing a distinctive pair of Mexican-style sandals. As Rafa walked past me to take his seat, I looked down and saw he was bare foot. I caught his eye as he smiled and said, "He needed them more."

I travelled with Rafael in both Africa and South America and we shared a connection with a rural community in Liberia, which we were both supporting in creating educational opportunities for some of the poorest and most underprivileged children in the world. We were doing so through the building of a school.

The school project is a part of the work of the Chickenshit Foundation, which a group of us founded shortly after Rafa's death to honor and fulfill his legacy of bringing empowerment, education, and transformation to all people through music, laughter, and compassion—and to help re-awaken waning or lost indigenous traditions, and support their sustainability and survival through the youth of the world. Two of the Foundation's principal projects focus on Rafael's vision to build schools for the Huichol people in Mexico and the people of Duan Town in Grand Bassa County, Liberia.

Robin, (who travelled with Rafael through Ecuador in 2015), and I have agreed to use the success of *Thresholds* to support this legacy. We are excited to commit 25% of any profits that we personally earn from the sale of this book to the school project in Liberia, to both complete it and sustain the school once it is built.

Learn more about the work of the Chickenshit Foundation here: http://www.chickenshitfoundation.org

PREFACE

THE CONCEPT for *Thresholds* was planted when Robin and I spoke of doing a creative project together after we met in Ecuador in 2015. We were on an adventure with a score of other coaches and leaders from around the world, which culminated in a two-day "Inspire" event at the University of Cuenca. However, the seed that was planted in Ecuador lay dormant until one day when I was asked to speak at an event at my local arts centre in Clapham, South London. The format was simple: tell a true story about an event in your life in no more than ten minutes.

The simple structure of that assignment that day had a profound impact on the audience. Ordinary people telling of the events of their lives, with no attempt to moralize or teach, had a galvanizing effect on the audience—creating real connection. People were connected to the storyteller, connected to others in the audience through a shared experience, and connected in their conversations afterward as they talked about their insights and emotions that the storytellers had called forth.

I contacted Robin the next day, saying, "I have a great idea! Let's get ordinary people from around the world to write about a true event from their lives and publish the stories in a book. Let's create connection and help inspire others through the sharing of personal experiences!" We honed the idea over several Skype calls between London and Dallas, Texas. Eventually, the blueprint was born. The book was to be called *Thresholds: 75 Stories of How Changing Your Perspective Can Change Your Life*, and the vision to co-create a book that inspires its readers to explore the *thresholds* in their lives took root.

Our vision included giving ordinary people the opportunity to tell their story—to share their experience for the benefit of others while creating something we would all be immensely proud to share. As Maya Angelou says in her book *I Know Why the Caged Bird Sings*, "There is no greater agony than bearing an untold story inside you."

A letter was drafted, and we started sharing our idea with people we knew and others we were introduced to—people we had met who intrigued us—people whose stories would inspire our readers. We asked people to step over their own *thresholds* and be transparent, exposing themselves for the sake of giving you, our readers, the courage to open up and speak of your own stories.

Finding the authors and editing the stories was a *threshold* experience in itself. But we persevered, buoyed by the beautiful stories that emerged, the skill and candor of the authors, and the vulnerability and authenticity of people willing to share intimate parts of their lives, perhaps for the first time. This book presents stories of love, of death, of birth, of motherhood, of fatherhood, and of childhood. It tells of struggles with addiction, pregnancy (planned and unplanned), of fears and adventures, and of insights and epiphanies and coincidences in weird and wonderful settings and locations from every corner of the world.

We envisage the book that you are now holding should become a cherished anthology of life experiences that its readers return to time and again. Robin and I hope that, as you read and reread the chapters that inspire you, you will create space to contemplate the messages and relate them to your own life and experiences. This process facilitates the loosening of attachments to how things "should be," promotes growth, and can lead to transformation—all of which contribute to making the planet a better place for all.

It is our desire that these personal narratives of ordinary people will engage you, the reader, as you share an author's epiphany or, perhaps, the victory they found in defeat—that the stories contained herein help you to overcome your own shadows by using the light cast from the writers' words. And, most of all, that you will feel connection: to self, to others, to life.

Love, Simon

ME, YOU, AND MY DIAGNOSIS

LAUREN POLLY

I COULD tell my dad meant business. He and my live-in boyfriend, Mark, were leaning towards each other, deep into a serious conversation. I caught Dad's eye as I approached the restaurant table. He leaned back and smiled in greeting. Mark, obviously ruffled by the conversation, jumped up and quickly kissed me before taking his leave for work.

"What was that about?" I asked as I sat and took a sip of Mark's untouched Coke, which he had left on the table.

"We were having a chat about your future. I want to be sure he takes care of you if you choose to get married."

I raised my eyebrows in question as my belly soured with the fear of what would come next—what always comes next after an expression of concern from my parents.

Dad, sensing my growing dread, smiled softly and patted my hand. "Lauren, I want to make sure he knows how important it is that you stay well. Paying for your psychiatrist, making sure you take your meds, supporting you so you don't get overwhelmed with stress—

those sorts of things. I want to make sure he's there for you the way Mom and I have been."

Yep. That is always next. No matter what I choose, this is still the conversation.

I moved out of state. I was doing well in school. I had a steady boyfriend, whom I loved. I was attending therapy regularly. And, most importantly, I was finding my feet and holding myself steady amidst all this growth and change. But no matter how much progress I made, or how often I proved myself, there was still the ever-present concern: Will I be okay? Will I be stable? Will I be sane?

My diagnosis still followed me. That dark sinister shadow left its mark with a stern warning and forecast of impending doom. *The shoe may fall again. Be prepared.*

That was fifteen years ago. To this day, I find it funny—and weird—that the entire "father to future son-in-law" conversation focused on my bipolar disorder. My dad meant well. After watching me struggle throughout my teen years, seeing me flip out during stressful times, and walking me through many a meltdown, he wanted to be sure that the next man in my life was equal to the task.

Had the circumstances of my mental health been different, I imagine this conversation would have focused more on my partner's financial worthiness, fidelity pledges, and the general "take care of my little girl" topics. But circumstances were what they were. I was bipolar. It was the pink elephant in the room that people were scared to speak directly to, yet unable to not consider in each interaction with me.

My bipolar disorder colored every relationship I had during that time. My family's constant hovering and caring through concern, the eggshells my friends learned to walk on, the forewarnings to my future spouse—this was the filter that people saw me through. Truthfully, at that time, it was the filter I saw myself through as well.

That's the thing with diagnoses—they become living, breathing entities unto themselves, so much so that each relationship is a strange threesome between the two people and the diagnosis itself. You don't just interact with the person anymore—you interact with them as a cancer patient, a clinically depressed individual, a person with PTSD, etc., making real and spontaneous connections difficult.

The anticipation of upsets hinders freedom of expression. Drama-filled moments suck the life out of the room. Unpredictable outbursts create hurt feelings and barriers to intimacy. And the individuals involved look at each other through the diagnosis fog, unable to see the other or the situation clearly.

Over the next fifteen years, emboldened by an amazing holistic psychiatrist, I challenged myself to explore who I was beyond the label of bipolar. Along this journey, my perception of myself began to change dramatically.

I had always heard that the most important relationship we have is the one with our self. I have found this to be a profound truth. Since I saw myself through the filter of bipolar and put that definition of myself first and foremost in my interactions, others had no choice but to follow. I would be angry that people would relate to me through my diagnosis, but I really wasn't giving them any other choice.

As I developed more life-affirming aspects of myself and gained the inner strength to pull away from destructive behaviors, the diagnosis faded into the background. I was able to show up more and more as me; and the kinky threesome of me, my relationship partner, and my diagnosis began to change into more direct and authentic connections.

In the end, I never married Mark. We were two young lovers who eventually grew apart. Recently, I told this story to a friend. She asked if the next "father to future son-in-law" conversation would play out the same way. I laughed as I acknowledged that no, it would definitely be different—if it took place at all. I don't see myself as bipolar. Neither do my parents. Neither do the other people in my life. After all the years of therapy, seeking, growth, and change, I am no longer Bipolar Lauren. I'm just Lauren. The filter is gone.

I have cultivated a trust in myself, an ability to thrive in this world, and a strong sense of self-awareness—beyond the diagnosis. Gradually, this new perspective of myself spread to those in my life. The caring through concern has turned into enthusiasm at watching me create a life that makes me happy. The tiptoeing to avoid a possible upset has turned into direct and intimate communication, and the hovering to ensure my safety has turned into giving me plenty of room to spread my wings and fly.

As Dad said to me recently, "Lauren, you've got this." My heart lifted and my lips spread into a broad smile as I happily replied, "Yes, Dad, I do."

THE NAKED TRUTH

SCOTT MURPHY

"GO STAND by the fax machine," my friend said. "Ya gotta see this."

To hear the enthusiasm in her voice, it must be something spectacular. My friend was an assignment editor for a local television station, so she received all sorts of unique requests from PR flacks like me who solicited the media with pitches for their clients. You had to be clever, relevant, newsworthy, and naturally of public interest. It was the only way to get your press release a first read, let alone a second.

The fax came out feet first. Initially, that was all I could see—two bare feet. *Uh-oh*. I turned my back to the machine as inconspicuously as I could, blocking anybody from seeing what lay behind me. As swiftly as the machine cut the paper, I grabbed the document and ran back to my office, clinging the facsimile tight against my chest.

I turned to face the door of my office so nobody but me could see what I could see. And there she was, this beautiful woman, smiling. Her back was pressed against a tree, the sole of one foot against the trunk. Her chest was jutting forward as she reached with both arms around the trunk behind her, just as naked as the day she came into the world.

I read the press release. The news station was one of several media outlets invited to judge the Mr. and Mrs. Nude North Texas Contest. Now that *is* a clever way to get the media's attention, though I couldn't say at first blush (and mind you, I was certainly blushing) if it was really in the public interest.

"Ya wanna go?" my friend asked enthusiastically. I could hear her smile on the other end of the phone line. "Come on. Go with me."

As modest as I was, she'd piqued my curiosity. "Okay. One condition," I said. "I don't get naked."

"No, no. I'd be there to judge this contest, not participate. You can stay dressed."

We made the one-hour drive northwest of Fort Worth. This place was remote. We followed the instructions, pulling up in front of an isolated, small wood-frame house, far removed from the noise of the city. Coming from behind the house was an unassuming, gentle-looking seventy-something-year-old man. Slightly frail, he was fair skinned and a bit hunched over. He had a white towel draped over one forearm, reminding me of one of the butlers in those British programs on PBS or maybe somebody on the show *Upstairs Downstairs*. Oh, and he was naked.

We asked for the individuals we were told to meet, and the man said he'd take us to them. But could we drive us there? It was later in the day on a summer afternoon. *Hotter than Hades*, as they say. My friend was kind to agree to play chauffeur for our new butler friend. I took the back seat so he could have the front. He very carefully laid his towel on the passenger seat.

We were greeted at the bottom of the hill by our host and hostess, two jovial middle-aged adults, perhaps a bit shy to physical activity. They told us we were the first media to arrive and were eager to offer us a walking tour. Naturally, we were invited to join them in the nude. I quickly said we were here representing our employer, so that would not be possible.

The host would stay behind, but joining the hostess was a short and spry little man with no clothing, just his black canvas high tops and a long beard, concealing a round, hairy belly. He was a truck driver passing through and was quick to cozy up to my friend, asking what the deal was between her and me. His breath reeked of alcohol.

"He's a friend of mine," she said. That proved to be a mistake on her part as she would spend the better part of the evening waving off his advances to have a drink in his rig.

Our hostess was a rotund woman with short hair and light tan. She walked confidently, wearing only her sunbonnet and yellow pumps with bows on top. We took a dirt road leading us to small cottages and RVs. As we passed each of them, she told us who lived there, how long they'd been coming to the camp, what had brought them, and why they stayed. She had a genuine love for each of the guests, each becoming family of sorts.

We stopped in front of one RV. It was surrounded by a decaying white-picket fence. The residents needed the gate to keep their dogs from running loose. Once invited inside, we were kindly offered some iced tea as they regaled on the virtues of the camp. As they spoke, a small-framed picture on the wall caught my attention. They didn't mind if I took a closer look, as I couldn't quite make out what I was seeing from across the room. It was an aerial shot of the guests, perhaps from a low-flying helicopter. They lay on the ground making shapes of the letters for the camp, all smiling and waving for the camera—buck naked.

Back at camp headquarters, we got a tour of the pool and the dining facilities. There we met several other guests, insiders who were curious of the outsiders, each with a cup towel over an arm or shoulder. Again, we were invited to wear only our birthday suits. *Um, no.* I was still in a bit of shock from the volume of naked people. I hadn't seen this many people in the buff before, probably two dozen at the least.

There were still no other members of the media in attendance, and as there was plenty of time before the contest was to start, we accepted an invitation to join our hosts for an early dinner. It was a very large potluck-style meal that was fairly typical of a Texas summer outing.

As a line of naked people filled their plates, the host made a few announcements from the stage set up in the dining hall. One was to welcome us, their guests. The next was to give a few reminders about the upcoming contest (there was still time to register to participate). Last but not least, was the announcement about the ever-important housekeeping rules, foremost the importance of the hand towel. *Always, always have your hand towel.* You *must* sit on your hand towel! That last house rule made a lot of sense to me. It was upward of ninety-five degrees, after all. I imagined they didn't want folks sweating all over the chairs.

It was a delightful meal, only to be surpassed by the company. Standing out as we did, was another dressed person. She was a young woman, perhaps in her early twenties. She was there with her boyfriend, one of the nudists.

The conversation was as you'd expect of a big event—lots of camaraderie among the nudists, lots of questions for us, and lots of invitations for us to disrobe for the rest of our visit. *Um, the answer was still no.* But it was no bother to them; they were very unassuming and glad we were there. And I was enjoying myself.

This was certainly a friendly lot. And by this time, I didn't even really notice that anyone was naked. Mostly, I was interested in what I was learning about each person there.

It was time for the contest. But alas, we were the only media to make it. These things happen. As a PR guy, there were a few times I'd scheduled events to draw the media and perhaps only a couple would show up. I wanted more for these kind folks. But that was just the way these things go.

"We're short on media attendance," the host observed. "Can you be one of our judges?"

"I'd be honored," I said.

There were a handful of female and male contestants. We, the judges, were told the rules of the contest. They were as follows:

1. Judge the nudists' tan lines.
2. Judge the nudist on her/his answer to the question, why did you become a nudist?
3. Judge the nudist on her/his response to the question, how would you convince others to become a nudist?
4. Lastly, judge the nudist based on her/his performance in the talent portion of the contest.

In this talent portion, each contestant was free to pull from a box of props to add to the authenticity of their lip-synching performance to the song *Rawhide*, the theme based on the Western show of the same name that ran on television in the early 1960s. Well, that seemed appropriate enough.

I think I turned twelve shades of red judging the tan lines, finding the responses to the question portion of the show much easier to observe. The last bit, the talent portion of the contest, didn't come without its challenges for the contestants. One got her bullwhip stuck in the ceiling fan above. Another got a little chaffed from wearing long-legged chaps in the buff.

Upon crowning Mr. and Ms. Nude North Texas, the greatest highlight of the show came when Mr. Nude grabbed the microphone during his acceptance speech, called his girlfriend up to the stage (the other dressed outsider), and got on one knee to propose to her. A roar of applause filled the dining hall when she said, "Yes!"

The night concluded with a dance, disco ball, and rolling colored lights. I joined in. And as modest as I was, I accepted a request from one of the women for a slow dance. It was getting late, but at nearly 10:00 p.m., it was still a balmy ninety degrees outside. I found it a bit challenging to hold my dance partner with my hands sliding down her wet back.

She was a pretty woman, and a bit modest herself. We talked after our dance, and she shared with me how important this event and the community was for her. She'd nearly died in a car wreck a couple years before. You could see the scar that ran across her abdomen. I hadn't noticed it before. How brave she was not only in sharing her story, but also in allowing others to see the scars clothing would readily conceal. She was far prettier on the inside than the package on the outside might lead you to believe.

This was a watershed moment for me.

The naked truth was, I was more susceptible to the environment than they were. Sure, I hid my body beneath my clothing. Lots of people are modest that way. But I also hid from myself. I was far too concerned with what I wore, what I drove, and where I lived. I dare not risk loving enough or voicing my opinion. Other people's opinions of me were more important than my opinion of myself. And I based my value as a human being in accordance with the expectations and judgments of others. I didn't want anybody to see my scars—scars we all carry.

GRAN

NATASHA MCCREESH

WHEN I was nineteen, I lived with my auntie in Mirfield and went to Batley School of Art and Design. Every day I walked up the hill to college past my gran's flat, and I never called in. I never even really thought about it. She was just my gran.

At nineteen, I was completely self-absorbed—making my choices, doing my thing, creating art, raving, and socialising. As I walked past her flat each morning, I think the only thing on my mind was the mushroom and bacon butty waiting for me at the top of the hill.

Even at the age of twenty-seven, when I moved back to West Yorkshire after some time away, I wasn't a particularly regular visitor. Gran wasn't on my list of priorities.

I don't know exactly when she became one. I don't remember how it all began, but at some point, she suddenly became a fixture in my week.

We ate a lot of fish and chips. There were moments when I think Gran loved fish and chips and me in equal measure.

We took our first selfie together when she was ninety-three. It was around the time I started doing her hair. She'd had the same hairdresser for forty years, and when her hairdresser retired, we struggled to find someone else to do her hair. So I learnt how to wash and set. Gran was graciously surprised each time I held the mirror up. I got better at it is all I can say.

I began to do her washing, and this opened me up to her obsession with airing. Whenever I took it back, I was asked the question, "Has it been aired?" Each time I lied, "Of course, Gran."

Cutting and filing her nails became a time for her to gossip about her carers and tell me about the latest goings-on in *Home and Away*. For me, it was a question of balancing kitchen roll on my lap to catch the clippings and watching where stray clippings flew off to as I snipped.

She could be a complete pain in the backside. There was always a list of jobs to do as I was leaving, and always the extra job that guaranteed I would come back (as if I wasn't going to).

She was stubborn, particularly as her mobility worsened. You wouldn't believe the names she called me when I was trying to help her stay independent by introducing equipment to her flat.

She drove me crackers with her constant requests. I was up and down like a yoyo from the chair I sat in whilst we talked, and we became very familiar as it got to a point where she required support with more personal needs.

The fact is, I only really got to know my gran when she was at her worst (and when I was too).

I remember, in January 2015, talking to Gran about resolutions. She was excited to tell me that when the weather improved after February, she was going to go to Sainsbury's with my dad to get her shopping and have some sausage and eggs in the café.

Instead, in February 2015, she was in hospital. Her heart was messing with her. The doctors gently told us to prepare. My dad, after a long conversation with the consultant, made the decision not to resuscitate.

Our hearts are so beautifully precious and really bloody contrary when they want to be. I took time to feel mine to understand its rhythm. Life suddenly felt even more valuable.

Gran improved, and before she returned home, we had to choose whether to additionally medicate her. It wasn't an easy choice as there were undesirable side effects and risks from taking the medicine, but there was a risk of heart failure without it.

It basically boiled down to a question of how we might prefer my gran to die when the time came—choices and risks. And so began a cycle of hospital to respite care to home and back around again.

One day, whilst cutting her nails, she asked me what the word was when you see people who aren't really there. I said perhaps you could call it a hallucination or vision.

She told me that for the last five weeks, she had regularly had visitors of this kind in her flat—a very tall man, a tall lady in an ankle-length black skirt, and two young girls.

She told me that she would stand in the kitchen and be aware of the man standing next to her elbow, over her shoulder. But if she turned, he disappeared. Whilst I was doing her nails, she told me a girl in a spotted dress was by my side.

We chatted about how she felt about them. They didn't frighten her. She knew that they were not unkind. She couldn't see their faces and was happy about that. They didn't speak to her, and she didn't speak to them. They coexisted. She was entirely at peace talking to me about this, and I felt totally at peace listening to her.

In one of the cycles, I noticed fear for the first time in my gran. She wanted to talk about funeral arrangements. She was upset because she felt that her religion had been taken away from her as she was not able to go to Mass.

There was a transition that my gran went through where she knew exactly what she wanted, yet was frightened to accept what she needed. It took us a while to persuade her to go to a care home. She fell out with me as I had some firm words with her, pointing out some harsh realities that I did not enjoy pointing out. I realised that sometimes, loving someone means that you have to be the bad cop.

I was just grateful she would be safe. Once, when I was leaving, I hugged her and told her that I loved her. She said, "I love you too." Then she said, "Actually, scrap the too. I love you." When I got in the car to go home, I cried because removing the "too" felt very important. It is a commitment rather than a response.

The next time in hospital, she asked me to pull the curtains around the bed because it was raining. She said, "Is there anywhere where it isn't raining?" She was reaching for it in front of her like a child does when they watch a 3D film for the first time. She asked for an umbrella, even though we were inside the ward. When I told her we didn't have one, she said, "Don't worry." And she carried on catching the rain.

Whilst the experience was surreal, it also felt very peaceful. I felt happy that she could feel the rain and that she wasn't in distress. This was a new stage in her life and it made me realise, yet again, how precious life is and that there may be a time when all I can do is feel the imaginary rain.

When the doctors moved her to a nursing home for end-of-life care, a vicar came to visit. She blessed and said a prayer for my gran. We established that before the lady became a vicar, she worked at the hairdressers that my gran went to for forty years. My gran used to bring cigarettes back for her whenever she had been to Germany to visit us. This was something we didn't know about my gran. I felt so overwhelmed by the love and respect that this stranger had for my gran that I had to leave the room.

A couple of nights before she passed on, I stayed with her through the night. She was upset, although at this time, she couldn't speak. It was all in her eyes. There was a moment when she woke up from sleeping, and I got a sense that she was disappointed to have woken up. I held her hand and told her she could go if she wanted.

On September 6, 2015, Gran had been Cheyne-Stokes breathing for nearly twenty-four hours. Cheyne-Stokes is a breathing pattern that indicates end of life. The nurse told us that whilst Gran was in a kind of coma, she could still hear us. We took it in turns to hold her hand and chat with her. I told her I was going to make some teas and whispered to her to hang on till I got back. I returned and sat holding her hand, watching her breathe in and out. A few minutes before 4:00 p.m., I noticed that she hadn't breathed in for a while and alerted my dad.

In the coming weeks, I didn't cry a lot. I had a sense of peace. I had held my gran's hand as she crossed a threshold. And even though I had given her permission to let go, in the moment when I asked her to hang on for me, she did. I will always feel peace about her passing on.

FINDING THE REAL DRAGON

HUGH OSBORNE

LOOKING BACK on my life, one of the hardest things I ever had to face was the death of my mother. I loved my mother deeply. She was one of the most amazing and influential people I had ever known. She taught me, through her way of being, the possibility of unconditional love. I was at her bedside as she left the world.

In one of the final conversations we had, she said that when my time comes, she would be waiting for me to welcome me home. I still have my work to do here in this life, yet the thought of death is perhaps more comforting with the possibility of once again being with the ones I love the most.

In the years that followed my mother's passing, I felt very lost. Nothing much made sense to me back then, so I did a lot of soul-searching and traveling in search for answers. Whilst living life on the road, my possessions got shunted around from place to place. And things inevitably got lost, damaged, or simply disappeared without explanation.

For many years, aside from memories, all I had as a reminder of my mother was a faded photograph and a pocket dragon statue that she gave me one Christmas many years ago. I remember her face when she gave me that dragon. I remember the excited conversation we shared about it. If I close my eyes, I can sometimes see her smile and feel the warmth that was between us in that precious moment. Over the years, my little dragon found its home on the shrine next to my bed, along with a few other things that I cherish in my life.

One night I arrived home to the news that there had been an accident and that the dragon had been broken. As the news hit me, I felt cold inside, like the life had been sucked out of me. I could feel strong emotion welling up within me. My first action was to move myself to another part of the house separate from my wife and son, as I knew from experience that I was best alone in times like this.

There was no story of blame, but there was raw emotion that needed to be released. I began to feel the emotions arise like a tsunami. Try as I might, there was to be no holding back. Any attempt at holding things together would have been little more than a lace curtain in the face of what was about to be let loose. The levees were about to be breached, and there was nothing I could do about it. Expletives burst out of me in anger and rage. I kicked a stool across the kitchen floor with my bare foot but felt no pain. My body shook, and a wail began to release itself from deep inside. It was like experiencing the death again. I broke down and sobbed.

The night passed in a veil of empty numbness. When sleep eventually came with its gift of brief respite, it was full of swirling and confused dreams as my unconscious tried to grasp for an angle. I awoke the next morning, feeling emotionally battered and bruised, but with a thread of hope that there would be some gold here somewhere, if I could find the willingness to see it.

I began to reflect on recent events in an attempt to join up the dots and make sense of things. Over the past days, my mother had been on my mind a lot more than usual, and there had been a number of random things that had made me think of her. I had noticed certain patterns of thinking arising within me that, whilst being familiar with my mother's psyche, were not usual within my own. Then it occurred to me that perhaps, somehow, she had had something to do with the dragon breaking. At first, I wasn't comfortable with this thought. I was not the sort to believe in such things, but somehow, this knowing was deeper than my thoughts and beliefs. And something inside of me let go.

The thing that I let go was a deeply held belief that my destiny was in any way attached to hers. This choiceless letting go was a big, beautiful relief. Whilst I loved and respected my mother, there was also something that I had resented her for. It was an old pattern of hers that, so far in this life, I had been unable to shake off. The pattern, which felt more like an imprint in my psyche, was an attitude my mother had towards money that I, at some point, had taken on as my own.

Like my mother, I had often seen money as a struggle. Money seemed to be a thing I had to fight for, something to grasp at that— like oxygen, water, and food—my life depended upon. No wonder I had rarely had more than a month's rent in my bank account and had lived much of my life hand-to-mouth. At the same time, there had been a fear of what money might do to me if I had it and, somehow, a belief that I was not to be trusted with it. There had also been a strong resentment against people who had money or who seemed to be relaxed around it. And whilst I have never believed anyone who said "money doesn't matter to me," I could see that, for some people, it flowed more naturally into their lives and bank accounts.

As I was reflecting upon all this, I came upon the age-old truth that, sometimes, things happen for a reason. I don't usually go too much into this type of thinking, but I do believe that each moment, no matter how painful, can contain valuable learning if I am willing to see it.

I sat for some time, wondering what the learning could be from all this. It seemed a very important moment that was potentially life-changing.

Mum wouldn't have wanted me to suffer over this, I thought. Then the question came to me: *What do I need to do to make sure this old mindset around money is fully and completely laid to rest?*

I realised that I was in a place I had so often seen others. I had suffered the loss of a parent many years ago, yet I was refusing to let her die. And, I was carrying my mother's unresolved issues as if they were my own burden.

Mum would never have wanted this, I thought. Suddenly, it became really clear that I was being given an opportunity to let go of my money fears, completely and for good.

I knew in that moment that doing so would require me committing to something outrageous and seemingly unachievable. Then it came to me, and I knew what I had to do. To let go of my fear completely, in a way that would honor my mother and myself, I would set out to become a millionaire by doing work that genuinely serves the world. And I would do so by the year 2020. I believe that the body doesn't lie, and my body felt like I had just put down a sixty-kilogram backpack after a twenty-kilometer hike. I'd had no idea of the weight I had been carrying until that moment when I let it go.

My path was now as clear to me as the light of day. And the best part was that all the things I would need to make this happen were projects already in development.

I knew that my commitment was not only about making one million pounds, it was also about ending an old pattern that may have been passed on over many generations. At the same time, this was very much about me stepping up and claiming a part of my own destiny.

My commitment is about honoring my mother in the truest way possible by making sure that a painful and unnecessary belief system travels no further along this bloodline. Really, it stops here.

The following night, I sat down with my wife and shared with her all that had been revealed to me in the fallout of this event. My wife is a wise woman, and on this occasion, her words really hit home. "Maybe it is time to find your real dragon," she said. I think she is right.

SPREAD YOUR WINGS

ALEXANDRA WENMAN

WHILE ON a holiday to Turkey with my old friend Steve, whom I grew up with in Australia, we decided to try out parasailing. Being in a country where there were no safety laws didn't seem to faze us, as we were in that carefree, devil-may-care holiday mode. And as far as we were concerned, we were invincible. We soon realised our folly. To get to the top of the mountain in Oludeniz—where our parasails, and therefore our bodies, would be launched into midair—we had to travel in an open-back truck with no seat belts. This truck was fishtailing and swerving dangerously around hairpin bends on a dirt road strewn with huge rocks, along sheer clifftops. There were no roadside barriers, and the driver was a total maniac. And all this while holding onto our parachutes.

I thought we were going to die, so I started praying to the angels to protect us. I specifically felt the urge to pray to an archangel named Ariel, who is supposed to bring courage. I looked up, and on the back window of the driver's cab was a bumper sticker with a pair of shiny outstretched wings with the slogan "Spread your wings!" I instantly knew we would be safe, but the following events were a big test of my faith.

Suddenly, the spare tyre, which was stored on the roof above the driver's cab, came loose when the bar holding it in place swung open and almost hit me in the head. The tyre started to fly out of its place towards me. If it had hit me, I would have been propelled out of the truck and over the side of the cliff edge to certain doom. But Steve was as quick as lightning. In the split second before the tyre actually left its cage, he leapt to his feet, and with all his might, he pushed the tyre back in place. For the remaining twenty minutes of the journey up the mountain, he stood there, holding the tyre in place with one hand and clinging desperately to the railing with the other, trying to balance and hold on as the truck swerved wildly all over the road. And all the while, he managed to keep hold of his parachute, which was wrapped by one strap around his left foot.

By the time we arrived at the top, my legs had turned to jelly, and I immediately went to the nearby toilet block to throw up. But any ideas I had of chickening out of the jump were put to the back of my mind. I truly believed, by this stage, that jumping willingly off a cliff would be a doddle compared to getting back on that hazardous truck.

There was nothing for it, so I put my faith in the angels and allowed myself to be strapped into the chute. Strapped in behind me was the pilot of my tandem parasail, who spoke not a word of English. As the sail started to fill with air, dragging us backwards, another man came up to give me a few terse instructions: "Do not sit down. When I say run, you run!"

And then he shouted, "Run!"

I felt like I was running to my death. My heart leapt into my throat as my legs began moving. But I was so weak from being sick, and the parasail was so full of air, that I was immediately swept backwards off my feet and into a sitting position in the harness.

The man yelling the directions ran up to me, dragged me back up to my feet, pointed at the edge of the cliff, and again shouted, "Run!"

I was freaking out, but I ran with all my might, thinking I was just going to plop over the edge. To my surprise, the parasail was swept into the air. And as it caught the wind, I was lifted ever so gently off my feet. I felt as though I was taking flight.

As soon as we were airborne, my pilot grunted, "Sit down now." I sat back in my harness and finally began to relax as we soared over the breathtaking turquoise ocean of Oludeniz beach. It was like touching heaven. I felt so safe and calm that the terror of the moments before now seemed hilarious, and I began to laugh. I felt euphoric. The adrenaline coursing through my veins must have been on overload.

When we swooped down over the beach to land, three men ran out to grab us. The landing was almost as smooth as the take off. I wanted to kiss the ground.

Thank God and the angels, I am alive! I cried out in my head. *What a rush!*

Our parasail was quickly bundled away, and I was unstrapped from my harness as we moved to the side of the landing area to watch Steve and his pilot come in to land. The usually cool-as-a-cucumber Steve looked wrought. As he stepped from his harness, I noticed he was shaking badly, and had tears streaming down his face.

"Are you okay?" I asked. I had been so sure he would enjoy his sail. He is way braver than I am, and seemed much more together after the previous horror of the truck ride from hell.

"No, Al, I am not okay. I could have been killed!" He pulled me away from the men to tell me that his parachute had not been done up properly. One of the carabiners connecting his harness to the parachute was missed and left undone when they strapped him in.

It wasn't until they were midair that Steve noticed his life was literally hanging by a thread. If the strap of his chute—which was merely hooked over the open carabiner—had come loose, one side of his chute would have slipped out, dragging the parasail sideways. They would have gone hurtling to the ground—to sure death.

I was utterly speechless. It was the second time that day that one of us had cheated death. There was no more doubt in my mind that I was receiving help from outside the realms of humanity. My angels had heeded my call.

The week after we arrived home, I popped into a little spiritual shop near Smithfield Market one morning after deciding to walk to work. I had noticed the shop the week before we left for our trip and I wanted to check it out. I wandered in and, straightaway, spied a new pack of angel oracle cards by Doreen Virtue. I bought the pack and excitedly unwrapped them that night when I got home. Upon opening the pack of cards and starting to shuffle them, one card came flying out of the pack and all but hit me on the forehead. The words written on that card made my heart stop.

Right there in black and white were the words "Archangel Ariel," with the message "Spread your wings!"

THE KAPOK

SIMON CROWE

MY LEFT foot slid awkwardly and made an ugly splash as I fell off the disintegrating trunks that lay partly submerged in the black water that formed our path through the rain forest in northern Ecuador.

Although my feet slid around in the oversized rubber boots that I had been issued by the guide, and the filthy water splashed my trousers, my mind was in a totally different space.

There was limited light under the dense canopy of trees and plants through which my group of companions picked its way. I was oblivious to their splashing and slipping. My mind was alert to the sounds of the magical jungle, and my body was alive to its energies.

My eyes peered into the thickest parts of the undergrowth, and my field of vision, a hundred feet wide, drew everything in. Everywhere was green—leaves of a thousand fertile shades, but nothing familiar. My eyes peered into the denseness, and my curiosity dissected the mass of branches and leaves and creepers, trying to learn the secrets of the forest—to make meaning and acquaint myself with this totally unfamiliar environment. My curiosity was gulping in the unquestionable energy of the nature that surrounded me. I almost forgot to breathe as I was so engrossed in the power and magic of the true nature of the million-year-old forest.

After maybe an hour of tripping and stumbling, we arrived in a small clearing. I became abruptly conscious of how tiring the walk had been as I became aware of my fatigued legs. We stopped to drink from our white and orange plastic water bottles, and began to tune in to the conversations that were breaking out about the unusual insects and plants that we had come across. A couple of people were resting on a basic bench that had been shaped from a large trunk. One of them adjusted her ill-fitting boots. I looked down at my feet, and we exchanged a smile of affiliation.

I was grateful for the chance to rest my limbs. I hadn't realised we had reached the point in the forest that our guide had been leading us to. I'd been so absorbed in the activity that I hadn't noticed we were standing at the base of a two-hundred-foot-tall kapok tree.

The kapok had a smooth bark and an almost metallic appearance. Its huge roots fanned from its trunk-like ten-foot wedged buttresses, whose job was to keep the tree ramrod straight as it rose through the leafy canopy and soared on above the reach of the other trees and bushes. It felt almost as if the forest had gathered around this alpha tree, leafy heads bowed in deference to its size and steeple-like majesty.

Now that I was paying attention, I caught sight of a man-made structure that stood alongside the columnar tree. It certainly was a sorry sight by comparison—a ramshackle tower of irregularly shaped wooden posts and planks held together with ropes and nails. It matched the kapok in height but compared in no other way. I smiled at the dissimilarity between nature's flawless beauty and man's rickety handiwork.

In effect, the hand-built wooden tower was a freestanding spiral staircase rising over two hundred feet to a point where one could cross a plank bridge onto the tree and enter a viewing platform that had been affixed at the point where the trunk divided out into thick boughs, branches, and leaves. The steps of the staircase were open to the forest on all sides. There were narrow runners but no risers, so it was more like a wide-rung ladder and a rope handrail looped along the length of each run of six or seven steps. The bridge between tower and tree was no more than five or six feet and was similarly unsound in its manufacture.

A few front-runners of the group had already started to climb up on it. The staircase creaked and swayed a little under their shifting weight. I looked up, saw it moving, and made a categorical decision that I was staying on the ground. Just watching them climb, my chest tightened. I felt a familiar giddiness and sickening sense of panic in my stomach and solar plexus, and the strength was syphoned from my thighs and into my rubber boots.

I had first become aware of my crippling fear of heights as an eight-year-old on a visit to the Post Office Tower in London. In the 1970s, it had a revolving restaurant that was open to the public. I had been so excited about visiting this place with my parents and remember, as we entered the restaurant, rushing to push my face against the window to the revolving platform to see the city of London in miniature. Instead, I hit a wall of fear that left me trying to scream through a constricted chest and throat. I was confused, but knew I didn't like the feeling of fear I had experienced. From that moment on, I lived my whole life with this fear.

I once had to be helped down from the fourteenth-century campanile in Siena with a coat thrown over my head. So I knew if I had been defeated by a stone tower that had stood for over seven hundred years, there was no way in hell I was going up this hand-built wooden structure, which reminded me of the closing stages of a game of Jenga—with all the solidity of the tower of wooden blocks already removed.

I once tried to describe my fear to a therapist. It frustrated me that I couldn't adequately convey my sense of terror so she could experience it, too, and understand that I was not just being "weak." The phrase "fear of heights" did not capture my fear. I had to make people understand so they could pity me. I wasn't afraid of what might happen if I went somewhere high up. My brain would actually create the same visceral dose of abject panic, and I would truly experience the fall to my death in all my senses. I would shut down, and someone would have to rescue me, like in Siena. That is the nature of all fear— it is designed and programmed into you to stop you from doing the things that provoke it. It is not pretty or sophisticated. It is just effective.

I could see the excited faces of my companions as they climbed the ladder, wanting to be part of the experience. But I couldn't pass the responsibility of me freezing and needing rescuing on to them. So I told the guide of my concerns. He assured me he had been up and down many times with many groups and that it was perfectly safe. But fears are not to be reasoned with.

I eventually let my desire to be at the top and experience the view tempt me, and I started to climb. I was fine for the first dozen steps or so, until I crossed the tripwire that triggers the alarms in my brain that shout "STOP! That's high enough." Cortisol and adrenaline then fired into my body to make me feel horrible, just in case I tried to ignore the alarms. Then a wave of panic swept over me as I realised that even if I got up, there was no way I could cope with the climb back down. I felt defeated and ashamed, and the thought of having to be rescued was too much to push past. So I turned around and told the people below me I couldn't go on.

But as I looked at the people below me and heard the people above reaching the summit, something totally unexpected awoke in me—a new voice of defiance—the voice of the desire not to have my life handicapped by this fear. I decided that if today was my day to die, then so be it. The thought that the fear of death was controlling my experience of life was no longer acceptable, and I vowed to face it down.

So I gripped the rope tightly enough to get friction burns, and I lifted my foot, taking one very deliberate step up. As I planted my rubber boot on the tread, I asked myself the silent question, *Am I dead?* Well, of course I couldn't have asked the question if I had been. So I took another and repeated the same questioning in my head, *Am I dead?* I continued this inner review after every step—the tone of my questioning growing more defiant—challenging the fear to show its face. Soon I found myself not asking but declaring, *I am not dead!*

I reached the two-hundredth step and inched across the plank that went from tower to tree and the viewing platform that spread above the canopy. *Am I dead?*

I stood with my friends and watched the sky as the dusk drew in and the birds and wildlife began to return to roost. There were a couple of scarlet macaws sitting in the nearby tree, with their long tails and vivid colours. Monkeys were sitting a few hundred yards away grooming each other, oblivious to us. A group of heavy-billed toucans could be seen just one hundred yards away through the binoculars. We held our breath as a group of toucans with bright yellow-and-black-striped chests landed in the branches of our tree, bobbing up and down as they fed just a few feet above our heads. I became mesmerised by the wonder of these exotic creatures and dazzled by the orangey-pink and blue sky, which painted the backdrop to the lush greenery of the landscape.

And I knew that death would always be near as I chose to live on my terms, and I embraced death as my companion on this journey of a fully expressed life.

WIDE OPEN

ROBIN VON SCHWARZ

I DON'T call my dad often. I'm not sure why. Maybe I fear feeling rejected on those days he isn't in the mood to talk. He can have a rather abrupt, nonemotional way about him at times, which I guess I've never really gotten used to. Then there are those special moments when he talks nonstop, relaying every detail of every doctor's appointment, visit with family, or mishap that's happened since our last conversation. I always hope that it will be one of *those* days when I call. I long for insight into the heart of this man I've loved from afar most of my life.

He was in the mood to talk this past Wednesday. In fact, he was in a great mood, even lighthearted. When he answered the phone, I gave him an out, if he wanted one, by asking if he was busy. He wasn't. Instead, he was eager to share with me the goings-on of his daily life raising his great-granddaughter—a precocious, intelligent first grader he and my stepmom have cared for since she was an infant.

He had an hour or so before he had to take her to Girl Scouts and proceeded to tell me all about their weekly Brownie meetings. One memory led to another, and soon he was talking about last year's chaotic father-daughter dance. It seems that sons were also allowed to attend, turning the event into a rowdy free-for-all. Eventually, the subject turned to the bond he shared with this great-granddaughter and how happy he was that she trusted him enough to ask for help with her problems. I could tell she made him feel needed.

At times, I've thought that raising a young child might be too stressful for my dad, given his age and health. At seventy-seven years old and a stent away from another blocked artery, he tires easily and often struggles to walk much past a quick trip to the grocery store. However, when I have traveled to Illinois from Texas to visit, I've observed how this little girl has given him a purpose, a reason to continue to struggle to overcome his physical ailments. When she isn't home, he seems sad and doesn't know what to do with himself. The second she walks through the door, his face lights up. This bubbly, active girl fills his life with love. That makes me happy.

Yes, this was one of those conversations I hope for, one in which my dad shares himself with me. And I can, for a moment, feel close to him. It was a great call until I heard him say "She is the daughter I always dreamed of having . . . the daughter I always dreamed of having . . . dreamed of having." His words hit me hard, echoing over and over again in my head, causing this surge of grief to rush my body.

The tears were immediate, filling my eyes then streaming down my face. Every fiber of my being wanted to retreat. I needed to get off that call so I could tend to my emotions before my dad figured out something was wrong. Growing up, my dad always lived states away from me, and I rarely saw him during the school year. When I got to see him in the summer, I just wanted his approval. It would have crushed me to upset him or think he was mad at me.

I didn't know what to say or how to feel but managed to keep my voice from quivering as the words "Yes, I'm sure you are close to her as you are retired now and have a lot of time to spend with her" came out of my mouth. He paused for a moment, as if reflecting on the past. "Yes, I guess I wasn't home much when you guys were around."

Though my heart kept going back to my dad's words, my brain was trying to be logical. *He didn't mean it the way it sounded. His words came out wrong. You know he loves you.* But my rational adult mind met some resistance as it battled old hurts and a lifetime of longing.

"I have to get off the phone, Dad."

He knew I was on my way to my daughter's house to babysit my grandsons, so I lied and told him I was already there. We quickly said our goodbyes and hung up. I didn't like lying to him but couldn't pretend to be unaffected any longer. I knew I needed to talk myself down before I made a mess of things.

Before I managed to get control, I chose to feed my misery by calling my sister. Selfishly, I wanted to commiserate with someone I knew would understand and validate what I was feeling. I also knew, when I called her, that our dad's words would hurt her too. Yet I didn't stop myself.

When I hung up the phone, I felt instant regret. I quickly pulled my car into a parking lot so I could send my sister a text.

"I am sorry I called you. I know Dad loves us. He probably just meant that he has the relationship with her he always wanted with us."

I was torn between needing understanding and being the protective older sister. Fortunately, my brain was making progress and breaking through a few battle lines. Unfortunately, the years without my dad's presence in my life forever created a small crack in the door to the room where unresolved insecurities are stored. Every once in a while, old habits swing that door wide open.

I got to my daughter's house and sat in my car, trying to collect myself. Here I was, fifty-four years old and upset over what? I felt silly. I knew that if I gave myself time, the emotions would give way to what was true and real. So I shifted my focus to the opportunity at hand and gave the rest of my evening over to playing and reading with my grandsons.

The next day, I sat down to write my dad a letter. I knew, while writing that letter, that I'd probably never send it. I just needed to put my thoughts down on paper so I could understand and work through them.

As I wrote, a memory from when I was about eight or nine years old came to mind. My dad was crouching in his driveway as I sat on his knee, holding our poodle. We were taking pictures together before my dad had to say goodbye to me, my brothers, and my sister. While he held me, my dad started to choke up, and I saw tears in his eyes. Though still a young girl, I understood my dad's hurt and felt his love. As an adult, I've often reflected on that memory, trying to put myself in his shoes. I imagined having to say goodbye to my own young kids, knowing it would be months before I'd see them again.

One memory triggered another, eventually leading me to one significant moment I shared with my dad on Mother's Day, May 14, 1989. I had just given birth to my oldest son and was resting in my hospital room when my dad came in alone for a visit. I don't remember the topic of our conversation that day, but I will never forget his words. He said, "I was always here for all of you kids when you were growing up, but none of you ever came to me with any of your problems. I don't know why."

His words seemed ironic to me and made me smile a little inside. My dad can be such a quiet, nonverbal man that it was always difficult for me to approach him about anything serious. He was so quiet that I once asked him why he never talked. He told me, "You learn more from listening than you do talking." I guess he was waiting to listen. If only I'd known.

These last few years of my life, I've found a lot of peace from learning how to find acceptance for what is. I try not to waste too much time backtracking in the muddy waters of yesterday as I don't have time to keep cleaning up the same old mess I make when I do. I'm getting better at keeping that cracked door closed.

Circumstances, time, and distance separated me from my dad for many years—and still do to this day. While it's too late to recreate the past, the present and future are wide open.

PUSHING THE EDGE

DAN MOSELEY

IT'S A beautiful, clear evening, and the stars shine bright against the dark night sky. The only other light radiates from my laptop screen as I sit in deep contemplation on the balcony of my apartment to avoid the stifling heat inside. It would be a beautiful tranquil setting if it wasn't for the insane screams of the child next door, the din of motorbike engines heading into town, and the faint drone of techno music overlaid with karaoke singing coming from the distance.

Only in Vietnam is what I'm thinking, but its cacophony of noise, which juxtaposed with the darkness, is a good reflection of what is going on inside my head.

It's been two days since I fired off a hastily written email to my friend Simon, the co-compiler of this book, explaining with multiple excuses that I did not have time to contribute. If I'm honest, I have only half-read the email about what is required, but the deadline for submission is eight days away. So I banged out my excuse without even asking myself if it's something I wanted to do.

It was the moment that I sent the email that I realised I had just met my most recent "threshold moment." And instead of facing it, I had disregarded it with the simplest of lies.

Initially, I thought the lie was to the book's creator, that I could just fob him off and crack on with my evening. But then I realised that the real person I was lying to was myself. I went from quietly sitting and reading to a state where my mind was spiralling out of control. I wasn't in a state of anxiety or stress before I'd sent the email. In fact, I'd spent the day cycling, reading, writing, and relaxing. But the moment I hit Send, I was filled with a sense of anxiety and unease. I found myself questioning my integrity and values. I immediately knew that time was not the real reason for not contributing to the book. It was just an excuse I had fabricated for myself, which masked the real reason: fear. The fear was somewhere in me, and I must have felt it to make the excuse. But I didn't even acknowledge it until I'd hit Send.

As I clicked Send on that email, the fear hit me like a hammerblow to the head. It swept over me. I found myself trying to think of my most inspirational threshold moment, one that would have real impact for the reader and offer a huge insight for the book. This sent my mind into a whirl of self-judging, negative thought. My mind was racing: *Your story won't be good enough. The compilers will reject your story. You haven't written an actual story since you were in school. You don't know what to write about. Your story won't have enough impact. You're not good enough.*

Now I could fully feel the fear. How had I masked it from myself when it was smashing me like a series of tidal waves to the brain? Wave after wave of crushing fear—fear of rejection, fear that people who read the story won't like it and, more importantly, won't think I'm good enough. There was fear and self-judgement galore. I asked myself, *What would I write? Will it make sense or just be a huge pile of rambling rubbish?* All I could think about was that a story should be structured with a beginning, a middle, and an end and that you can't just pick up a pen at 11:00 p.m. and write one. But that's what I did.

I was so taken aback by the clarity with which I saw my lie that I had to right the situation. So I wrote the story. It was not my biggest threshold moment but my most recent. Within the hour, I'd penned the story and sent it across to Simon. The whole process was freeing. It felt great, and I felt energised. I knew I was up against an edge and decided to push against it. Every other piece of writing I'd ever submitted, I had spent hours procrastinating; but this just flowed. And then it was done.

Or so I thought. The email dropped back into my inbox. "What could I do to more fully engage the reader? How could I make the story flow better?" It was only a couple of questions but enough to fill my mind with doubt.

I knew it, I thought to myself. *Not good enough.* The email said nothing about not being good enough. In fact, it started with, "I like your story." But my mind decided to completely ignore this information, choosing instead to focus on a negative narrative that I had completely made up. I concluded that I could not be bothered to reread, let alone rewrite what I'd written. I disregarded the challenge to make the story more interesting and engaging, decided it was not important, and closed my computer.

And that is what has put me in this dark place, both figuratively and metaphorically. For two days, I've felt this hanging over me. I've had that anxious feeling that you get when there is something pending that you must address. Try as you might, you can't escape it. And eventually, you have to face it.

This has led to me sitting on the balcony, not to avoid the stifling heat, but because it's a complete change of environment, and I'm hoping it will inspire me. I'm looking for the clarity that I need to write my story, but all I can focus on is the noise and the din. Again, it's a reflection of what's going on inside my head. All I can hear are the negative stories in my mind. I'm questioning myself, *If this is not important to you, then why has it been on your mind for the last two days? What do I stand for? What are my values?* I'm seconds away from sending a second email to the editor, saying that I really don't have time to go back over this as the deadline is even closer now, after all. But I've already been there, and I know what's going to happen.

I've written countless different stories and countless versions of the same story, and I start to question, again, what is preventing me from finishing this project. I know that writing is not the issue. I love writing. I write every day. It gives me clarity when I don't have clarity. It allows me to visualise and create. It also allows me to talk to myself about my fears, values, and integrity on different aspects of my life. I write without fear of judgement. And that's it, my moment of clarity. I usually write for my eyes only, and this leads me to write without constraint. I like what I write, so why am I now judging what I write? I decide that there is value in this story for me and that it is worth finishing. I have come up against a threshold moment, and I like what I've learnt from it.

As I sit and the darkness in my head begins to clear, I question myself on whether life is just a series of threshold moments. Are some moments so big that they require facing and others less easy to identify? I ponder how often I've stopped myself taking action by asking a "how" question. "How long will it take? How much does it cost?"

I am amazed that the simple act of writing a story caused so much inner emotion, and by the realisation that I can mask my fear behind a simple excuse. I'm left thinking that I always need to have the awareness to challenge myself when a situation that requires a decision arises. I vow never again to hide behind time as an excuse and instead ask the questions "Do you want to do it?" and "Is it worth the effort?" I would have to conclude that the learning about self from this simple exercise was well worth the effort and a whole lot more. I feel invigorated and feel like I've found my voice.

THE GRANDMA SITTER

LEAH LUND

WHEN I was nine years old, I became my grandma's babysitter. Some might consider leaving a nine-year-old to care for an eccentric old woman as skirting the edge of child abuse, but I was raised in a third-generation farming family in the Upper Midwest plains of the US, and everyone did their part. That was just plain practical.

Sometimes, I wonder how my grandma ever became a farmer's wife. She seemed misplaced out there on the lonely homestead. She'd been a career woman in her twenties, teaching school in the same one-room schoolhouse that my dad and his siblings eventually attended. She was also an artist with a passion for worldly artifacts, who could be found strolling around the house in a bright-colored kaftan and turban with its jewel-encrusted broach. She wasn't exactly cut out for the menial tasks or mundane routines of a farmer's wife.

When my grandparents were dating, it was custom to keep an autograph book in which one's friends would write an inscription. My grandma cherished the book in which my grandpa (a stern, stoic Norwegian) had professed his love, in poetic style, for the Icelandic princess he was courting. I guess my grandma was wooed. Maybe she didn't think past the infatuation or consider that his willingness to express affection might someday wane. Fifty years and six home-birthed children later, there she was—still isolated in the same simple wooden house that her husband's father built—surrounded by the treeless, windswept prairie and miles from her closest neighbor.

My grandma really was a princess by blood. She was the twenty-seventh-generation descendant of a Viking princess named Bergthora. A saga written about her namesake was published by Penguin Books. My grandma was also a princess by style. Her farmhouse decor ranged from bird's-eye cane colonial to Egyptian tapestries to abstract art.

Despite her education, intelligence, and artistic talent, Grandma had a severe fear of being alone. I imagine it developed in her later years, and I don't remember a time when this wasn't the case. She might have preferred the brutal winter months because my grandpa was always at her side—the benefit of a farmer's schedule. Every year after Christmas, they would travel to California to see their daughter. Grandma would return home giddy as she shared her adventures of dancing with Lawrence Welk on his TV show and shopping for foreign treasures. She always brought back gifts like fresh oranges, abalone shells, or puka-shell necklaces. Great material for show-and-tell at school.

But in the months between planting and harvesting, Grandma's mood would vary. While Grandpa and my parents worked the land, Grandma could never be left alone. Grandpa used to pay neighbor ladies to come for coffee and spend the afternoon with her. That was until I was old enough for the job.

Most days, babysitting Grandma was not much different from playing at her house. She'd tell me stories and show me her paintings and ask me to play her a song on the piano. The natural wood of the beautiful carved upright was painted the same yellow as the outside of her house. Not everyone's cup of tea, but it was my grandma's favorite color. I'd lift my fingers off the keys and hear her shuffling her house shoes across the kitchen floor, putting cookies and lemonade on the table. She was known to have a little cookie when no one but me was looking. We wouldn't tell Grandpa as her diabetic blood sugar might get out of whack. She was also known to have a little sip of wine and a cigarette.

I never really understood what caused Grandma's mood to shift. Sometimes it seemed that she became more anxious if it got late and Grandpa wasn't home from the field yet. Other times, her eyes just glazed over with tears in the middle of a sunny afternoon. I'd soothe her by saying, "Grandma, don't be sad. Why don't you show me another painting?" Occasionally, I'd manage to distract her.

Other days, it would be an hour-by-hour process of counting down Grandpa's arrival. On the very worst days, she would slip into uncontrollable, inconsolable, hysterical crying. The sound was gut-wrenching. I could only compare it to the bloodcurdling shriek of a peacock or the guttural moan of a cat in heat. I've never heard anything like it. I hope I never do.

My grandma was afraid that something would happen to Grandpa in the field and she'd be left alone forever. When my hugs and encouragement didn't calm her, I'd reason with my nine-year-old intellect. I'd explain how everything was fine and remind her that Grandpa was careful with the machinery. I'd also explain the farming process and the likely duration of each activity. When my conversation wasn't enough, she'd ask, "Can we just go see him?" Often, I'd give in, and we'd pile into her enormous Chrysler Sedan.

I'd been driving since the age of eight, but I still needed to sit on the edge of the seat to navigate down the gravel road to the southern section. We'd turn onto the dirt prairie trail, the tall grass scraping the undercarriage, and journey far enough to catch a glimpse of Grandpa on his tractor or swather or combine. During harvest season, my mom would be in one of the other combines, and I'd envision her frustration with me for driving all this way, even though she plowed with a team of horses when she was six. If it was coffee time, we'd bring a thermos and a few sandwiches so the crew could join us for a break. If not, Grandma's fear was appeased by simply watching her love from the distance for five to ten minutes, and then we would return home.

I didn't know that my grandma's *condition* was ever diagnosed as anxiety or depression. I wouldn't, as a Scandinavian family doesn't really talk about those things.

A psychologist might say I missed out on my childhood. I disagree. I grew up in a house where I never once saw a key for the front door. My parents and grandparents lived on the same farm and worked the family business together. I learned life skills in caring for Grandma, and these have served me well in my life and my career. I inherited a love of big ornate jewelry and fun, eccentric clothes and even had a career in fashion.

Every now and then, I will slip on my kaftan and channel my inner Bergthora.

MENDING BROKEN HEARTS

AYN CATES SULLIVAN, PHD

WE WERE traveling due west as the sun set over the Celtic Sea. Perhaps we should have pulled over, but we decided to keep driving straight into the light. It was blinding, but somehow, we felt as though we needed to follow the golden road. Straining to see as he navigated each hill and around each bend, my fiancé, John, drove my daughter and me successfully to the small Cornish village of Illogan, where we were to attend the wedding of a young friend named Hannah.

Weddings and funerals invite us to travel long distances. There is something satisfying about celebrating major passages of life with our loved ones. We enjoyed hugging the family, dressing up together, and collectively offering our best wishes to the new couple. Freshly married couples are a symbol of life and hope for the family. We always want the best for them, even while knowing that not all marriages last.

After the wedding, my daughter, John, and I decided to explore the southern coastline of England. We took the back roads and wove our way through sunken lanes lined with stone walls and hedgerows to the seaside resort of Brighton, where we chose to spend the night.

We live in California, and since we were in the United Kingdom, my daughter wanted to see her father in Scotland. Our divorce had been painful, and the mere thought of a visit brought up old memories that I would have preferred to forget. I stayed up most of the night trying to book her flight, but no matter what airline I tried or what ticket agencies I clicked on, it seemed that all the flights were full. I began to grow increasingly annoyed with technology, and my mumbling must have disturbed John, who asked me to turn off the computer and go to sleep.

In the morning, John met me in the lobby of the hotel for breakfast. He had been out walking along the beach, considering how he was going to share what he was feeling.

"You have to go to Scotland and make amends with your ex," he said. "What?" I asked.

I need not repeat the list of accusations that I had been narrating about my ex for the last fifteen years or so. I was furious, and I felt wronged and justified in my anger. But my current fiancé was a yogi and long-term meditator. He was committed to peace and conflict resolution, which I admired but was not embracing fully. He was challenging me to let go of a story that no longer served me or supported the person I had become. I had to look at what sort of life I now wished to embrace.

"The way you feel about your ex will be taken into our marriage. You need to forgive him, or at some point, what is unresolved will be turned against me."

I sat looking at him with an open mouth. "But he—" I started the old rant then watched as tears began to flow down John's cheeks. He looked at me with gentle eyes and an open heart. I wanted to hit him. Instead, I closed my eyes and took a few deep breaths.

Is he right? I asked my own inner guide. Then I began to feel the hard shell of my heart melting. I understood that there was no reason to continue to blame myself or another person for the mistakes we had made long ago. It was time for me to accept the role I had played in the divorce and to put it all to rest.

"Let's go and do it," I said, taking John's hand. "I'll make the amends."

The first phone call did not go well. My ex said he didn't want to see me, and so I flew into yet another rage. The young mother in me was still hurt, and I had to make peace with her before any progress could be made. My daughter was now a lovely young woman in her own right—so really, somehow, I had survived being a single mother. We were both healthy and leading successful lives. If anything, the experience had made me a stronger and wiser person. John called him back and explained that I wanted to make amends. That was acceptable.

Divorces always have two sides. Neither of us had been angels, and two young attractive people living in London have plenty of opportunities to make mistakes. I had expected a man who would show up for his wife and daughter. He was a musician and wasn't sure how I ever got such an idea. Unmet expectations can cause a lot of heartache. In hindsight, we should have discussed what we wanted from each other before we married and decided to bring a child into the world.

Once we decided we were all going to Scotland, it was easy to book the hotel and the flights. As we were preparing to board the flight from London to Aberdeen, we were stopped by security guards. We watched as Prince William and his then fiancée, Kate, walked onto the flight in front of us. Since my children were named William and Kat, I had a little chuckle. When you choose the road that leads to your highest destiny, you know, because it seems as though a red carpet rolls out in front of you. The way becomes clear and miracles start to happen.

"I guess we are all taking a royal flight," I said to my daughter, who was curious about what it would be like to see her parents together.

Luckily, John was radiating a field of peaceful presence that we were all benefitting from.

When we arrived at Norwood Hall, we discovered that the hotel had some interesting history. Pitfodels Castle had once stood on the site, but the Roman Catholic clan who lived there had been lost to history. It reminded me that, eventually, all stories are laid to rest. And there was more. In the nineteenth century, a merchant by the name of Colonel James "Soapy" Ogston, who made his money selling soap, remodeled the building. And today, three ghosts are said to haunt the hotel. It seems that James had a mistress, and he could not decide between her and his wife, which caused them all a great deal of unhappiness. I just had to laugh. It was the perfect place to make amends.

My ex entered with his new wife and a few of his family members. My fiancé, who was then already many years sober, decided to order a round of drinks at the hotel pub for everyone, as is the custom in Scotland. We all sat around in a circle, looking at each other. All the faces were familiar, and I realized as I looked around that I actually liked them and no longer bore any ill will. From the looks on their faces, they weren't quite sure how to respond. We are taught to take sides, but relationships are much more complicated and intricate than the black and white lines we generally draw. Actually, we are all engaged in sharing life together.

Eventually, I took my ex's hand and said, "Let's do this." He followed me out of the pub into another room but asked, "Why are you shaking?"

"Because this is hard to do," I said truthfully. He didn't respond, so I assumed he agreed with me.

We wound up sitting in the hotel library, which was filled with many tales. After nearly fifteen years of not speaking, we sat there looking at each other. Even though years had passed, he was still familiar. I knew his smell, his movements, and his habits. After all, I had lived with him and slept in the same bed with him for eleven years. So he knew I was genuine.

I took his hands and looked into his eyes and said, "I want to make amends and ask for your forgiveness. We were so young when we married and made so many mistakes. I'm sorry for any way I hurt you and myself. I am willing, in this moment, to let go of any way I felt hurt by things you did and did not do also. I no longer need to carry the burdens of the past. I have learned from my life, and that is enough. And I want to thank you for giving me the greatest gift any man can give a woman, and that is my beautiful daughter."

He responded in a way I did not expect. He burst into tears.

"I'm so sorry," he said. "I wasn't ready to be a dad then, but I am now."

What else needed to be said? Years of sleepless nights, fury, and frustration melted into a tidal wave of compassion. We were both just kids trying to figure out our way in a chaotic world. We hugged, and the story of pain and suffering was over.

All family members' eyes were focused on us as we walked back into the hotel pub holding hands. Our daughter's eyes were the widest. I feel there was a split that healed in her soul that day too, a wound that she would not need to spend her life trying to resolve. Instead of bitterness and division, there was wholesome gathering of people bound together by blood and marriage. We were all in this together.

Kat stayed with her Scottish family while John and I traveled together through Ireland, where he began to rediscover his ancient roots. But that is the subject of another story. What I knew was that my heart had healed, and it was time to love again.

That was eleven years ago, and I am still deeply in love with John. I also am happy to report that our young friends who married in Cornwall are still happily married. When we choose to forgive one another, and mend our broken hearts, we can love again.

THE ROAD TO ACCEPTANCE

TREVOR THOMAS

"YOU CAN'T go on the high dive. You're too fat," said the kid in front of me. I was ten at the time, standing in line with other kids for the diving boards at the local swimming pool. I had never interacted with large groups of kids outside of school before. His friend snickered, and I remember thinking, *These kids are older than me, so they must know what they are talking about.* Looking back, I know that I was an average-sized kid, but I believed them when they told me I was fat. And it stuck with me.

Flash-forward about twenty years. I'm six feet four; I wear size 17 shoes; and I weigh around 380 pounds. I remembered what it felt like to be bullied as a kid, so I decided long ago that I never wanted to make anyone else feel that way. So I learned how to look harmless. That's a really hard thing to do when you're such a big guy.

I've spent most of my life apologizing for my size—not wanting to get in the way, hurt someone's feelings, or accidentally express any feeling that wasn't good. I was afraid that if I ever let it out, I might lose control. My father gave me the nickname Gentle Giant, but there was a part of me that always felt trapped by that name. I mean, what good is a giant if they're always gentle?

It wasn't until I attended a self-empowerment event about telling your personal story that something finally shifted for me. The man leading the event told me that there were strengths in my size that I had never tapped into before. He said that when I stood tall and confident, I made those around me feel safe and powerful. He showed me a side of myself that I had never really tapped into before, because I was afraid of it. He was telling me that my size was actually a good thing.

It was an amazing revelation. All I had to do was accept my size, then what I thought was a weakness could be turned into a strength! I didn't have to apologize for my bigness; instead I could stand tall with confidence and give people a sense of safety and security just by my presence alone. That was a gift I wasn't able to give before, and it taught me a valuable lesson: acceptance. I spent so long denying who I was because I let some kid in line at a diving board define me. And I thought there was something wrong with me. I never realized I had been given a gift, and all it took was accepting who I was to be able to step into my full potential.

This realization, however, was just the beginning of my journey.

I got to go to Liberia a couple of years ago with a group of transformational leaders teaching self-empowerment messages. The first thing I noticed when I got there was this "look" the locals would give me. It was sort of a "What the f——" kind of look, each person stopping what they were doing to stare at me. I learned that Liberians are very much into eye contact, and they would look me straight in the eyes with this quizzical stare on their faces. Before I went there, I had imagined I would fit right in, surrounded by tall African people. Instead, I was bigger than any of them (and pretty white besides), so I stuck out like a sore thumb.

I quickly realized that there was no blending in for me. I needed to choose how I was going to show up. And what I chose was to stand with confidence in my bigness. I chose to stand up straight, look each of them in the eyes and stand for my greatness. I projected that sense of safety and confidence that I had only recently unlocked, but which I knew was an innate part of who I was. It was like learning how to swim by being thrown into the deep end of the pool.

With every person I made eye contact, I was saying, *I am just a metaphor for you to step into your bigness too.* And it was amazing. Some people smiled and laughed. Others waved. And some stood taller. It was like they were waiting to be given permission to shine. I think the truth was that I had been waiting, and they were giving me permission. When I left Liberia two weeks later, I had many new friends and was affectionately known as the Big Guy.

I went to Ecuador last year on a similar trip. I thought it would be another opportunity for me to "step into my bigness" and share my greatness with those around me. I also thought I'd get another cool nickname, like the one I got in Liberia!

Our first stop was an ecolodge in the Amazon rain forest, where it rains pretty much every day. I grew up in Arizona, so naturally, when we arrived, I ran out to stand in the rain. When I came back in, someone told me that one of the natives had said, "Tiny really likes rain." I thought, *Yes, I got my nickname.* It's an ironic one, but it is a nickname. There was a little part of me, though, that felt fear. I couldn't figure out if they were acknowledging me or making fun of me. It brought me back to that moment in line at the diving board, getting teased but trying not to express how I felt so I wouldn't hurt others.

During our stay, we took some jungle treks where we would go with a guide deep into the jungle along these narrow paths made of boards stretched over marshes and mud pits. Because of my size, I kept breaking the boards and people started saying they were worried about me getting hurt. They didn't know if they could carry me back to camp. In my head, I was thinking, *This is ludicrous!* I wanted to show them I was this big strong guy, and they didn't need to worry about me. I wanted to pick up a log or wrestle an alligator or something. I wanted to step into my bigness, but I kept finding myself in these situations where I felt small.

The next week, we went up into the Andes, to a village near the top of one of the mountains around 9,000-feet elevation. The villagers then took us on a "short" hike, which none of us were prepared for. It was about two thousand feet down the side of the mountain to a river. When I finally got to the river, I thought, *I guess this is where I live now because there is no way I am going to make it back up that mountain.* I thought that I was afraid of trying to get back up the mountain, but I figured out that what I was really afraid of was asking for help. Asking for help meant that I was inadequate, that I couldn't do it on my own, and that I wasn't really in my "bigness." Instead, I was in my "smallness."

I finally realized that if I was going to make it back up the mountain, I would need support. The whole group jumped into action. Some of the health coaches in the group stayed back to help me, and villagers ferried water down the mountain to everyone walking back up. When I finally got to the top, a friend asked me, "How does it feel to know that everyone was focused on sending you love on that trip?"

At first, the question hurt. Deep down inside, I thought everyone was pitying me. I was scared they had all believed I couldn't do it. Then I realized that there was another side to stepping into my bigness, and that was stepping into my smallness—my vulnerability. There is nothing wrong with asking for help. Everyone has things that they can't do. In fact, there is nothing I can do that doesn't require support of some kind. I wasn't born by myself. I didn't grow up by myself. And I didn't get to where I am without the help and support of others.

I learned two lessons that day. One was that if I just take it one step at a time, I can do pretty much anything. The other was that it is okay to accept support from others.

THE UNLIKELY BIRTHDAY GIFT

JAZZMYN BLU

IT WAS a Friday, about ten minutes after midnight on December 5, 2008.

I was awake because it was my birthday. I had plans for later that night, so I was putting my outfit together. This was my first birthday away from home, and although I didn't grow up celebrating birthdays, excitement and anticipation for the good time ahead kept me optimistic and looking forward to going out with my high school sweetheart.

I had just turned nineteen, and as the clock struck midnight, I squeezed my eyes shut and fervently prayed about the good year I wanted to have. The previous month had been hectic with roommate struggles on top of the regular demands of adjusting to university life. I just knew that my birthday would be the silver lining that I was taught to seek out in the midst of a storm.

"Things will be greater later," my mother often reassured me.

After my last prayer, I grabbed my cell phone to text my mom. I sent her this message, "So happy and so proud that I said my first prayer at nineteen." Maintaining my faith and adherence to religious tradition outside of my parents' supervision was a source of pride for me. She replied, "Happy Birthday," then said she was happy for me. She then texted me a message that I will remember for the rest of my life.

"Yah is real. I know of his blessing through you. Peace, Princess."

I texted her goodnight and went to bed, excited about the day to come.

Those would be her last words to me.

My dad called me around 7:00 a.m. He said, "Normally, I would be calling you to tell you happy birthday. Instead, I am calling you to tell you that your mom didn't wake up this morning."

I could not gather the strength or the vocabulary to respond. I always had something to say, especially when it involved my dad. But this time, my mind was grasping for words, and my body was gasping for air and meaning.

"Your mama is dead, Jazzmyn. I tried to wake her up this morning, but she wouldn't wake up. I'm sorry. I'm sorry she died on your birthday."

I don't remember ending that conversation with my dad. All I know is that as soon as it clicked in my head that my mother had passed, on my birthday, no less, I began to scream frantically as I ran up and down the hallway of my four-bedroom apartment, every bit of me a sweaty, nervous wreck. I ran from my bedroom to the living room and back again, not realizing that I'd awakened my roommates, who had been sound asleep. I completely lost it.

I found myself crying and rocking back and forth on the floor in front of the couch while my roommates attempted to console me the best they could.

"Was she sick? When was the last time you talked to her? Are you going to be okay?"

"No, she wasn't sick. My dad said that he had heard her cough the night before, but that wasn't unusual for her to do in her sleep since her blood pressure medication would make her cough."

I had just texted her at midnight, right before I went to bed, I thought. *Why didn't I call her? Why didn't I opt to hear her voice? How could this happen?*

So many questions swirled in my head, and I condemned myself for not seeing her the week prior, when I had the chance. I blamed myself for her untimely departure and, irrational in my thinking, convinced myself that there was something that I could have done to keep her here with me longer.

As the stream of tears slowed down, I found myself remembering funny things that my mom had said over the years. She once said she planned to grow her dreadlocks so long that she would have to wrap them around her waist like a belt. And when she had grandkids, they could use her hair as a jump rope. Then she would laugh at the thought of us taking her outside in the backyard and washing her hair with the water hose.

Once I got over the initial shock, a strange but familiar calming peace came over me. I had always been the strong one, the person that others leaned on during difficult times. It was uncomfortable for me to not assume that position now. So I wiped my tears away and hugged my roommates. I tried to convince them to go back to bed, telling them I would be okay. I then tried to convince myself that I would be. I went back to my bedroom and got dressed for the day.

About an hour later, my boyfriend showed up at the door with flowers and breakfast in hand. I opened the door to him telling me "Happy Birthday!" He sensed something was wrong. I accepted the gifts, took his hand, and walked him to my bedroom, closing the door behind us. I sat him on my bed and told him about my mom. His eyes got big in disbelief, and seeing his reaction, I started to cry. This time, I wasn't hysterical. Instead, I was able to comfort and reassure him that everything was going to be okay. I watched him struggle as he called his parents and told them the news.

As we packed up and headed to my parents' neighborhood hospital, where my family was meeting, I knew I had to gather my strength so I could be strong for my family. I saw my mother on the table—my dad holding on to her hand for dear life. It all seemed surreal. All I could manage to say was, "I am glad she doesn't have to work anymore, and I'm glad she will no longer know pain."

Unfortunately, my boyfriend was meeting most of my family for the first time. When he "met" my mother, I tried to convince him of the beautiful person she had been before that day, and how she would have loved him simply because I loved him.

I cancelled my plans for that night and stayed home to comfort and mourn with my two younger brothers and the rest of my family who were visiting. As we settled in for Sabbath, I remembered my older cousin putting his hand on my shoulder and giving me the best advice that anyone had ever given me. He told me that I didn't have to be so strong for everyone. He told me that it was okay to take time for myself—to process and heal.

"There's this peace that I've seen daughters have when their mothers pass on, and this isn't the first time I've witnessed it. It's like you all know that it's going to be okay. But you don't have to be so strong for everyone," he repeated.

The next day, my niece was born, and I wondered if she had met my mother on her way here.

As the days passed and we shared stories about the good times that we'd had with my mom, I felt a shift in my personality. My mom's death had forced me to grow up, and I knew I had to do away with self-centered motivations and self-absorbed behaviors. I had to realize how important family was and how we needed to enjoy each other while we had the time, because we just never know.

When my mother passed, it was the most beautifully complex and painful thing that had ever happened to me, and I have forever been changed by it. Who I am today is absolutely because of who she was while she was here.

I used to be scared that I would forget her laugh or the sound of her voice. And sometimes, I do. But I will never forget how she made me feel or the impact she had on those around her. Almost nine years later, people can't help but smile when they speak her name. I can only hope that I leave the same impression with my life.

Now when my birthday rolls around, I am full of reflection. I check in with myself, *Are you having a good time? Are you being a good person?* Knowing and being aware of my status has fundamentally changed who I am and how I show up for myself and others.

For my nineteenth birthday, my mother gave me the most precious gift—the freedom and ability to cry and be vulnerable. I am now more complete and have learned to balance strength with vulnerability.

My mother's memory has become a practice of self-care. And her death gave life to my need for interdependence and shared strength.

I couldn't have asked for a better birthday present.

Z"L

REDEFINING PRIDE

JEFF HARMON

I'M SITTING in this office, waiting for them to roll in my wheelchair. *My wheelchair.* Those two words seem a bit surreal. I'm nervous, excited, terrified, and relieved, wondering, *How did I get here?* It's not that this moment is a surprise or unexpected. I've been waiting for the wheelchair for almost eight months now. But as I sit in this quiet room, my thoughts race back to all the events that led to this moment. My life will never be the same.

A few short years before all this, I completed two triathlons: a 1,500-meter swim, a 24-kilometer bike ride, and a 10-kilometer run. Now I'm here.

In 2006, I started to get noticeably clumsy. I didn't pay it much mind since my size 14 feet had always made me a little clumsier than the average person. But my wife finally said, "Would you please have it checked out?" So I did. After weeks of poking, prodding, researching, and conversing, I was diagnosed with adrenomyeloneuropathy (AMN). I'll save the technical details of AMN for your Google search, but in simplest terms, the coating (myelin) on the nerves in my legs is deteriorating. I jokingly say that my brain and legs aren't on good speaking terms, thus, the clumsiness.

AMN is a rare congenital disease in boys and men for which there is no cure or conventional treatment. I'm fortunate that it didn't decide to show up until adulthood. Boys diagnosed with it don't typically survive past the age of twelve unless they have a stem cell transplant. I breathed a sigh of relief when my doctors told me that it was unlikely that AMN would affect my brain and take my life. Despite the potentially devastating news, I am grateful there was never a "Why, God?" moment. This was just my "deal"—and everyone has a "deal."

Life was pretty normal after my diagnosis. Early on, the symptoms of AMN were subtle and progressed very slowly. My daughters, Maddie and Gloria, were born in 2007 and 2012, respectively, and life got swept up with our being new parents. I also started my entrepreneurial journey in 2011, and life marched on. My wife tells me that I was in denial—not denial that I had the disease, but denial that it had to change anything about how I lived my life.

By the beginning of 2013, to her and the outside world, my walking was becoming more labored. I was regularly questioned about my leg. "How did you injure it?" "When will it get better?" And when they saw I wasn't getting better, "What's the deal with your legs?" I had been a very active person up to and immediately after my diagnosis. Running, playing basketball, hiking, and biking were all part of my life. When the questions came, I'd laugh them off and claim it was an old basketball injury. There was no reason to go into a long explanation. While I knew it would only get worse over time, life was pretty normal, and I decided not to face the reality of my condition if I didn't have to.

That all changed on July 11, 2013. That morning, I made the hour-long drive to Princeton, New Jersey, for a business-plan meeting with two colleagues. Since I was in denial, I parked in a spot that would require a bit of a walk. I walked about fifty feet, took one bad step, rolled my ankle, and fell to the ground. I immediately knew something wasn't right. I first realized I could not get up and then saw the bump of a bone on my lower left leg. It was definitely broken. As I lay there, waiting for the ambulance, my main thought was how inconvenient this was going to be.

So began the wild three-and-a-half-month journey of surgery, recovery, and rehabilitation from the injury. Once cleared by my orthopedic doctor, I began to work and travel, but my mobility was never the same. The injury had pressed the fast-forward button on AMN, and in the blink of an eye, I needed a cane to stay upright. I remained in denial about the reality of my condition, but it quickly became obvious that I needed near constant assistance to walk. While my youngest daughter was "surfing" on tables, walls, and people as she learned to walk, her dad needed to do the same.

In the midst of all this, my business continued to grow, and life carried on. I took on increased leadership responsibilities in my church and took on new responsibilities in the local not-for-profit community. I wasn't going to let AMN change my life. That included looking good, hiding my cane when I took pictures, and avoiding the real reason for my physical limitation. My recently broken leg was a convenient reason for my problem with walking. While I wouldn't allow AMN to change the basic framework of life, life was indeed changing. I was making different choices, and my family was silently (and sometimes not so silently) in a state of concern of another fall and the worst-case scenarios that could accompany that.

I conceded that we needed to move from a three-floor home to a single-story home in 2014. We chose not to go places or do certain things. I stayed on the sidelines while my daughters and others were active. I agreed to see a new neurologist who had experience with AMN and who suggested additional support in the form of leg braces.

Leg braces? There was no way! We would also discuss the possibility of getting a manual or electronic wheelchair, but my six-foot three-inch pride always shut down the discussion, leaving my wife shaking her head and wondering when I would wake up to reality.

The wake-up call finally came in November 2015. Lying in bed one night, my wife handed me her smartphone and said, "Look at this guy." It was a story about a man named Chris Kaag. Chris served in the US Marine Corps and was diagnosed with AMN at twenty-one years old. He is a business owner and founder of the IM ABLE Foundation to help create fitness and movement possibilities for people with disabilities, and he does all this full-time from a wheelchair. I immediately contacted Chris and made the two-hour drive to visit him in person.

Almost immediately, I could see and experience the choices Chris made in his life. He owned his disability and his wheelchair. Through his choice to view his own disability as a personal stepping-stone and not as a crutch, he inspired me to redefine the way I viewed my AMN.

I began to see the freedom that was possible through using a wheelchair. I had been challenged for two years to swallow my pride, but on that cold December day in 2015, I realized that I didn't need to swallow my pride but define it differently. I also left that day committed both to a manual wheelchair that relied on the strength of my upper body and to being an athlete again.

If I could have, I would have gotten in a wheelchair that day, but the process took much longer than that. As the ordering process unfolded and I told people about the decision I had made, it was typically followed by a response of "I'm so sorry" or an awkward smile and uncertainty of what to say next. My response to them was —and still is—that my chair means *freedom*.

My body continues to break down little by little. Because of AMN, I can't be too far away from a bathroom, and the prospect of adrenal insufficiency is real. Deciding to use a wheelchair was not only the right thing to do, but it was the right time to do it.

So I sit here today ready to receive my wheelchair, and I'm still in a little disbelief that I'm here and about to embark on something I never believed would happen. The truth is that I don't know how much or how little I'll use it, and I'm completely freaked out by the prospect of wheeling up and down inclines. And, I wonder how air travel will work out. With that said, I'm not stopping. I'm building a business that has a huge impact on leaders living more consequential lives. I'm serving others in my faith community. I'm physically stronger than I have been in fifteen years, and I'm exactly where God wants me, doing what he wants me to be doing.

SHEDDING MY SKIN

KAREN GEDISSMAN

IT WAS a Saturday like any other, and I set out to go to my weekly musical theater workshop at the Skylight Theatre Company on Vermont. I began taking this class in the spring of 1987, and it was now 1998. And I was going strong, attending whenever I was in town and not away working in my field as a musical theater professional. The Skylight Theatre Company was part of the infamous Beverly Hills Playhouse, run by the renowned acting teacher, Milton Katselas. He was also my acting teacher. Gary Imhoff taught the musical theater workshop on Saturdays. Now years later, I am in Gary's master class, which is now its own entity. Gary has always played a pivotal role in my life as a teacher. He said to me just the other day, "You are a fixture in my life." And I replied, "As you are in mine."

There were two fateful Saturdays that changed my life forever. The first one was on a day when I was feeling particularly bad, scared, and uncertain of my future as a performing artist. I had just been hired to be a headliner for Princess Cruises, and I didn't know how I was going to navigate the high seas, literally and figuratively, with a skin condition that I had that was the bane of my existence.

I had been diagnosed with parapsoriasis, a more moderate form of full-blown psoriasis, at the end of 1992. My entire life, I was completely free with my body. I was comfortable in my own skin internally and externally. And then in my twenties, an age when any woman wants to feel beautiful and confident, I began to get this rash, this hateful skin condition that changed my existence and my sense of self. Although it was not a life-threatening illness, my life turned upside down because of it. As I was getting ready to go work on the ship five years later, in 1998, I didn't think I could manage my skin without people noticing. What was I to do?

At the Beverly Hills Playhouse, there was an acting exercise that Milton would assign an actor when they had something very personal getting in the way of their life, their career, and/or their artistry. This exercise was called a personal monologue. The concept was to write and/or create a monologue wherein the actor only had to use the truth of their conflict or issue once in the piece. The rest of the monologue could be made up. It was up to the actor. In doing this personal monologue, students would have tremendous breakthroughs on many levels, both as a human being and in their work as an artist. Gary, one of Milton's core group of teachers, would assign this exercise as well. Only in the musical theater workshop, a song would be included with the assignment.

Back to Vermont Avenue in Hollywood at the Skylight Theatre Company in the summer of '98—I happily went to Gary's class, only to find myself churning all day with the thought of my psoriasis, and whether or not I could accept this wonderful cruise ship job with the hell of my skin condition.

Gary was and is a very perceptive person and teacher, and at the end of class that day, we took a walk down the sidewalk, where our cars were parked. As I began to speak to him about my concerns, he immediately assigned me a personal monologue.

I could not have imagined the sheer defiance, rage, and pain that came flying out of me. I began screaming and crying that there was no fucking way that I was going to do this personal monologue. It was enough that I didn't want people to see or touch my skin when my rash would break out on different parts of my body, but I certainly wasn't going to tell a class full of people about it. No way, no how, absolutely not! Gary calmly stood next to me as I wept with passion and tears flew out of me with great fury. Like a true spiritual master and a fierce teacher, he began citing examples of famous singers and actors that performed with challenges greater than mine. He stood strong in his conviction that this exercise would help me overcome my concerns and fears, and cause me to succeed instead of give up.

We stood on that corner down the street from the Skylight for at least a half an hour, and I finally gave in and accepted his request. I was going to attempt to fulfill the assignment of the personal monologue. Was I happy about it? No. Did I think it would help me? No. Did I give in because I was weak? No. I trusted Gary, and I reluctantly agreed to put my best foot forward. He hadn't led me down the wrong path before. And what was the worst that could happen, right? I walked away from that tumultuous exchange, exhausted and not knowing how this was going to come together. I guess on some level, I felt it could help me.

I knew I couldn't do this alone. So I went to my good friend at the time, Robin, and asked her if she would work with me and direct/ guide me with the ideas that I brought to her. She graciously said yes, and we began this adventure.

I told her how I had always loved my body, felt free with it since I was little, and that how now I was afraid a man wouldn't find me attractive or sexy. I told her that I couldn't always go to dance class, and that I had to figure out, every day, whether I had to cover up my skin with clothes or not. I also told her how I had tried a million ways to make the psoriasis go away, ranging from medications (topical and oral) to diets and gurus, and everything in between. Living with this condition was exhausting, and I hadn't found my way out yet.

I had reached my limit. I couldn't take it anymore, and I didn't know how I could relay this to a class full of people, let alone take a job, where it might be too hard to manage. Still, I kept meeting with Robin and having long talks with her during our rehearsals until I came up with a creative and artistic format to set my scene.

I made three collages that contained pictures of me throughout my life, especially my sexiest and most beautiful pictures. Some of the pictures were with boyfriends and some of me performing, but all taken before I developed my dreadful skin condition. Then I recreated my bedroom on the stage and hung my collages. The concept was to bring my most personal environment to the scenery, capturing my innermost feelings for the monologue and song I would be performing.

Three weeks after my fiery discussion with Gary, my assignment was ready to go, and the second fateful Saturday had now arrived. I created my bedroom set for the scene and sat on my bed in a robe and began to tell the story of the time in my life where I felt beautiful and free. Then I told of how my skin condition began robbing pieces of me as it got worse. Suddenly, I was immersed in this powerful and artistic experience, and before I knew it, I was singing my planned song to go with my monologue, "I Dreamed a Dream" from the incredible musical *Les Misérables*. Being the emotionally expressive and truthful actor that I am, I brought all the colors and layers of my pain and hell and put them into the song. As I did so, Gary interjected his keen and insightful direction at key moments to move me deeper into the experience. You could hear a pin drop as the room was so quiet with support, surprise, and care. My voice soared on the wings of my pain, and slowly, I was being liberated of the layers on my skin that had been burning my soul for all those years.

What followed was the culmination of my friend Robin's gentle guidance from the ideas we exchanged during our rehearsal process. I had decided to take my robe off, being fully undressed, as I had the lighting fella lower the lights slightly. While sitting with my back to the audience, on a black box, I dropped my robe. I had next to me, on another box, a framed black-and-white photo of me that I was recreating, with me in the same pose. My dear friend, Wendy, had taken it before I developed my parapsoriasis as part of a series of sexy photos that I made as a Valentine's Day gift for my boyfriend. In the picture, I was wearing three-fourth-length white gloves. And I was sitting on a glass table with my back to the camera and my head turned slightly to the side, and you could see the back of my naked body to my butt. It was artistic and beautiful.

I sat in that very pose and disrobed for the class, and slowly, the lights came down. The personal monologue was completed, and my fellow classmates roared and cheered for me as I felt my heart beat in a way I had never experienced before. I had changed. Something in me had shifted in a way that went beyond words. In the core of my soul, I found relief and a new sense of acceptance for who I was as a woman, as an artist, and as a person who was living with a condition that might not ever change or go away.

It was glorious. I felt a ton of bricks lifted from my shoulders, and it became the unbearable lightness of being personified.

In the twenty-four hours that followed, I let a man touch me again after going a few years without that kind of connection. And in turn, I kept the job and was ready to sail the ocean with a newfound courage for all that I had to offer in spite of my skin. I grew a thicker skin, and at the same time, I shed my old dead skin that had been keeping pieces of me buried.

After two fateful Saturdays, a relentless and loving teacher, a good friend, and my own courage, I found that I had grown new skin that gave light to new opportunities, a new love, and a new life.

BEAUTIFUL DEATH

CHRIS GARDENER

I LOST my wife eighteen months before she died. We spent every day of those eighteen months together. It was beautiful. It was intense. It was important. It changed my future. But I lost her eighteen months before she died.

After twenty-two years of being together and aged just thirty-nine, my wife was diagnosed with a brain tumour.

"Incurable," they said. "Uncertain prognosis."

Our kids were eight and six at the time. *What do we tell them? How? What's going to happen? How is Mum going to be? What does this all mean?*

I had my own questions, of course. *Will she be in pain? What can I do? Can I cope?*

How would we tell her parents? It'll be incredibly hard for them. Your children aren't supposed to die before you.

I was running my own business at the time and was "successful" in anyone's eyes. And in one conversation with a neurologist, everything changed.

Over the next four years, we had amazing support and treatment. There were two operations to remove parts of her brain, radical radiotherapy, and chemotherapy.

All of it helped.

None of it cured.

As her condition deteriorated, she became unable to do anything without help. Getting out of bed, showering, using the toilet, getting dressed, standing, sitting—even talking and stringing words together became impossible. When your brain is affected like hers was, your abilities get seriously limited. And in what turned out to be the last eighteen months of her life, the tumour impacted her ability to think and understand too.

Back when all this started, once we'd gotten over the initial shock of the diagnosis, my wife and I agreed on a few things. We had clarity and certainty about what was important. We had each other. We had our kids. And we had loving families and close friends. In a perverse kind of way, we even realized that we could look at this as some kind of twisted *gift*. We had been given the opportunity to *not take life for granted*. Certainly, we sure as hell wished this situation was *not* happening; but given that it was, we could wish it wasn't or we could make it beautiful.

"Quality, not quantity" became our watchwords. It was no longer about how much longer she would live but about how beautiful that life could be. Out of the blue, we had a different perspective about life. It was as if the lenses had been polished. Until that point, we hadn't realized they'd been slightly blurry. It all became very clear.

Life mattered.

Here we were, still feeling young in our late thirties, forced into a situation where we didn't know how much longer we'd have together. The statistics for her particular tumour suggested that the median life expectancy was seven years.

That didn't mean that people lived for an average of seven years. It meant that 50 percent of the people with this tumour died within seven years.

I have a math background. My wife was a musician and an artist. From my perspective, a median of seven years didn't tell us anything about my wife in particular. After all, it's also true to say that 50 percent of people are still alive after seven years. Some of those might still be alive after ten, twenty, or even thirty years. They could be. We just didn't know. As an optimist, I wanted to hold on to that thought. But it wasn't me who had the condition, and my wife just couldn't get her head around that possibility. For her, seven years became the goal. It was not long, but a lifetime for our kids right then. It was not long, yet plenty of time to live, love, and enjoy.

Of course, we'd assumed, up until the diagnosis, that we'd have at least fifty more years of life together. There was no rush. Well, we weren't looking at fifty years anymore. It was time to make the most of life. So we thought about what we would do. What does "make the most of life" actually mean?

There were brutal constraints of treatment—brain surgery, radiotherapy, more brain surgery, and chemotherapy. There were also the practical constraints of having two children at primary school. Heading off to the sun and travelling with carefree abandon wasn't a realistic option. It also would not have been fair to her parents and family. They would want to spend time with her too.

So for us, the choice was clear, and it was beautiful. We would treasure the time we had, treasure just being, and treasure the love we shared. We would find joy in ordinary things, like playing music together, eating meals, and cuddling on the sofa.

For most of the three and a half years after the diagnosis, my wife would be herself—not a victim and not someone to pity. She was just someone getting on with life as usual. Then as she deteriorated and could no longer speak or understand things clearly, it became my privilege to care for her in every way.

I was a professional, a successful man with my own business. I had a strong reputation. People perceived me as business-oriented. And I loved the work I was doing and how I was impacting my clients. But I was happy to drop it all. My wife needed me. Practically and emotionally, she needed me. Our kids needed me. And that was *all* that mattered.

I found myself in a totally new world. And I actually really enjoyed those months I was home with my wife. Of course, we wished things were different. Of course, we wouldn't have chosen to face what we faced. But we didn't get to choose. Things were what they were.

And it was beautiful.

We didn't need travel, trinkets, or sympathy. We had each other, and we were all together.

It was time for Dad to do the cooking. Most of the time, that worked out well. And when the food was rubbish, we would all laugh. When spaghetti bolognese went wrong, it was funny. And the capable man messing up tea was a perfect recipe for our kids' hilarity.

Yes, it was beautiful.

I surprised myself too. Whilst working, whilst building a business, and whilst being a professional, I had defined happiness as success. And I'd defined success as something external. Now it was very different, very real. Happiness was no longer defined as success. Happiness was love. It was connection. It was about treasuring moments and experiences.

I was able to look after her for the whole of those last eighteen months. My wife died at home, beautifully peaceful, surrounded by her family and loved.

In the next few days and weeks that followed, I thought I would feel emptiness and loss. But I didn't. I felt content and peaceful. I recognized that I had mourned while we were still together. As my wife lost her mental abilities, I lost my wife.

After she died, I didn't feel empty. I actually felt full—full of love. I still had plenty to share and plenty to give. I was ready to love again, knowing that like one candle lights another, sharing love with someone new doesn't extinguish a previous love.

We shared nearly twenty-eight years together. And even though I'd lost her, those last eighteen months were some of the most precious. I was privileged to experience and share such deep connection, such tenderness, and such beautiful moments with someone. It was as if a microscope had been turned on us so we could see with crystal clarity what really matters.

That was over four years ago. The kids are now approaching the end of their school days, with exciting futures ahead. I'm back working on my business, but things are different now. I'm not seeking success. I'm enjoying the game. I can have a bigger impact on my clients now because I've been lucky enough to experience what really matters.

I've learned to not take life for granted.

CHILDREN RAISING CHILDREN

KAREN VANBARNEVELD-PRICE

IN THE winter of 1969, in a small desert town of Southern California, I gave birth to my daughter. I had celebrated my sixteenth birthday on August 1 of that year with some of my high school friends, and as far as I and my parents were concerned, my child would be given up for adoption. In those years, the law stated that your parents could decide whether or not their minor-aged children could keep their own children. This was my second pregnancy, the first having been terminated. And although my parents were not onboard with me keeping my child, I wanted her. I had long since broken any contact with the child's father and had no intention of keeping him in my or the child's life as he was an addict already at eighteen years young. I had broken off our relationship after he asked me to tie his arm off while he shot heroin.

My parents had separated, and I lived with my mother and younger sibling. I had watched for many years as my family broke apart at its core, my two older sisters and brother already having gone their own ways in their late teens. Maybe it was a need for my own little person to love and be with that subconsciously brought me to become pregnant a second time. I always blamed my father for not being around much. It was easier than looking into my own young heart and soul, finding whatever lacked there. I have long since forgiven him for any conceived wrongdoings as a parent.

My mother and family doctor had already found suitable parents through whatever avenues were used at that time, and they were at the hospital, waiting for the child to be born. In those days, we had no ultrasound to determine what the sex of the child would be, but this couple didn't care.

I remembered my labor being intensive but relatively short, given I was a month late. After four hours, my daughter was born at nine pounds four ounces. While giving birth, they had draped a sheet across my abdomen so that I couldn't see the infant or know the sex. I remember crying when she cried after being slapped on her little bottom. I knew then that I would never see this little child I had held so close to me for almost a year. It broke my heart.

After I was taken to my hospital room, no sleep would come, only thoughts about my baby—their baby now. After a few hours, my mother came into my room to see how I was. She told me that she had gone to see the baby and how beautiful "it" was. She then told me that if I wanted, I could keep the child but with conditions. I would have to finish high school, then go to work to support us both. My immediate reaction was an unequivocal yes.

I should have known that after having five babies of her own, she couldn't bear the thought of giving away any of her progeny. My child was indeed a beautiful one, already being a month old out of the womb.

I could say now that the rest is history, given that my daughter is now in her late forties and has her own grandchildren. But life is never that simple. Throughout my daughter's younger years, being the child of a child was not easy for her. I still had my penchant for needing the attentions of men due to my own self-loathing. A consequence of that was hiring a lot of babysitters, while I was out doing God knows what. Well, I know what, but that is not part of this story. I was also a recreational drug user. I thought that cocaine and alcohol were more socially acceptable as long as I kept my job, paid my bills, and put food on the table. I stopped all that nonsense around the age of thirty-two, after becoming aware of the havoc I was wreaking in our lives.

Although I did fulfill my obligation to finish high school and work, I did not fulfill my own tacit obligations as a parent to the best of my abilities. I loved her more than I loved myself, which is not a good way to start parenting. I have learned, over the second half of my life, that I needed to love myself more, so I could know self-actualization and could have the capacity to share that with her during her seminal years. It is difficult to say whether or not a child of sixteen has the capability and experience to understand themselves well enough to become a good parent. While I now feel that my decision to keep her was a selfish one, not considering how I was going to properly care for her, I would not change that decision. However, I would not advise others to duplicate this path.

Over the last twenty-five years, I have taken responsibility for my deficiencies as a mother, apologizing profusely. And, I have sought to guide and help my daughter as much as humanly possible. Having been through so many hardships together, we are as close as any mother and daughter could be, maybe even more. We have a mutual love, respect, admiration, acceptance, and reverence for each other and ourselves that we might not have come to under what is considered to be normal circumstances.

I could not even imagine what my life would have been like had I not made that decision over forty-seven years ago. I have had the fullness and richness of a life lived outside the lines, learning every step on my path how to love myself for all my limitations and flaws, as well as my generosity and compassion. I now understand the importance of sharing our nascent gifts with those around us. As we are given these gifts unique to us, it is our responsibility to contribute those gifts to our families and communities. Mine has been a life well lived and continues to be well learned.

MAGIC TREE

HEATHER DUKE

WHEN I was nine years old, my family and I would visit my aunt and uncle in Dallas almost every weekend. They lived in this tiny house in a neighborhood that was old and crowded with huge trees and narrow alleyways. In the backyard, there was a small koi fishpond that was overflowing with tadpoles. Certain times of the year, we enjoyed my aunt's lush garden, where sweet honeysuckle and blackberries lined the back fence. There was a huge tree in the yard that had branches and leaves that reached all the way to the ground and formed a little hiding space for us to play. My little brother, cousins, and I called it the magic tree.

We loved to hide within that tree and play a game we called nature kids. We each had an element that we represented. I was wind. My brother, Mark, was ocean, and my cousin, Jessica, was earth. It was Jessica's responsibility to make sure we were fed every day while in our fantasy world. She would collect honeysuckle and berries from the yard, as well as sneak food from inside the house, such as sweet pickles and cheese. We always pretended the food was something else, something we grew in an imaginary garden. It was my job to fan Mark and Jessica with leaves from the trees. This would always get them running in circles as I chased them with tornadoes of wind to get them excited. Mark's only real task was to run our errands and make up stories so we could laugh.

My heart aches for those days, for so many reasons. Things were simple then. It was so easy to entertain ourselves all day long, pretending to be fairies living in a tree with nothing but berries and flowers for food, stumps of logs for furniture, and baby frogs for companions. How fun it was to make up stories and songs and perform them for each other, dancing and smiling with nothing but the sun in the sky leading the way.

Mostly, I long for those days because my sweet-natured younger brother is no longer a part of my life. Several years ago, Mark lost his sensitive life to a heroin overdose. When he died, I lost one of the most profound people in my life. I lost my favorite soul.

Every memory from my childhood involves Mark—memories of us playing in my mom's backyard on our spring-mounted horse, memories of us eating watermelon under the sprinkler in nothing but our underwear, memories of us fighting over who ate the last chip out of the bag and had to throw it away. There are so many memories— memories frozen in time.

Mark and I drifted apart in our teenage years. I was always at a friend's house or was sneaking out with a boyfriend. I was never there for him when he needed me. I was a horrible sister. From a distance, I watched him get wrapped up with a bad crowd of people and head down a path of destruction. I would laugh when he would stumble in drunk or stoned when he was only fifteen. Though it is hard to admit now, I was entertained by his antics. I didn't know then that I needed to help and protect him. Looking back, I often feel like I abandoned my best friend. I left him to figure out this polluted world on his own, allowing him to self-destruct.

As the years went by, Mark got darker and more distant, becoming someone I didn't know. It was then that I tried to get him back.

Selfishly, I wanted my brother back. I wanted him to ask for free desserts at restaurants again and to strike up random, hilarious conversations with strangers at the park. I wanted him back for me and for my family. In retrospect, I should have wanted him back for him, so he could feel better. I had ignored his pain, unaware of the personal struggles he was having. Instead, I would argue with him because he would keep Mom up at night trying to steal her car keys or trying to convince her to take him to dope houses. I was so angry with him. I often lashed out, calling him names like loser and druggie because he would pawn my dad's tools for spare change.

Mark was hurting me and our whole family and was missing out on seeing his bright little nephews grow up. They needed their uncle, just like he needed me. Mark needed to be heard, understood, and helped. He needed his sister, not the angry, spiteful person I had become. He needed me to guide him through the grim days and push him along to a better path. He needed me to see the depth of the ocean that he was drowning in, and I didn't. He needed his wind.

Though Mark died when he was twenty-seven years old, I have always felt like I lost my brother when he was fifteen. I mourned his life long before his physical body left this earth, crying many times over the loss of my sweet and innocent playmate. For most of the last ten years of his life, I felt like he was, for the most part, a stranger. Mark's addiction caused so much turmoil in my family's lives, turmoil that consumed us with so much fear and pain that when he was gone, we didn't know how to hold it together. We all fell apart —separately.

Reflection is a powerful thing. It's a shame that we can't look into a pool and see what lies ahead in our lives. I now see how I've taken on blame and carried guilt for things I honestly had no control over.

I have, however, learned to be more present in my relationships, and to be aware of the needs of others. More importantly, I've learned when to accept that the path someone chooses to take isn't my decision to make. I savor the memories I had with my brother, and it's a hard reality to know there won't be new ones to make. Although sometimes, when my eldest son walks through the room with a goofy look on his face, or my youngest cracks a joke that has me laughing for days, it will hit me out of nowhere—there are indeed new memories. My brother lives on in those smiles.

A SEA OF ANXIETY

STEVE BOLLOCK

AFTER DAYS of delay in the tiny bush village of Bettles in northern Alaska, three of us got the sudden call to get ready to fly in the late afternoon. The expected break in the rainy weather pattern, impinging on our late fall river/wildlife expedition into the Brooks Range wilderness, had finally arrived. Many of those in our group had been here in 2008, avoiding the mosquitoes by traveling in autumn. We had great weather then, dry and chilly. My intuition had warned me that this year might be different.

We had volunteered to act as a probe to see if the smaller floatplane, the Beaver, could get through the high mountain pass in time to radio back for the Otter to come on ahead with our seven companions. Bettles is just south of the Gates of the Arctic National Park, the least visited and largest of all US national parks. Our flight headed up the Alatna River drainage, seeking passage to the Noatak Valley. The ninety-minute trip was as good as we could have imagined with fair visibility and little turbulence. Our young pilot saw an opening through Gull Pass and seized the opportunity. We landed on Nelson Walker Lake to a gorgeous fall tundra frosted with light snow.

I felt so happy to be back. My anxiety back in Bettles was transformed into pure joy. As we hurried to set up tents and kitchen shelter, I fell into the beauty of this wild place, enjoying not only the colorful tundra and snowcapped peaks around our lakeside camp, but the awesome silence and solitude after the bustle of the Bettles's airstrip and hangar.

We had spent three days exploring this strange outpost—a blend of the historic Koyukon village and the national park headquarters. The bad weather found us watching nature videos in the park's theater, wandering muddy dirt streets, and sleeping on tarps in the hangar. The time in Bettles was a training ground for all of us, a workshop in waiting and adjusting to the truth of what was real. The good news was that we were time-rich with sixteen days to raft only forty-five river miles.

At last, here we sat—Scott, Leslie, and myself—under our nylon shelter, cooking some dehydrated soup and marveling at the contrast in our recent homes. My excitement neutralized all sense of exposure to the cold and snow. The prospect of being alone for a few days if the storm was to persist was just fine—an unexpected chapter in the adventure we had signed on to. There was an immediate bond amongst the three of us, as well as a deep and soulful connection to this Arctic landscape and its yet unseen four-legged inhabitants.

Something very special had just happened.

Later the next day, the Otter made it through with our companions, three river rafts, and the rest of our gear. Two days later, we portaged from the lake to the river. The weather turned clear and cold at first with calm days that slowly warmed into gorgeous vitamin D–collecting, sunbathing afternoons. Clear night skies meant 'Aurora borealis' sightings. Those up during weak-bladder moments between midnight and 3:00 a.m. often burst into oohing, aahing, and occasional cheering, as at the end of a great fireworks display. The dynamic movement of curtains and spirals of light urged everyone to brave the subfreezing temperatures, though we often had the inclination to simply open the tent door and take a partial view from a warm sleeping bag.

On the second leg of our river journey, we entered a stretch of major side-creek tributaries, where salmon were making their way toward spawning grounds. The bears were taking full advantage of this late autumn food supply. During one eighteen-mile day, we had eight grizzly sightings from our rafts. These were great opportunities as there was little danger of interaction and full viewing until the bears caught our scent or motion.

After rejecting a nice camp at the mouth of Kugrak Creek due to numerous fresh large grizzly tracks in nearby bushes, we found ourselves camped in the middle of a serious gravel-bar wildlife corridor. The next morning, a large bear came around a blind corner into face-to-face contact with several of our people. Being the "good" bear he was, or due to our bad human smell, he immediately waded to a midstream sandbar, scrutinized the intruders, and then swam to the far bank to continue his search for fish.

On our final river day, before the portage to the lake where we would rendezvous with the floatplane, we spotted a grizzly on the bank downstream from our landing place. Up came the binoculars and the logical maneuver to give wide birth. By the time we passed the bear, it dawned on us that we had floated too far and missed the portage trailhead. The bear had distracted us in a serious way, which led to the need to drag the rafts over a half mile back upstream before the anticipated portage. In spite of this extra effort, we felt honored to be in the bear's furry presence and in awe of our good fortune to have had these great ursine encounters.

Floatplanes need to land on lake water, and the quarter-mile portage to Lake Matchurak was arduous. Each of us needed to make four or five trips with as much gear as we each could carry. While there was a trail of sorts, the terrain was uneven and wet. The rafts were most difficult, particularly the long skinny one, which only had handles on each end. Three of us carried it overhead (or more accurately, on our heads), walking single file. It was an exhausting day.

We'd spent three nights at our previous camp. The Brooks Range Aviation floatplanes were in the air daily and our SAT phone contact with them indicated *reasonable* weather ahead. There was no indication we needed to alter our schedule to beat bad weather to Matchurak. We cleaned the rafts the afternoon of the portage, organized our gear, and intended to fly out the next day. The morning of our anticipated departure, we awoke to a light snowfall. And when we contacted Brooks Aviation, they told us that Bettles was fogged in.

Then it began . . . the waiting.

As the snow subsided later in the morning, we were in a mix of feelings amidst awesome beauty and impatience to catch our flights back home. When we contacted the air service in mid-afternoon, news was they were clear to take off and would make a run at getting through the pass. We moved right in to breaking down camp.

We waited and waited, watching the eastern sky toward the passes. Finally, around 6:00 p.m., we began to lose hope. Another call to Bettles confirmed that they'd been unable to get through the pass, and we moved into setting our camp back up once again.

By the third day of our wait for the floatplane, our minds were adrift on a sea of anxiety, fearing more bad weather while hoping for a clearing—just three hours would do. The weather pattern was fickle. *Perhaps the pass was clear, but what was the ceiling in Bettles? Could the planes even get off the ground?* With the snow flurries and the wind coming and going and the hours of anything resembling warmth diminishing daily, we spent many hours in the tents. Most of us read a lot and traded books back and forth. And, we played a lot of Rummy 500 and cribbage (without a board).

Reading was not a big part of how I spent my time. My mind tends to go where it will and I just watch, to see how seriously I will take it. Distraction is not much of an exploration. So when the fears began to rise to serious levels, and I wondered if I would live to see my grandchildren again, I turned to my journal and began to write.

Our food supply is not too worrisome yet. We have eaten the emergency food packed for two extra days of waiting and have rationed what is left into two small meals a day. It seems that three more days of "some eating" is possible. I now appreciate the extra insulation of my 190-pound chubbiness! I recall expressing a desire to return to my optimal "playing weight." Voila! A golden opportunity to manifest my imaginings.

I know how to fast; I have done it several times before. But as low blood sugar arrives, look out! Recent reality checks reveal a strong trend toward crankiness.

I am choosing not to fill my mind with the written thoughts of others. I prefer to simply watch my own. I sometimes call this my meditation practice, lacking any other formal, spiritual discipline. The one book I did throw into my dry bag was Buddhist Anam Thubten's, No Self, No Problem*. Waking up to a snow-covered tent for the third straight morning is taking my monkey mind to that most definitive No-Self Possibility. Fearful thinking is nothing new to me, but these circumstances are pulling up thoughts of worst possible outcomes. Death seems uncomfortably near.*

What are my lingering attachments that impede letting go? What relationships have not had adequate expressions of love? What remains in need of my forgiveness?

What future experiences are still deeply desired?

Suddenly, the NFL opening game does not seem too important!

Paul was up at first light every morning to make the coffee. "The good news is that the weather cannot get any worse," he announced cheerfully one morning. The next morning, he shared "The bad news is it can only get worse. We have a five-thousand-foot ceiling and twenty-mile visibility." But Bettles and the pass each had their own conditions, so what it looked like where we were was not very relevant. My internal mechanism was to avoid further disappointment. I just wanted to hear the roar of the Otter's engine and see it breaking through the skyline into my view.

Buzz, one of the camp "worker bees," decided to break out his fishing gear and before we knew what he was up to, he landed an eighteen-inch lake trout. The word rang out through the camp, and Scott joined him. Within a couple of hours, they decided they had enough and threw back a sixth, equally large fish. They shifted gears to gathering brush, both for warmth and the fish fry. The fish tacos filled our bellies and provided a much-needed lift for our spirits.

By this time, we were thinking about possible emergency rescue measures—jet helicopters dispatched from Prudhoe Bay, national park choppers for search and rescue—but the sad truth was that those things never happened up here unless someone was actually dying. In truth, we were nowhere near such extreme measures, much to the dismay of those who might pay whatever the cost.

The bad weather finally broke on day five. By noon we heard the welcome sound of a float plane clearing the pass, and we scurried to break camp as the pilot circled and landed on the lake. We found out from our pilot that Brooks Range Aviation had forty people stranded in the bush—some of whom had been out longer than us. One group was at a lake that had frozen over, requiring them to hike across tundra to a larger lake where planes could land. Others had food but no fuel or firewood to cook it. One party of hunters watched their food (caribou) disappear to a hungry bear. All things considered, we'd had it pretty easy.

We all missed our flights back home and were prepared to spend one more night in the Bettles's hangar. Much to our surprise, the folks at Brooks Range Aviation had a plane waiting to scoot us back to Fairbanks. It seemed they'd had enough of us whiney flatlanders who didn't quite understand being at the mercy of the elements the same way Alaskans born and raised as part of the food chain did.

A few weeks later, we received an email from our favorite bush pilot, who was back home in Texas. He and the other pilots were laid off ten days after we got out. Everything was frozen. It was the earliest winter they could remember. This was yet another reminder of our vulnerability and extraordinary good fortune.

Of course, most people would never choose to have the experience we'd had if they knew it was coming. Interestingly, I have never wished I had not gone, neither during or in the aftermath of the adventure.

There is no predicting how much longer we could have maintained our equanimity. Clearly, we misjudged the likelihood of an early winter; but then life is actually quite unpredictable—even though we do our best to plan, prepare, and control it.

Since the trip, I make it a practice to express every bit of love I feel, when I feel it. I try to let go of disturbed feelings when they arise and challenge the fears that inhibit my adventuresome spirit. And, I choose to treat death as a future great adventure into the unknown. As one favorite poet, Rebecca del Rio, says, "Live the life that chooses you . . ."

ONE POWERFUL DECISION CHANGED EVERYTHING

JANE BYTHEWAY

I COUNT myself lucky that until June 2007, I'd always enjoyed meeting new people—and public speaking, for that matter. I loved connecting and sharing ideas, helping others to feel at ease, and finding out about them—what makes them tick, why they do what they do, what their hopes and dreams are, and anything else they are open to sharing.

Whether I was at a party, a new zumba class, or a business networking event, whatever the occasion, the conversation usually followed a similar pattern, "How is the weather?" (What else, in Britain?), "How do you know the host?" etc. Then the discussion would become a little more personal, "What do you do?" and "Do you have children?" These were all pretty safe and easy territory—or so I thought—as I loved talking about my boys, Liam and Matthew, and the adventures that we had together.

I had negotiated my corporate marketing role down to three days per week when Liam was born in 1995. And after Matthew arrived two years later, I started my coaching business—ultimately transitioning to full self-employment in early 2000. My job suited my idea of how I wanted to be as a mum.

I loved the walk to and from school every day, catching up with my boys about the day's events, having their friends over for tea, and watching and helping them learn and grow. Sometimes, we'd cycle to school. Or they would ask me to bring scooters at home time, and I'd ride on one scooter with the other one folded up in a bag over my shoulder, much to the amusement of the secondary school children I would pass on the way.

Sadly, one part of family life did not turn out as anticipated. The boys' father and I had separated and divorced in 2003 when they were just five and seven years old. I felt sad that we had become a broken family, and we made every effort to ensure that they had a good relationship with both of us. At my place, we became a gang of three—Jane and the boys. I was determined that life would still be an adventure, weaving in some wonderful trips that included camping, youth hostelling, celebrating New Year in London, and saving up for holidays in Florida and Italy. I had plenty to talk about whenever I met new people at networking events.

And then everything changed. On June 20, 2007, I had to say the hardest words of my life. In the entrance hall of a Sikh temple, where Liam was on a school trip, I knelt down, took him in my arms, and told him, "I'm so sorry . . . Matthew died this morning." Matthew had been in hospital for four days after having his appendix removed. There were complications because it turned out that his appendix had been leaking for some time before it was removed, but it was a shock to everyone, including the medical team, that he had died.

So instead of enjoying those getting-to-know-you conversations as I had in the past, I found myself not knowing how I would answer when the topic focused on children. It felt like such a huge thing to say that I'd had two little boys and that my younger son had died.

I remember saying to a friend that I felt sorry for the other person when I did share what had happened as I could see that some people didn't know what to say, though people generally responded really well. Sometimes, they would say "I'm so sorry" and "I don't know what to say." Some reached out to touch me with tears in their eyes as they tried to imagine how I might be feeling or how they would feel in the same situation. I would often find myself weighing up in the moment of the conversation whether I would see this person again. Should I tell the whole truth or just tell them about Liam, my son who was alive? Sometimes, I did that. And then later in the conversation, I might talk about a holiday with the boys and wonder whether the person I was talking to would pick up the fact that I had only said I had one son yet also referred to the boys.

But whenever I held back from telling the whole truth, it never felt right. At first, I thought it was because I was in some way dishonouring Matthew's memory, but what I came to realise over time was that it was me that I was dishonouring by editing out a part of who I am. Some months after Matthew had died, I remember a friend saying to me, "What I don't want for you is that you are defined by this." I didn't want that either. But it is part, a significant part, of who I am. And what I came to realise was that each time I didn't say the whole truth, I was defining myself as someone who edits out parts of myself in order to fit in and to make other people feel okay.

In 2015, I made a decision: whenever the subject of children comes up, I will always answer with the whole truth. Instead of being on edge and wondering how I would handle the question if it came up, I knew what I would say. That decision was liberating. I no longer edit my story to make it easier to be accepted and to make it easier for others. I feel whole and free. In fact, the connections I make now are often far deeper as other people share the whole version of who they are with me too.

FREEDOM ROYALE

MIKE WEEKS

THERE WERE hundreds of promotional flyers and posters clinging to the walls as tenuously as the people who placed them were clinging to their partially formed dreams. They were tattered, folded, torn, and mostly collected from the exits of nightclubs at 4:00 a.m. or from stacks that tottered for attention each week in record shops. Everything and everyone within the walls were crying out for some yet unknown fulfillment.

The predominant theme of this leering wall mosaic was psychedelic. It offered assurances of long nights of erupting bliss on the dance floors, driven via a total loss of inhibitions as each reveler vibrated to the rhythm of a gazillion megawatts of heavy battering-ram-base electronic music. I was just one of millions of young people taking part in a regular, mass, and uncontrolled experiment in which we gladly marched to a new drumbeat in the hothouse honeymoon embrace of British rave culture.

The space that existed within the walls of the apartment reeked of a deeply unpleasant odor. It hadn't been cleaned in many weeks. And most of the overflowing makeshift ashtrays, cut as they were from plastic water bottles, sat next to empty beer cans that had just enough fluid remaining to emit a heavy odor of sour, rancid yeast and hops, mixed with yet more cigarette and unmentionables.

The single mother of the current occupant had upped and walked out two months previously to live with her new boyfriend. Her son, Mark, had shared five years of school with me, as well as a number of now incomprehensible skirmishes. I disliked him more than I cared to admit. I went along with the general appreciation for his sanctuary from adulthood, solely out of desire to remain amongst other members of the informal gang of friends and misfits, who were my world. Most of us depended upon each other for entertainment, stimulation, and in many ways, emotional survival.

I was envious that at sixteen years old, Mark was now the official occupant of this tiny apartment block squat and would remain so until the council found a way to remove him for nonpayment of rent. That sorry residence represented freedom and had become the focal point for my friends and me. On any given day, there might be a dozen or more 50cc mopeds scattered outside, along with an excess of that number of teenagers within its walls. We drank cheap alcohol, smoked marijuana, and ate as much junk food as we could afford. This combination was our midweek opium that provided disconnection from the need to consider our futures.

And yet we still planned, mostly our attendance, at one of the raves that were sweeping the country and whose advertising adorned the walls. It was both simultaneously liberating, as well as an oppressive period in my life. All my friends were sixteen or seventeen years old. We had mostly all dropped out of further education and were passing our days playing cards with the money the government allotted us under the title of bridging allowance, which was code for half of what we'll get on the dole at eighteen years old.

We were a volatile bunch. Most days saw some form of physical infighting amongst us. And verbal abuse wasn't just common, it was the creative extent of our communication. In some way, either individually or collectively, we were all horribly passive. We were waiting for something to happen to us, or for us, or because of us. But until something happened, the pattern was repeated: We'd meet at the flat, go to the betting shop, return, and engage in the same activities as the day before and the day before that until a dispute or real-life crime drama came our way—including police chases that were becoming a common form of exercise to some of our more defiant friends.

Most of my friends and I were still living at home for one reason only: we couldn't afford not to. In my home, overbearing parental control and daily fights were reduced only by my committed absence. It was an elegant solution to the anger and contempt I felt for the grown-ups in my life. I simply stayed away from them all as much as possible. The gods were thanked regularly for the freedom afforded me by a beat-up Suzuki moped. Whilst fuel slopped in its tank, it enabled a mode of exploration unmatched by feet alone.

A week before my seventeenth birthday, I'd allocated a morning to shop for a new pair of trainers. Near to the sports shop was a camping and outdoor store. I had twenty-five pounds in my back pocket when I curiously entered to inspect their camping and rock climbing equipment, with a dream of soon owning my own rope and harness. I had rock climbed with a school teacher and a friend's father on a half-dozen occasions and was hooked on the idea of one day being a climber myself.

I knew I was naturally competent at the movements that make a good climber, and I appreciated, rather than feared, the buzz it gave my nervous system. However, I had yet to lead a climb in which the risk from a fall makes the ascent all the more meaningful, exciting, and dangerous. This step in progression required considerably more knowledge and practice, but I knew instinctively that it held a form or pattern of experience that suited me.

When I left the YHA store, I no longer had enough money for shoes. I held in my arms a coffee table photography book called *Rocks around the World*. The book documented a year in the life of a legendary German climber named Stefan Glowacz as he undertook a global rock climbing adventure like no other.

The first picture I gazed upon left me slack-jawed. And most notably, for the first time I could remember, I experienced wonder or maybe it was awe. The images in my new purchase were crisp, richly colored windows into an exotic world I could never have imagined to exist. Each chapter told the story of Glowacz in a dazzlingly different location, clinging waterdrop-like to a featured wall of limestone, sandstone, or granite.

Successive images lit up my nervous system to the point where I believed I could feel the texture of each pocketed rock face and viscerally sense the expansive void of exposure that comes from moving confidently on fingers and toes despite being thousands of feet above the ground. Images of rope-free ascents triggered the shadow tremors of fear in my muscles that in real life would paralyze me in positions where paralysis meant death.

Picture after picture punched a hole of awareness into the claustrophobic enclosure that had, until then, been my reality. The lid was lifting on the container for how I thought the world was and might always be. I converted the information from the body positions, facial expressions, and muscular tension of climbers in those images and made it into meaning that would fit my own deepest desires. This was not just a book to me, it was a clarion call— one in which images of the protagonist blasted a form of message into my brain's visual centre, the reverberations of which were experienced throughout my entire body.

The message was clear. Rock climbing could be my liberation and path to freedom from this monotonous vacuum I existed in. A seismic shift occurred in my nervous system, heralded by a deep discomfort in the form of an ever-increasing impatience for anything that was not represented in this new vision. Above everything in my life, I craved freedom, and now I knew what it looked like.

With my impatience on hyperdrive, I would not and could not wait. The tinder had received the spark and was now consuming all the oxygen around me. By the time I'd got home, without new shoes, the book had been scanned twice, cover to cover. By the time I'd owned the book for a week, I had read and absorbed every square inch of every page. I knew every caption and held my truth like an evangelist holds a Bible. Untouched as I was by any god, I lay awake at night, ablaze with visions of distant lands and high adventure.

In the first wave of excitement, I had attempted to translate what this all meant to my friends. Maybe one or two of them would appreciate the message and then join me with their own dreams of foreign places and exotic adventures. Alas, my friends were more interested in the promises from their immediate world, not least of all the posters and flyers on the flat's wall.

I arrived to see that wall on a sunny afternoon and entered to low-key greetings. My discomfort was elevated to and perfectly matched by the usual stench and disorder. For ten minutes, I tuned out to the usual chatter whilst tuning in to the silent wondering that was my constant internal voice. It questioned over and over, *How am I going to travel the world as a rock climber?*

No member of my family had ever been on an adventure or labeled himself or herself as a climber or traveller. In my mother's case, she had rarely left her hometown of Bristol for more than a day of her adult life. My family and circle of friends had little desire to step beyond their comfort zones, and certainly, no member of my family had conjured a dream and then committed to living it. Instead, they bought football pool cards, smoked endless cigarettes (my adult lungs still sometimes remind me of the sixteen years of daily passive smoking), and watched endless TV—morning to night.

It was assumed I would follow suit and adhere to an unspoken constraint that people like me from places like mine stayed right where life had landed us. I sat in one of the haggard chairs as my mind offered up a particularly compelling image from the book. Each time I recalled the images, it would trigger a synesthetic rush, charging my neurology and nerve endings to experience the tiny sandstone edges under my fingertips. With eyes open but not seeing, I sensed the vast void of space under my feet and connected to the shifting of bodyweight as I delicately balanced up the ladder of crystals that my climbing German hero balanced on in the photos. Those photos now seemed to be absorbed deep into my neurons.

Except now, as I dropped into another daydream trance, there was no photo or book to look at, only me, experiencing what I assumed such moments of near levitation would be like. In a way, that moment was my step into a new world, whilst remaining sat in the old. The rush of images and sounds was *it*—the signal. Desire for freedom now trampled any illusion of binds. Clarity came in two words, "Go now." All previously conceived hurdles to my dream could be ascended as my version of reality heaved open, and my agitated self came alive as if on a rock face painted with anarchy symbols.

Clarity and certainty make an impressive cocktail. This blend might be called a Freedom Royale and would be consumed in celebration of my departure from this place and any other that held the faintest hint of my young seventeen-year history. Each of us in the room had longed for an "anything else," and now at least one of us was clear what that was.

I stood to the sensation of another debut. Congruency: my thoughts, words, and feelings met and matched my actions in one effortless motion for the first time. I smiled and spoke neutrally to my friends, a number of whom I'd grown up with since we were little kids.

"I'm done, lads. I'm leaving to travel the world and become a rock climber. I want to go live in France and America and Australia and . . ."

I trailed off to allow for the laughter and sarcasm.

I gave it one more chance. "I'm serious. This is it. I'm out of here. This is my goodbye to you all."

One of my friends quipped, "See you tonight then, Weeksy?" More laughter.

I smiled, took one final glance upon my past, and then walked out, never to see any of my friends again.

THE POND OF FREEDOM

JOHN ODA

AS A child, I ran freely through wide, flat orchards of almond trees and explored a sparkling pond filled with cool green water. I observed with amazement the cycle of life as tiny tadpoles grew into round, fat frogs, sitting contently along the quiet shores. I would lie for hours under broad willow trees that surrounded the pond, gazing into the light that filtered through the swaying branches as the wind whispered songs of freedom to me. Life was simple in those early years.

My childhood was filled with safety, warmth, and peace. But at some point, around the age of thirteen, things began to change. There was a voice that started to grow louder in my head and it began to vibrate the core of my being. That voice said something like this, *This is a racist, cruel world.* It was no coincidence that around that same period, I learned for the first time what had happened during WWII to my parents, all my aunts and uncles, and my grandparents. They were unjustly thrown into prisons. Their only crime was being of Japanese heritage. That mass incarceration was the crucible in which much of my anger, negativity, and fear were forged.

Although I was of above-average intelligence, my grades started to slip, and darkness surrounded me in a thick shadow. Anger and rage became my everyday companions. The chatter became more pronounced, *It is an unjust, unsafe world. Watch out.*

In high school, my perspective on the world shifted. I discovered the key to a safe and secure life—alcohol. That amazing elixir could make the grayest mornings bright. When that same voice whispered in my ear, *This is an unsafe place*, I was now armed with a way to change my view of the world. I had found magic in the bottle.

For the next twenty years, I ran far, fast, and hard. I created a whole lot of wreckage with my disregard. I would do anything to stay in orbit, floating above this prejudiced world and its harsh realities. I lied. I cheated. I stole. But as false gods do, that amazing key to life turned on me eventually. I swung closely by some near misses, some dark caves, and some thoughts of ending it all. I knew it was only a matter of time before that darkness would take me out. I knew something had to change. Out of desperation, I decided to put down that once magic elixir and clean up my life just in time for my thirty-fourth birthday. In the ensuing process, I decided I needed to clean up the mess I made in the preceding years of my chaotic life as best as I could.

With the help of a spiritual director, I made a list of the people and places that I had harmed. Most of the names at the top of my list were family members and friends, but also near the top of my list was a grocery store in my hometown. I had to calculate how much I owed that store due to my prolific shoplifting. The amount, which included interest, was in the thousands. I was willing to pay the money back because I wanted to change my life. I yearned to get back to some modicum of the freedom I felt as a child.

It was a sunny summer morning when the time came to travel back to my hometown and make things right with the store in question.

The drumbeat of fear began to mount as I got closer. *They are going to arrest you and throw you in jail. It is an unjust world, don't you remember?* I pulled into the parking lot and completely froze. Unable to move and barely able to breath, I sat there and prayed, something that I had not done in many years. I mumbled a plea to God for help. I remembered at the age of six how one Sunday school teacher tried to teach us how to pray.

"But who are we praying to?" I asked.

"God, of course," replied the teacher.

"But how do I know God hears me if I can't see him?" I wanted to know.

"Oh, he hears us. It says so in the Bible," she said with a sense of assurance that even at that age, I knew I would never have. Her answers were completely lacking for me. Soon thereafter, I decided I would never pray to a god that I could not see.

But sitting in that car on that sunny summer afternoon, I prayed with a fervor that only a desperate man can do. Suddenly, I had a sort of out-of-body experience. I was looking down at myself from above my car. My childhood flashed in front of my eyes. I remembered the pond and sitting under wide willow trees. I could almost feel and hear the breeze through the branches. I still could not move.

And then a small voice whispered to me, "Let go of the steering wheel. Open the car door. Put one foot out. Put the other foot out." And so it went, "Open the car door. Close the car door. Walk to the front door." Before I knew it, I found myself in the store in front of the store manager with my heart pounding, my hands sweaty, and my mind racing.

"What can I do for you, son?" he asked, pulling me back into the reality of the situation at hand. I slowly explained that as a young kid, I had stolen a lot from that very store, and I was there to pay the money back. For a moment, that familiar negative voice popped back into my head, *This is where he calls the cops and has you arrested.*

The store manager stared blankly at me with a look of disbelief. Finally, he responded, "Ummm, we can't take your money, son." My spiritual director and I had anticipated this answer, so I said back to him, "Is there a charity where I can donate the money I owe in the name of this store?" Again, I got the blank stare.

"No there is not. I'm sorry," he said. The manager fidgeted as if he had other things to do. "Is there anything else I can do for you?"

I said, "No that is all I needed, I suppose. Thank you for your time." As I turned to walk away, I was secretly overjoyed that I did not have to shell out the money. I exhaled for what felt like the first time in days.

"Hey!" I was about thirty feet away when he shouted, and I knew exactly what this meant. This is where he finally calls the cops. *They will haul you away, and there is nothing you will be able to do about it.* I slowly turned to see him walking toward me. His puzzled look had turned into a slight smile.

"Hey, son, I don't know what you're doing with your life, but you are on the right track."

"Thank you," I managed to say. I walked back to my car and sat. There was no chatter. The world, even with its imperfections, was a fine place to be. I felt solitude. I felt free. I closed my eyes, and suddenly, I was filled with a childlike wonder. I was sitting by that quiet pond, the water's glistening and fat frogs sitting serenely along the shore.

I could feel the warmth of the sun shining through the window. Years of tightly held and constricted emotions came bursting forth. I don't know how long I sat there in my car, but I quietly sobbed for what felt like a lifetime. I could almost hear the sound of the wind through the willows singing to me, *You are free.*

Since that moment, fear has come and gone through my life. But that voice, that fearful part of me, has never returned with the same fierceness. When it does return, I simply say, "Thank you for sharing, but you're wrong." And I continue along this journey of life.

EPIPHANY ON EPIPHANY

DEB CELEC

IT WAS thirty years ago—on January 6, 1987, Epiphany—that my mother took her last breath. She was fifty-six.

Many years before, when I was eight years old, my mother was hospitalized for what we now know to be bipolar disorder. Her initial hospitalization was for a few weeks, and the second time in 1974 lasted for a month. I have no recollection of third grade.

I do have vivid memories of visiting my mother in the Northside Hospital psych ward with my father in October of 1974. We walked into her room one evening and witnessed her waving to an imaginary person outside the window. She was diagnosed as having both manic-depressive and schizoaffective disorders. Her psychiatrist told us he had never seen both of those present at the same time. I struggled to understand it all and wondered why my mother couldn't just get a grip on her life. *Why couldn't she control her emotions? Why couldn't she stop this nonsense?* I was crushed, but I held back my tears. I had to be strong and in control. I was never ever letting go of control.

As my father and I walked down the cascading concrete steps to the car that day, I looked over at him and said, "I would understand if you wanted to leave her. It's okay with me." He took my hand and, without hesitation, said, "Debbie, you don't leave someone who is ill. Your mother has a mental illness, and she needs treatment." I didn't appreciate his commitment to my mother until years later, when he demonstrated his love and devotion once again as she battled breast cancer.

My mother was a beautiful woman with a creative gift, an expressive nature, a contagious laugh, and a kind heart. And she loved her five children. However, with any given episode of mental illness, her joy would be sucked out of her, leaving her flat and emotionally exhausted for weeks at a time. Ultimately, her illness affected our relationship as she was incapable of expressing kindness and love or expressing the most basic maternal instincts.

Difficulties arose as I struggled to reconcile my feelings for my "normal" mother with my broken mother. As I tried to understand her invisible disease, my defenses grew stronger. Maintaining control over my life was imperative.

During the summer of 1968, when I was in that stage when a young girl experiences physiological changes, I made a vow to never have children. For years, I didn't completely understand where my decision came from. It wasn't until I was forty that I finally recognized it was connected to my mother's inability to nurture me.

I worked through most of my childhood/parent issues and came to the same conclusion so many others have: my mother had done the best she could at the time. Yes, I had forgiven her, though I'd made a conscious decision to be anything that my mother was not.

My mother's days of depression outnumbered her days of mania, and they came and went until her diagnosis of breast cancer in 1979.

Oddly, the mental issues virtually disappeared once she began the cancer fight. While confronting this new disease, she demonstrated courage, fortitude, and faith. It was as though her desire to live and enjoy her family and her life had been awakened.

On this past anniversary of my mother's death, I wanted to honor her memory with a Facebook tribute as most of my FB friends and acquaintances had never met her. As I shuffled through dozens of old photographs that varied in size and quality, some faded color and a few black and white, I saw a glimpse of my past resurface.

Some photos triggered good memories, and others, not so good. Hours passed as I teased a few pictures out from the pack and put them aside, using other photos to create an album that depicted the way I remembered her, a glamorous, expressive, one-of-a-kind woman. My mother's smile was beautiful and, when she was happy and content, her eyes glistened. She was genuine and transparent, so whether she was happy or sad, it was real and it showed.

I posted the album to Facebook with a heartfelt tribute. I then looked at the photos I had put to the side. The pictures were from a trip to the Bahamas and a stop in Miami at the Fontainebleau Hotel. One picture was of my dad and me, and the other, of me and my mom. Those photos, taken in April 1970, revealed indisputable evidence. Looking at them, I observed that though my mother and I were standing together about six inches apart, there was no physical contact. In the picture of my dad and me, he had his arm around me and was holding me close.

I stared at the pictures in utter amazement. I was not imaging this. I had been right all along. My mother was not nurturing. The more pictures I examined, the more evidence I found to support how I'd felt. Suddenly, I saw her differently, and a piece of the puzzle fell into place.

In that moment, I thought of the analogy where life is compared to a tapestry. The tapestry's underside has a chaotic array of colored threads with no rhythm or reason, but when you turn the tapestry over, you see the beautifully woven picture on the top side. That is what I see now, a beautifully woven tapestry of my life.

Looking at those pictures was an epiphany for me. I realized my mother couldn't give me what she didn't have. Something in her past must have contributed to her inability to show affection. Although I may never know the event in her life that affected her, I believe with all my heart that my mother loved me deeply. And I loved her.

Until we meet again on the other side of heaven, her beautiful spirit lives on.

TEA WITH MS. SOPHIA

RICHIE CASTRO

"OUR NEIGHBORS are jerks. How am I ever going to learn to sing if they keep calling the police when I practice?" I continued to grumble to myself as I packed away my microphone. My roommate, Tom, had been sitting quietly at my bedroom desk. When he finally spoke, he asked, "What did the police say this time?" As I struggled with the mic cables, I said, "They warned me that if I get one more noise complaint, they are going to write me a ticket. Stupid neighbors! My mic wasn't even turned up loud." Tom paused, then replied, "Well, maybe they're not complaining about the volume." I looked up at him, puzzled. "Well, dude, you sing out of key a lot." I had no idea what that meant as I had no musical experience. I couldn't tell if I was singing in key or out of key. Tom was a saxophone player in our college marching band, so I figured he was probably right. That's when I asked Tom to help me to learn to sing in key.

I had Tom sit in front of me while I sang along with my favorite Bon Jovi song. I asked him to signal me every time he heard me sing out of key. I figured this would be a good way to hear or feel what I was doing wrong. Tom pushed play on my stereo. The Bon Jovi rock guitars rang out, and as the lyrics came, I started to sing. I wasn't two words in when Tom yelled, "There! You're out of key. There! You're out of key again. There, there, and there!" Man, I couldn't sing more than a word without Tom yelling "There!" It was all pretty discouraging. And the worst part was, I couldn't hear the difference between when I was in key or out of key. It all sounded the same. After we finished, Tom tried consoling me a bit, "Dude, it's not really your fault. You're probably just tone-deaf." And there it was. That was the story I carried for years. I liked to sing, but I was tone-deaf.

In 1993, I graduated from college. On my drive home to Denver, Colorado, I had my windows down and the radio blasting. I was singing at the top of my lungs and felt as free as a bird. School was behind me, and I knew I could do anything I wanted. On that drive home, I decided to take a hard look at that old singing story. I liked to sing, so why couldn't I learn to be a good singer? I decided I was going to take my first real step toward doing just that.

As soon as I got to Gramma's place, I flipped open the yellow pages and started calling different voice teachers. It was all just too expensive. I was about to call it quits when I spotted a tiny ad at the bottom of the page. It read, "Learn to sing from Colorado's most experienced voice teacher." I dialed the number. When it picked up, I could hear someone fumbling with the receiver. Finally, an old woman's voice said, "Hallo?" I sat up straight. "Yes, hello. I'm calling about singing lessons." The old woman on the other end began to speak. It was a bit difficult to understand what she was saying because of her thick eastern European accent. "I charge fifteen dollars for one hour." I tried to control my excitement. That was half the cost of the other teachers. "I would like to take a lesson from you. Are you accepting new students?"

"You can come this afternoon," she said. She began to give me her address, and before I knew it, she was saying goodbye.

I said, "I'm sorry, I didn't catch your name."

"My name is Sophia, Ms. Sophia."

I got out of my car and slowly walked up the sidewalk to Ms. Sophia's house. When I reached the front door, I kicked away some old newspapers and knocked. I heard the locks unfastening from the inside. When the door opened up, the sunlight spread across Ms. Sophia's face. She had white hair, pale skin, and was around five feet tall with a slight hunch in her posture. Her eyes were a dark blue, and one of them drifted far off to the left. She looked like she was in her late nineties, but she moved and spoke as someone much younger.

She invited me into her house, and the first thing I noticed were all the shelves covered with books and record albums. Against the wall near the kitchen was an old piano with a mountain of sheet music piled on top. Ms. Sophia asked, "What type of tea would you like?" I said it didn't matter. She responded, "Okay then, I will give you my favorite. It's good for the voice." She motioned for me to sit at the kitchen table. I remembered feeling strangely comfortable with Mrs. Sophia because she talked to me as if we knew each other from before and as if I was a singing colleague from her past. I liked that.

Over an hour passed before we finished off the last bit of tea. Ms. Sophia talked nonstop about everything from knickknack collections to philosophy. But no matter what she was talking about, she always seemed to bring the subject back to singing. I enjoyed listening to Ms. Sophia's old stories. At one point, she shared some photos from her time as a professional vocalist. They were old, cracked, black-and-white promotional photos. She also busted out some old opera records and played them on her turntable. As I flipped through her music collection, to my surprise, I found three Frank zappa albums. She said Frank zappa was a true artist.

Before I knew it, three hours had passed. Ms. Sophia announced that it was time for her dinner. I was a bit disappointed because she never asked me to sing. As I was getting up from the table, Ms. Sophia said, "I'm not sure if you can be my student." I looked at her curiously. She continued, "I don't know if I like your voice." I perked up, thinking she was going to ask me to sing, but she didn't. She only said, "Next lesson, I will evaluate." I paid Ms. Sophia for three hours of singing lessons, and we said our goodbyes.

I was a little bent on my drive home. I paid all that money, and I never even came close to singing. All she did was *talk* about singing. The following days, I thought a lot about the things Ms. Sophia had said. "Artists are the closest people to God. Singers are special, as they don't need any tools to create their art, just their voice."

Ms. Sophia explained that our voice is a divine tool for connecting. She said, "When we sing, we open to the heavens and all that is around us. You can find people from small village tribes to big city neighborhoods singing in ceremonies of celebrations. Singing projects human expression, sorrow, anger, joy, and love. Singing is something all people desire. Singing is the purest expression of the soul." I guess this explains why most people are scared to death to sing in front of anyone. It exposes our depths.

During my second lesson, I once again found myself drinking tea at the kitchen table. There was more talk about life and how it all related to singing. Ms. Sophia believed that everyone could sing. In her opinion, it was only a matter of confidence. I thought to myself, *How can this be? After all, I was tone-deaf and sang out of key.* Ms. Sophia said that small children naturally open their mouths and sing. These little artists are with true expression.

"Somewhere along the way, children tend to have their confidence taken from them. Someone says to Jonny, 'Your voice is loud' or 'You sound strange when you talk or laugh.' These types of comments are confidence killers and lead to a person closing their voice off to the world and the divine."

Ms. Sophia continued to explain that most adults are too shy to sing. They say "I can't sing" or "I only sing when no one is listening." However, it was these words that stayed with me: "It is important not to forget that singing is an art. There's no right or wrong in artistic expression, only truth."

Ms. Sophia got up from the table and walked over to the piano. She sat down and placed her hands on the keyboard. She turned toward me and said, "For a teacher to build confidence, they must like the art of the student." She motioned for me to stand next to the piano. "I want to hear your voice."

I felt my throat tighten up as I stood from the table and awkwardly walked toward her. Ms. Sophia, noticing how nervous I was, pulled her legs from underneath the piano to face me. She placed her hand on my forearm and said, "Relax. I just want you to sing to me."

I felt completely off-balance. "Uh, okay. What do you want me to sing?"

She gently squeezed my forearm and said, "I want you to sing 'Happy Birthday' just like you've sung it your whole life. Just sing me 'Happy Birthday.'" She closed her eyes and sat back.

I was confused, but I took a deep breath and started to sing. "Happy birthday to you. Happy birthday to you. Happy birthday, Ms. Sophia. Happy birthday to you."

When I finished, it felt like an eternity before Ms. Sophia opened her eyes. When she finally did, she smiled and simply said, "Good. I like your voice."

I wish I could say that I ended up as Ms. Sophia's favorite student and that she turned me into a singing Jedi. But the truth of the matter is I was a restless young grasshopper, impatient and full of expectations. I couldn't get over the fact that I had spent hours with Ms. Sophia, and all I had done was sing "Happy Birthday." At the end of that second lesson, I concluded that Ms. Sophia was merely a nice, lonely old woman—but not the singing teacher I was looking for. I wanted a do-re-mi drill sergeant.

Unfortunately, I never went back to Ms. Sophia. Instead, I took the long way around to becoming a singer. Yes, I did learn to sing. I have been making a living with my singing for twenty years now. But it has only been in the last five years that I really stepped into being a singing artist. Ms. Sophia was light-years ahead of me. I could have shortened the road to becoming an artist if I would have recognized that the nice, lonely old lady was a singing guru, speaking truth.

Today, whenever I hear people say, "I can't sing," I imagine myself at Ms. Sophia's kitchen table, listening to her stories and to every word she is saying. But this time, I am really hearing what she is saying. "Every person can sing. The voice is a divine gift. It is important to unblock and free your voice because the expression of the human voice can move mountains. The world dances to those who sing."

VEGETABLES, A RABBIT, AND ME

RUSSELL DAVIS

I AM aware that many men who are diagnosed with infertility can feel less of a man in some way, unable to fulfil their primal role. Personally, my primary response was more a shock and a blind panic of realising that my subconscious strategy for happiness had come off the rails. I genuinely believed that having children would bring the contentment I had been seeking all my life, and now I was being told it was not an option. This prompted a lot of deep reflection and a strong desire to take myself away from life, to retreat, and to go to a place where I could just be alone.

In the beginning, my wife and I had told ourselves that infertility wasn't a problem. We worked with young people running youth groups, summer camps, and respite foster care. Our lives were full of children. We also believed that there were many children in need of love and care, so we could always explore fostering or adoption at some point.

Then seven years into the journey, we were told having children of our own was a genuine possibility. We allowed ourselves to become excited about this again. When I thought about being a father, my insides lit up and became tingly with excitement as I allowed myself to recognise my deep desire to be one. I realised I could stop kidding myself, stop trying to protect myself from the pain and heartache, and allow myself to be honest about my deepest desires.

So we began trying. But after almost another year, we found our initial diagnosis had been incomplete. And I was, in fact, infertile. I shall never forget the doctor asking me whether I had been exposed to dangerous levels of radiation. It felt like I was in a parallel universe — that it wasn't really happening to me. I already thought that life could be cruel, and then it dealt us this card. As if eight years of heartache were not enough, having thought we had finished running that particular marathon, it was like being told we had to do it all over again. Only this time, it was far more difficult, and the chances of succeeding were far smaller.

So I retreated and found myself as the guest of a community of nuns at a convent, contemplating their vegetable garden and life.

As I sat in the beautiful gardens, my gaze moved to two vegetable patches. One full of succulent vegetables—row upon row of lush green vegetation. The other—a scrubby patch of soil—a few lonely weeds were the only sign of life.

Struck by the stark contrast between the two, my eyes came to rest upon the empty one. It felt like my life—barren and empty. Everyone else's life seemed to mirror the other one—vibrant and full of things that bring them happiness. Life appeared to be easier for them. For some reason, true happiness and contentment felt harder for me to achieve. *Perhaps I don't deserve life to be easy, or perhaps I haven't worked hard enough for the happiness they appear to access so effortlessly*, I thought.

I was not truly happy. This was a revelation for me. I had many pleasurable things in my life. I worked really hard, striving for the things in life that I believed would bring happiness—the school grades, the degree, the successful career with the good pension, a lovely wife, plenty of friends, and a spiritual faith.

How come I have so studiously done all my homework, been the good boy, and yet life seems like a continual struggle to just keep from feeling like something is missing?

So I sat, contemplating the difficulties of life. Suddenly, one of the nuns approached me. Out of the blue, she handed me a small bundle of fur. It was a baby rabbit that had been caught by one of the nun's many cats. She didn't know what to do about it, so she brought it to me. At first I was annoyed. *Why has she given it to me? I am here to get some space for reflection and to be left alone.*

I looked down at the tiny rabbit cupped in my hands with its soft brown fur and its eyes closed. It was panting rapidly. I could not see any obvious signs of injury, but it was clearly in a state of distress. I was pretty sure it was going to die.

As I looked at this beautiful, helpless little creature, I felt an immense wave of sadness. I couldn't bear the thought of it dying alone. I know I was engaging in anthropomorphism, but I couldn't help the wave of sadness and grief building up inside of me. *Does this little baby rabbit know it is loved?* I didn't want it to die alone, not knowing. I began to cry. The crying turned to sobbing. It surprised me because I usually live in my head so I don't have to feel my emotions. I sobbed for this rabbit, but of course, I was really sobbing for me.

Do I feel loved? Do I allow myself to be loved?

I knew on a conscious level that my wife loved me, as did my family and friends.

But how loved do I feel? Do I really know it in my heart?

The answer was a resounding *No!*

After what felt like hours grieving for this rabbit and grieving for myself, a feeling of peace began to grow in me, like the calm after a storm. All was quiet within. It was a feeling of space, so restful and soothing.

As I continued to sit, these feelings manifested an even deeper sense of peace. I felt loved and lovable. I felt alive in a way I had never experienced. I felt both a grounding and a calming sense of peace and love. I felt so alive to my senses and the moment, in a more vivid way than I had ever experienced.

For the first time, I could see through the illusion I'd created in my mind—the illusion that my happiness was dependent on something else I had yet to achieve or create in my life.

Subconsciously, I had been getting more and more desperate for this elusive happiness and deep fulfillment. Having children was simply the latest condition to which I had attached my happiness. I had believed that having children was a sign of a new season for my life and was going to be the gateway to true contentment.

With the rabbit in my hands, I made a decision: I am going on a journey. I am going to start living the life I want rather than the life I think others expect of me. I am going to do more things I enjoy just for the hell of it, and I am going to play more. "Follow your bliss" is my mantra from now on.

I looked up at the vegetable patches. I looked at the empty one.

Yes, that is my life. It's not full of thriving vegetables, but it is a blank canvas—a fertile soil ready to support new life.

HOW CHANGING ONE WORD CHANGED EVERYTHING

ANN SKINNER

I SAT at the dinner table, trying to eat the food my husband had prepared that evening, but I just couldn't. Instead, I was swallowing the tears that were sticking in my throat.

I had come home that day feeling confused and misunderstood as a conflict at work had escalated. The conflict had been brewing for some time, but until then, I had not been able to talk about the situation to anyone, not even my husband. I felt ashamed, sad, and confused; and I didn't know how to wrap words around what had been happening.

Up to that point, I had thought I could handle the situation by myself. But a lifetime of sorting out problems on my own without asking for help was about to cause my downfall. By the time I was ready and able to ask for help, it was too late as the momentum created had carried the conflict past the point of no return. A couple of weeks later, I felt forced to leave my job.

As is so often the case with our deepest, darkest moments, the most painful experiences of our lives can often become the most liberating; and although it didn't feel like it at the time, this was such a moment.

To this day, I am grateful for two things that helped me recover. First, I am grateful for my husband's support. He did not try to judge or fix anything but reassured me by just being there for me whilst I tried to give some sense of meaning to it all.

Second, I was given the gift of time. The gift of contemplation and reflection, which allowed me to create a deeper understanding of why what happened had happened. It also allowed me to slow down and acknowledge the sadness and even the anger at the unfairness and the powerlessness I felt.

I was upset with my colleagues for their backhandedness and disappointed with my manager for not providing the appropriate support. But above all, I was angry with myself for my inability to express myself in a way that might have resolved the situation.

I realised quite quickly, however, that wallowing in sadness and anger wasn't going to help me in the long run. I understood that I had to take a closer look at myself. How had I allowed my voice to be taken away from me? How had I managed to put myself in that position? What had been my "response-ability" in this story?

There was one thing that had confused me throughout the conflict. I thought I had been well-liked. I was known for my empathetic nature. So what had gone wrong? Why had they not believed my good intentions?

After much reflection, it dawned on me that despite my concern for others, my greatest concern had been for myself. At a deeper level, I knew I had been doing things and pleasing people in order to get recognition. I wanted to be certain of my colleagues' appreciation of me. And whatever I did, at some level, I needed to hear that I was good enough. This need for approval made me very uncertain about myself. Over time, it caused me to lose my voice and, with it, my influence.

The other reality was that I had not been happy at work for some time, and I had been trying to hide it. For someone like me who is generally blessed with a happy disposition, feeling unhappy was hard to acknowledge as I felt I had no real reason to be unhappy. I had a decent job, a loving husband and family, good friends, and a comfortable home. Still, I felt unhappy, and this unhappiness had filtered through in my work. Although I had still been putting the work in, in every other way, I had been lacklustre in my participation.

I had initially taken the job because it gave us the financial security we needed at a time when we needed it, but I had felt out of place. And I knew I had outstayed my welcome. A lack of purpose beyond making money kept me from feeling energised by my work and prevented me from contributing fully. For a while, I had been trying to figure out what to do next, but all I knew was that I needed to create more meaning in my life.

For years, my main career question had been "What do I want to do?" It was an ever-persistent question nagging away at me, and one I never received a satisfactory answer to other than "I don't really know." Instead, I just did what I thought I could or should do; and after two-plus years, when the excitement of a new job wore off, my eyes were on the "next adventure" (as I liked to call it). The upside of this was that I had a lot of adventures and had gained a wealth of experience. The downside was that I often felt like a fraud who was about to be found out.

To help ease my troubles, my husband and I went sailing on a beautiful, crisp winter's day. Getting out in nature is always good for gaining perspective, and as I was reflecting on what I was going to do next, I suddenly wondered if instead of asking myself "What do I want to *do*?" I should be asking myself "What do I want to *be*?"

It was a change of one word, but in that moment, I knew everything was going to be all right. As soon as that question popped into my head, I heard the answer loud and clear—I wanted to be wise.

Wow, wise! I thought. *That's a tall order.* But somehow, the answer made perfect sense to me, and it made me feel more excited and alive than I had felt for a long time.

This new insight prompted other questions, such as "In order for me to be wise, what do I need to do?" Ultimately, the questions helped me figure out my next steps and the wisdom I needed to find my way back to myself and reclaim a sense of self.

It's a funny thing about life that when things are right, the Universe gets together and creates magic in the form of opportunity. Not long after that moment of revelation, the perfect job presented itself to me, and I leapt at the chance. This job gave me the scope for the growth I needed and helped me learn more about what motivates and inspires us to act and live the lives we choose to live.

Now, at the time of writing this story, I am exactly ten years older, and I wonder whether I have become "wise." As I reflect on this question, I realise I am now wise enough to know that the more I know, the more I know I don't know. I have started to understand that being wise has little to do with knowing in the conventional sense.

This is a wisdom I am relearning every day as not knowing is still an uncomfortable place for me to be. Not knowing means letting go of control. It means asking for help when I need it, and daring to be vulnerable, which I still find challenging. Wisdom, however, has taught me the truth about vulnerability—which is that vulnerability takes courage even though it feels like weakness.

With wisdom also comes compassion, and that includes compassion for self. Nowadays, when I feel the tears coming, I no longer try to swallow them. I simply let them come and remind myself that I am human and that dark times can turn to light by changing something as small as a word in a question.

THE PROSECCO MOMENT

STACY LYNN FLOYD

IT WAS a typical Upstate New York winter's eve, wet and cold. Somewhere between 5:30 p.m. and 6:00 p.m., I sat on the edge of my single bed, exhaustion from the day's work rising. My heart was heavy with the decision of going or staying. I mentally flipped through all the previously used excuses in search of a new angle or anything that would squelch the building angst and guilt. First the waves of nausea, then the anger began its boil, the guilt taking over and tumbling out.

"I can't do this anymore. I'm tired of making excuses and feeling sick, guilty, and wrong."

My rant was quickly followed by heavy tears. But between the heaving sighs, the arrival of a new angle appeared, not at all what I expected. It felt bold and empowering. The tears and guilt vanished.

And in that moment, I made a decision that would change the path of my life forever. I crossed over a cavernous threshold.

"I'm not going ever again. In fact, I'm going to do whatever I want right now." As a giggle escaped my lips, my head started to fill with a rush of effervescence, exactly the feeling you get when drinking prosecco, like the way it rushes down your throat and fills your body with tingles and joy. But I wasn't drinking anything.

I felt free—a freedom that was so expansive I remembered getting up and swirling around the room. "I can do whatever I want, and I don't care anymore." That initial experience was connected to two decades of fear that just evaporated.

Later I realized that some of the fear was still lingering, but not enough for me to care what they would think or say anymore. I was truly free.

I don't care if I get in trouble or if I get reprimanded. In fact, I'm going to do something really fun this Thursday night. Yes, I'll go to the movies and do the complete opposite of what I'm expected to do. And I'm going to choose a movie a good Christian would never see—an R-rated movie.

An evil, delicious laugh escaped from my throat, and I declared out loud so all of me could hear, "I can do anything I like whenever I want!"

"Really, Stacy?" the little voice replied.

"YES!" I announced even louder. But this time with an inner power that even now as I remember pulls my spine straight and fills my body with breath.

With my heart beating in anticipation of freedom, I pulled out my 1988 newspaper and located the time and location of a movie I'd dreamt of seeing but had not dared to until this moment. As I dressed for the weather, the guilt began its creep back like a composed script inside my head.

At the time, I lived in a private apartment complex that housed many fellow friends of my then religious faith and following.

I was a very, very devoted young Christian woman, who was

awakening to an effervescence of change in my life that I'd never experienced before.

It was like my first glass of prosecco—the effervescence of the bubbles; the rush of that beautiful golden liquid filling the glass; and the bubbles tickling my nose, bursting open on the tongue, and filling me with magic.

In my mind, I didn't care who saw me getting in to my car and going in the opposite direction of where we usually headed on a Thursday eve. But I had my well-rehearsed script ready just in case. I let the fear of being caught fuel me into my car and off to my local cinema.

The cinema was located in a newly built shopping plaza, which added to the taboo of breaking my two-hour, Thursday-night ministry Bible school ritual—a ritual that had been in place since the early years of my life. At that point, I was at least nineteen years indoctrinated in the structure that included guilt and rules.

I can remember the excitement of driving my car into the city with the lights and traffic of other cars out and about on a Thursday night. I was sure many were not on their way to Bible class but, from what I could see, to the shopping mall with me. As I parked my car, I pulled my coat up around my neck, breathing in the cold icy rain as the thrill of entering the theater and buying a ticket increased with every step.

Sitting in the dark theater and sipping my cold soda, the inner bubbles rising in me, my cheeks were bursting from the smile on my face. "I did it! I broke the code." My mind wandered briefly to my friends and family sitting in the hall in service. Once more, a giggle escaped as I sunk down deeper into the seat, letting the flickering shadows of the scenes before me draw me into a world I had only dreamed I could inhabit.

Little did I know, I would be stepping into and through many changes —steps that would profoundly alter the course of my life over the next two years.

I know now that I had a choice. The idea of having a choice may seem ordinary and simple to most, but this new freedom catalyzed the beginning of many roads I would walk and traverse throughout this life. This power of choice would push me up against many fears over and over again, and it would shape who I was always becoming. It also spurred a relentless desire to break a few more taboos—taboos that freed me from a way of life that was no longer resonant with who my true self was aching to become.

I walked away from a religious structure that my parents entered when I was three. I was excommunicated, casted out, shamed, and ignored until I saw the error of not just my actions, but also of the thoughts of freedom and choice that now burned hot. My decisions severed deep connections that ran right through intimate family connections. I excommunicated me from my parents.

As I continue to become, never have I regretted that moment, the choices, or that ultimate decision that rather painfully released me from foundations of guilt and shame into multiple and ongoing prosecco moments of well-being, inner peace, and joy.

I do miss the connections I grew up with for the first twenty years of my life. And as I look back, I am grateful. I am grateful for the experiences I gained during that period of my life, grateful for the beautiful people that nurtured me that I still hold in my heart, and grateful for *every* challenge that occurred in that strict religious environment. I now have tools of inner discipline, a thirst for truth, and the conviction to listen to my inner bubbly.

More than anything, I am grateful for the realization of choice in every moment to respond differently to everything and anything. And I have an innate trust that whatever needs to be done to support that response will show up in grace and love.

What has arisen is a clear commitment to let life flow through me.

It's not always easy, but it is gracefully perfect for me.

These moments, I often sit and wait for that inner voice to arrive and say, *Yes, Stacy. You can.*

And I open to the next experience of life.

RUNNING FREE

NEIL SKINNER

RUNNING FOR me was never an absolute must but always a niggling thought at the back of my mind, like an awkwardly located itch that was difficult to scratch. Why that should be the case took many years and one defining moment to discover.

Several times during my life, I have changed into T-shirt and shorts, laced up my trainers, and headed outside for a run. Full of enthusiasm and purpose, each time I felt I was destined to succeed in becoming the runner I thought I was. Inevitably, by week 3, I was tired, my knee hurt, and the doubts and excuses had crept in; and I would quit again. The gaps between failed attempts went from months to years and then to decades, yet somewhere deep inside, the runner in me was still waiting for another opportunity to succeed.

The opportunity arrived in 2008 when I was forty-nine years old, and living and working in Amsterdam. It came in the form of an invite from my employers to join the newly formed company running team and take part in a local ten-mile business run. With six months to prepare, I added my name to the growing list of volunteers and set about getting fit.

It soon became clear that all those previous attempts at running were not failures but lessons. I resolved to learn from them, follow the advice I'd previously scorned, start slowly, and build up distance gradually. I admit to feeling a little self-conscious as I set off around our local sports field, running for one minute, walking for one minute, increasing the time spent running little by little. Once up to ten minutes of continual running, I found myself enjoying the feeling of setting targets and reaching them, proud of the improvements I was making.

During this initial period of training, I continued to learn from my previous mistakes. I had seldom, in my past efforts, reached the point at which my body had adapted to what it was being asked to do. In my youthful ignorance, I had believed that my body was there to do what it was told and what I dictated and that any negative feelings were my body telling me it was not cut out for running. It was extremely liberating when I understood that during the first five to ten minutes of a run, my body needed time to adapt before it would begin to feel better. I began to listen to my body and work with it toward our common goal—in partnership as opposed to dictatorship.

Race day duly arrived, and with a mixture of excitement and nerves, I set off to run farther than I had ever run before. An hour and thirty-one minutes later, I crossed the finish line, exhausted yet elated at having managed to run ten miles. By this time, I was well acquainted with Mr. Runner's High and enjoyed hanging out with him, following most long training runs. What I had not expected was a visit from his cousin, Mr. Post-Race Runner's Low, who informed me that if I wished to carry on hanging out with his cousin, I was going to need a pretty strong reason to continue running.

Over the next few years, not wishing to lose my newfound fitness, I continued to run and compete in occasional races. I had progressed from ten miles to a half marathon and had my sights set on the Amsterdam Marathon scheduled for October 2012. *Could I really run*

26.2 miles? Would that then fulfil the as yet unexplained need in me? Was the itch about to get scratched?

In August 2012, my wife and I went on holiday to Australia, visiting old friends on Great Keppel Island at the southern edge of the Great Barrier Reef. This beautiful island boasts seventeen white-sand beaches along its forty-three-kilometer circumference, as well as numerous bushwalks through its interior, all just waiting for me to put on my running shoes. Having enjoyed two short runs and several walks with my wife to get a feel for the island, I planned a more adventurous run from Fisherman's Beach on the west coast to Bald Rock Point Lighthouse on the east coast.

Under blue skies and sunshine, I set off at a steady pace, first on road, then on a dirt track leading to narrow trails that weaved their way through the bush to the top of Mount Wyndham, the island's highest point. The views were spectacular and revealed that the onward route to Bald Rock Point was going to be more challenging. It seemed most hikers turned around here and retraced their steps, leaving the trail ahead overgrown and indistinct. After a slow and tricky descent, I picked up the main track leading out to the lighthouse at Bald Rock Point. Once there, I sat with my back against the lighthouse wall and ate the few snacks I'd carried with me, enthralled as a white-breasted sea eagle hovered over Red Beach to my right, while several humpback whales passed close to the shore in front of me on their annual migration to the north to breed.

Feeling blessed, I set off running home, shirtless in the afternoon heat, cooled by a faint sea breeze. Almost immediately, I knew something was different. There was a spring to my step, a lightness more akin to skipping than running. I seemed to be floating over the ground, overwhelmed with joy when the realisation struck me that this was why I run. This was the feeling imbedded in some early memory that caused the itch I'd been unable to scratch.

Here I was at fifty-four years of age, a child again, reliving the joy from doing something for no other reason than the sheer joy of doing it. I knew then, as I ran, that while physically able, I would always be a runner. It was also very clear to me that this had little to do with running and everything to do with the freedom to feel and express joy as a child does when at play, unencumbered by the baggage of adulthood.

Running had been the route I took to reconnect with my inner child and once again feel what it is to be truly free, free to be just me and running free.

FROM ONE LIFE INTO ANOTHER

LEIGH TILLEY

S-DAY

IT HADN'T occurred to me that I was not happy.

I'd been stuck in a routine for so long—wake up, drive to the station, get the tube to work, firefight problems, and deal with tricky and technical situations all day long, day in and day out, because the job was well paid, and I had a big mortgage.

Autopilot.

Habit.

Now it is a totally false expectation to believe that one can be ecstatic 100 percent of the time. However, we should feel comfortable, relaxed, and safe for a large percentage of it.

It was July 2, 2013, and I was driving to work. I was sitting in traffic, and I felt shattered. I was exhausted in the tired-but-wired style rather than merely sleepy. I was anxious, edgy, and nervous. I did not feel like myself at all.

I had not slept properly for months. The erosion of my previous relationship weighed heavily on my mind and deprived my mind of calm and stillness. We were at different points of experience in our respective stories, and it was clear that we approached life differently. I had begun the process of selling my house and buying a new apartment closer to the city to start a new life—a life full of clarity and positivity.

My mind snapped back to where I was. I sat there in the traffic, constantly rubbing my sore neck as my gaze wandered to the other people all stuck there too, all becoming more and more impatient as they were probably late for work.

I saw an opening and decided to leave the traffic on the approach to the Blackwall Tunnel. I knew a different route to the car park that I drove to each day at North Greenwich. I moved quickly under the dual carriageway and made my way around the back of the superstores. As I encountered some more traffic, I began to feel really, really hot. In addition to feeling anxious, tense, and worried, I now felt as if I was burning up.

What was happening?

What appeared to be grey and black snowflakes began falling from the sky towards me. They continued to fall, looming ever closer and expanding as they approached, filling up my vision. I started to blink rapidly, hoping that they would go. They didn't disappear though. Instead, my sight began to become obscured. My vision became darker and darker, and in no time at all, my remaining perception of the external world was governed by a triangular shape around my right eye.

I was extremely scared as I sat there in traffic, and I knew that I had to get to the car park as quickly as possible. I didn't know what was happening to me, and I was concerned about getting into a wreck and hitting something or someone. A gap appeared in the traffic, and I cautiously negotiated the roundabout and the road leading up to the car park at North Greenwich. I edged the car into the parking space slowly and then breathed a sigh of relief as I sat there, trying to comprehend what was happening.

I tried to speak, and nothing but a muffled sound came out. I gripped the steering wheel as I began to feel dizzy. And then just like that, my torso fell backwards into the seat like a lifeless doll, and I could no longer control it purposely anymore.

I felt so heavy, as if constructed from lead. I tried to lift my arms, but it took so much effort. I used my right arm to lift my left arm so that I could hold the steering wheel in order to pull my torso up. I managed it, but then I fell back into my seat again.

My god, what is going on? Am I dying?

My head was spinning, and the slightest movement from my physical body made my brain and mind feel as if I was riding a roller coaster. I began to feel very sick—very sick indeed. Suddenly, I felt as if I was going to vomit, and I had to get outside for some air. Sadly, I was worried about getting sick on my work clothes, and on my car too. How pathetic, as they are just things. I used my right arm to lift my left arm once again, and after three attempts, I managed to successfully open the car door.

I had to lift my legs out of the car one at a time. Sitting sideways, I tried to stand but fell to my knees, vomiting violently onto the concrete floor of the car park. All that came out was a green foamy liquid. I had rushed out of my house without eating, having only a green health-powder drink made with water. I watched as the trails of green foamy liquid spread out between the cracks and tiny gravel stones on the concrete floor. I continued getting sick, unable to control myself as I tried to remain as still as possible. I was on my hands and knees when a passer-by stopped.

"Are you okay?" he asked in what sounded like a Scandinavian accent.

I can't remember what I said, but the man seemed to understand my urgent need for an ambulance. I managed to prop myself up against the car, slumping sideways—unable to maintain an upright position. I must have lost consciousness for a while as the next thing I remember is being picked up by two male paramedics, who lifted me with ease and carried me swiftly to the ambulance.

Each time I moved, I was violently sick. I was promptly given a small cardboard bowl, which I clung to as if it were my key to life. At this point, the light began to hurt my eyes too. As the ambulance started up, I clung to the shiny metal rail at the side of the bed they had strapped me into. I just wanted to lie as still as possible. The vibration of the ambulance, as it raced along, rattled through my entire body. I was sure that I was dying.

This couldn't be it, could it? I had worked so hard, securing well-paid and sought-after roles in software at good companies. But what had it all been for? It didn't seem right at all.

Aftermath

Three days went by before the hospital staff told me that at the age of thirty-eight, I had suffered multiple strokes—six in total, causing six areas of brain damage and impacting my sight, speech, and movement. I would later dub that fateful day *S-Day* or *Strokes Day*. I was told that it was akin to being hit very, very, very hard over the head and that my fitness, my physical and mental strength, had kept me alive.

I walked out on July 12, 2013, ten days after my emergency admission to hospital. Little did I know I was about to embark on the first steps of a long and hard recovery, rebuilding and reshaping what was to become Life 2.0.

I continued with the sale of my house but had to pull out of buying the new apartment as I could not work and was medically signed off. Ironically, the apartment was opposite the hospital, and I was buying it as a relatively short-term option in order to get to my day job more quickly. I never saw the apartment or my old office again. It was an odd but strangely liberating feeling to go from having a house, a car, and a relatively high-flying job to be living in my friend's spare room.

Perhaps in my old life, I had become caught up in identifying myself with my career. We are not what we do, but it is easy to get wrapped up in this illusion. This exceptional and unforeseen event had shifted my focus from work and material possessions to looking at, and after me for the first time that I could remember.

I moved in with a good friend and began to reassess my situation. Across the next two and a half years, I learnt so much about myself, perhaps pushing myself too much at times. I oscillated between being extremely enthusiastic and depressed, which brought on feelings of gloom from the dark shadows that surrounded my upper vision. It seemed as if it would stay this way forever.

Eventually, I rebuilt my sight with daily eye exercises. Refining and improving my vision is a daily practice for me now. Bright lights and glare can still be an issue for me though. For my speech, I perform a daily series of sentences provided by my singing and vocal-coach friends. My confidence was affected when I could not articulate my thoughts clearly. I had always thought of myself as a relatively well-spoken and articulate person.

My movement, my body shape, and my physical strength have improved by leaps and bounds due to the use of vestibular exercises and yoga. When working on neurological exercises, I was taught to stop as soon as I had dizziness or any kind of pain, which can come on very quickly. I began to realise when enough was enough. It is very satisfying to be carving out my own physicality.

My perception of self, others, and the external world was altered completely when I worked on myself from the inside out. I had never tried meditation but found myself in a short formal course, where I quickly found that it was of great benefit to me. Meditation especially helped me in my quest to rebuild my life swiftly, which often led to me overthinking or trying to move too quickly.

The popular phrase "Let go of what no longer serves you" resonates deeply with me now. During my recovery, I gave a lot to charity and sold many of my possessions. I was able to put everything I own in one room.

I am so much lighter now in body, mind, and spirit. The weight loss occurred on three levels: emotional, material, and physical.

Now that I am lighter, I feel as if I have come full circle. How I remember the feelings I had as a shy, imaginative boy with the knowledge of adventures from Life 1.0.

Why am I here? What is my mission?

How can I be of service in Life 2.0?

THE FIGHT OF MY LIFE

LACEY DOWLING

WHEN I walked in the house after a long day at school, I was not prepared to handle what I was about to discover. My mom had not mentioned anything to me on the ride home about what she had done. So when I opened the door to my bedroom, a flood of emotions and intense panic took over. It was a panic I had never known before. My mom had cleaned my room. It was spotless.

My laundry was done, and all my belongings were reorganized. It freaked me out. It was not like I enjoyed my room being messy. In fact, I typically spent all my free time cleaning. It was a never-ending process. If I dropped a piece of clean clothing on the floor, it had to be rewashed. If the non-contaminated items touched the contaminated ones, they had to be cleaned. And if they could not be cleaned, they were disposed of. If *any* of my stuff ever went into the outside world, it could never come into contact with the other items in my room again.

Though my mom was trying to help, she had no idea which items were contaminated and which items were not. In my mind, everything had been cross-contaminated, and I felt like I could no longer live in my own room.

My emotions quickly turned to rage. "How could you do this to me?" I screamed. Overwhelmed by the task ahead of me, I couldn't imagine how I would conquer all the cleaning I had to do to feel safe again.

Her kind gesture felt like a betrayal. *Why couldn't she just respect my feelings? Why couldn't she understand my methods or the process I used to keep everything clean?* I knew there was no way she could ever truly understand my irrational thoughts as it was hard for me to understand what was going on in my head. And while I hated to see my mom hurting, I just wanted someone who would give in to me and support me in my compulsions. She wouldn't.

It all began the summer after my freshman year of high school. Fear and anxiety began to take over my life. When I look back, I know now that there were times before then when I felt afraid or anxious, but this new fear was different. It consumed every moment of every day. I felt like I was drowning in my thoughts, and I could not find a way to push past them. For a long time, I was able to keep others from knowing what was happening. But eventually, hiding it became impossible.

I wish I could say I knew what led me to believe that I would be contaminated by my environment or that I would be harmed, but I can't. The fear was just there. I feared for myself and for my family, often staying awake all night to check on my parents and siblings to make sure they were all still breathing. I wanted everyone to stay healthy, and I could not understand why they did not fear the same things I did. However, no matter what I did or how hard I tried, I could not seem to keep myself and everything around me safe and germ-free.

My mom and I began to do some research. We needed answers. It did not take us long to realize I was dealing with a debilitating form of obsessive compulsive disorder or OCD. The obsessions were the reoccurring thoughts I would have. The compulsions were the behaviors I felt the urge to repeat over and over again. The behaviors would bring me relief, but only for a moment, before another obsessive thought would occur.

I did not want to fight my thoughts. It was too painful. And despite my state of mental exhaustion from constantly trying to keep my world in order, it seemed easier to give in to the compulsions and fears than to confront them. Though on some level I was aware that my fears were unfounded, a stronger voice was able to convince me they were real.

We sought help from many people—pastors, counselors, psychiatrists, and medical doctors—but we received very few answers. Those who didn't turn us away just wanted to prescribe medication. I tried a couple of times to take the medication, but within a few days of taking it I felt worse, not better. To this day, I do not remember much from the many appointments we went to, though there was one appointment I will never forget. It was the last one my mom ever took me to.

She was a counselor—a woman who was clueless as to the impact she would have on me by making unfounded conclusions about the rest of my life. I remembered sitting with my mom in her office on the verge of tears—the whole visit. I listened as she described my future in detail. She said that my life would never change and that the OCD was a life sentence. She went on to say that I would either be hospitalized or on medication for the rest of my life. She also told me that I would probably suffer from other illnesses as well, like anorexia—diseases associated with the same part of the brain as OCD. She even told me I would never get married or have children. She took away all my dreams.

I could not breathe. All I could think was that if she was telling me these things, they must be true. Had my thoughts and fears really crippled me to the point that my life was already over?

Devastation quickly turned to anger, and I decided that I was not going to let that lady tell me my life was over. I was going to fight. I knew it would not be easy, but I was finally ready. As terrible as that appointment was, I was truly thankful I went to see that woman that day.

Having to fight my own thoughts constantly, every day was an exhausting battle. I knew I could not do it on my own. It took a lot of prayer and a lot of faith in the Lord to conquer my fears. I also had to rely on my family for help. With every obsessive thought I had, I would have to choose not to follow through with the compulsion.

My family supported me by not catering to my patterns of behavior. As mad as that would make me at times, we all knew it was what I needed to overcome the disorder. From time to time, I still have an irrational, fear-based thought pop into my head. I am now equipped and able to quickly push those type of thoughts away.

As I sit here today with my wonderful husband and children, I am even more thankful for that day in the doctor's office. I would like to think that at some point, I would have made the decision to fight, regardless. But having someone take away all my hopes and dreams for the future gave me the courage I needed to tackle the OCD.

FEAR, GUILT, AND LOVE

ANONYMOUS

I WAS very excited to be moving to Australia in January 2010. In fact, I couldn't wait to leave. In my early twenties, I was exhilarated by the endless possibilities of traveling.

Warming up to my dream trip to Australia, my good friend and I went away for a week on holiday in Spain in the summer of 2009. I met this pretty girl on the last day of my trip and told her I would keep in contact. Her name was Hannah.

On our return to the UK, I drove down to see her and stayed over a couple of times. After spending time with her, I realised that we were completely different people. I told Hannah I wasn't going to be seeing her anymore. I couldn't wait to leave for Australia.

November that year was wet, cold, and grey. I remember looking out of my office window at the misery. I received a text out of the blue from Hannah, whom I had cut ties with a couple of months prior.

It read, "I have something to tell you. Can you talk?"

My heart rate immediately started to skyrocket. I looked around the drab office to see if anyone had noticed my sudden internal horror.

Nothing, just the faint tapping of keyboards and mouse clicks. Getting up from my chair, I walked outside to make the phone call.

"Hello, Hannah, what's going on? What do you need to tell me?" "I am pregnant, and it's yours, Aaron."

Immediate rage started to sweep up my torso.

"What the fuck are you talking about? You told me you couldn't have kids and that you were having a hysterectomy. You fucking lied to me."

Hannah had a disease of the womb called endometriosis. She had told me that her problem was severe and was the reason for her two previous miscarriages. She had told me that she couldn't have children and that her doctors were removing her womb in a hysterectomy because of this.

All she ever wanted was to have children, but she had been denied that dream. Now it all made sense. I had been set up.

I was absolutely furious and was trying to contemplate what I had just been told. "Fuck you. Fuck you. Fuck you!" She was trying to trap me; she never wanted me to leave. I exploded all over that call, not even sure what I was saying. I denied it was possible. After all, she had told me about her condition. She was lying. I knew she was in a delicate place after an abusive previous partner. But would she make this up for me to stay?

If this was true, I was now trapped in this situation, and my dreams were going to be crushed. Part of me thought she was lying about being pregnant. I felt ridiculously stupid. The feeling of being trapped evoked a predictably immature response: resentment. I was angry because I felt I had been baited—hook, line, and sinker. I was angry because I had been so blind. I was angry, ultimately, because of fear.

I told her she was sick and to never contact me or my family again.

I pushed the information to the very back of my mind and buried it. I didn't even want to think about it again. I told myself she was lying and that it wasn't true. I believed my story. But it was there in my mind, eating away my energy, my gifts.

Guilt and shame were slowly building up, waging a war against the fury and fear. A feeling of unconditional love and connection wanted to make an appearance, but it was being strangled by this compound of prehistoric emotions. It was a cauldron of conflict and unsolved truths within me. All I could think about was Australia.

Get me there now!

Arriving in Australia two months later changed everything. Proximity, they say, has power. Well, I solved that problem. I went about as far away as possible. It didn't feel like I was running away from it because it didn't feel like it was real. It was just a bad dream, which was over. After all, I *had* been set up. Out of sight, out of mind. I worked hard, traveled, explored, and tried not to think about it. I had been offered sponsorship to stay in the country and live—a ticket to an Australian passport. I absolutely fell in love with the place.

One evening, my phone began to ring; it was my sister. I jumped out of the van I was sitting in and walked away from the camp as I answered the phone. She was crying. Something was wrong.

"Hello, Kim? What's the matter?"

"You have a daughter," she sobbed, her words setting off a powerful chain of emotions inside of me.

It's true. I was shocked at how surprised I was to truly embody this fact. The truth had been floating around in my consciousness, its grip squeezing my core truth, holding it prisoner. Guilt and shame, being the dagger, pierced this truth into my consciousness in short punctuations a few times a day before being forcefully discarded.

My sister was crying, and tears were flowing down my face. I dropped the phone down by my side as I tried to breathe, walking away from the campsite towards the pink desert sunset.

I felt sadness, followed by outrage. "Why are *you* crying?" I asked my sister.

"Because it's such a sad situation," she cried. Every cell in my heart ached.

I felt trapped.

I stubbornly exploded again, swearing I was never going to see the baby or have anything to do with her as Hannah had lied to me. I said I didn't care at all. Over the next few days, my parents called to talk about it. I didn't want to talk. She had lied to me; therefore, it was up to Hannah to explain everything to the child when she grew up. I was not going to be her dad because of the circumstances under which it all happened.

I knew what my family was saying was right. In the midst of everything, I knew this child was completely innocent. But I had my ego to protect. I had been lied to, and now my dreams and aspirations were at risk of being taken away. My story in life was going to be ripped from me. It was Hannah's fault. I had been planning on going to Australia for years, and she set me up.

Nearly two months had passed, and my heart was aching more than ever; an internal battle raged.

I was scared. My fears were rooted in the despair from the shame and rejection leading to the horror of not being enough and feelings of doubt of someday being loved. All this was wrapped in more shame and guilt.

The thoughts running through my mind were aggravating a plethora of emotions. Like an endless loop of scenarios playing out in my head, they were driving me crazy. Future stories were dominated by delusional negativity, like movies of my future life playing on the cinematic wide screen of my mind. The principle of being misled into something so life-changing made me upset.

But she told me she couldn't have children. Yes, but that is what she believed as it was what her doctor had told her. Of course, she would tell me this too. All of this internal dialogue was a process at play from my limited perspective.

Well then, I have given the most precious gift to this woman. What if this was all meant to happen like this?

Maybe, but it feels like I have been deceived. My mind was at war.

You have to take responsibility for your part in this too, even if you think you were misled.

What will everyone say? What a scandal! What shame and guilt I feel.

My friends and family know who I am, so I shouldn't care what everyone else thinks.

But maybe this is all happening for me. What if this is a precious gift?

The suppressed unconditional love that was always there had an escape plan. The raging fear was not as fierce anymore. Burying it and keeping it to myself allowed no room for me to see it from anyone else's perspective. It allowed me no room to forgive, no room to confront shame, and no room to release guilt. Talking about it with my parents and family was hard at first, challenged by my stubborn fear, but it evolved into therapy for my heart and soul.

In the months after my sister first called, I started to enjoy the thought of becoming a father. It excited me. Every time I thought about it, I would have a warm, loving, exciting feeling bubbling away in my gut. I had been longing for this feeling for over two years.

I spent time in the coming weeks hiking up to my favourite viewpoint to think. Overlooking the breathtaking panorama of the iron and ore–rich red landscape in Northwest Australia, I was finally free. As free as the majestic eagle-hawks circling in the blue sky above. I knew this moment would come. The gratitude was overwhelming. I am a father —a dad-to-be. Through anger and frustration came my breakthrough. I made *the* decision in that moment. Maisy is innocent. It's not her fault. She needs me. I need her. I am going to be Maisy's dad.

I am coming, sweetheart. I promise.

Even though the fear, shame, and guilt were still there, the power of love was now infinitely stronger, liberating me beyond belief.

Later that year, I was back in the UK. It was the first time we would see each other. There was excitement, peppered with anxiety. I knocked on the door, and Hannah opened it, smiling. I looked down and saw Maisy, my sweetheart, for the first time.

She jumped up and down and let out an uncontrollable squeal of excitement and screamed, "There's my daddy!" She then ran up to me, and I picked her up for the first time, squeezing her close with no sign of fear, just unconditional love and pure euphoria. A perfect moment I will cherish forever.

Our relationship has blossomed. And it is better than I ever dreamt it could be.

I will always be here for you, sweetheart, no matter what.

We see each other every week. We laugh until our faces hurt. She loves me, and I love her. We are daughter and daddy.

And you are the greatest gift of my life.

NO WHITE KNIGHT NEEDED

JEANINE BECKER

LAST FOURTH of July, Independence Day in America, I was reflecting on how one particular hike in Ecuador forever changed my concept of independence.

The night before my unexpected adventure, I was out to dinner with almost thirty others. We were seated at a large table, and behind us was this life-sized mural. Right behind my head was a white knight on a white horse. I laughed—partly because I had been thinking a lot about wanting a partner, ready for my own white knight, and partly because the idea of being saved felt so ridiculous. Me as the damsel in distress? Nope, it's not going to happen.

I take pride in being a strong, independent woman—definitely someone who could take care of herself. My motto might have been "I've got this." So I had a picture of me taken in front of the mural, laughed at the idea of my white knight, and thought, *I'd rather be riding my own horse beside him than to be whisked off wearing some big dress, riding sidesaddle, and unable to steer.*

Early the next day, all thirty of us who were on this volunteer adventure together left our hotel to deliver clean water filtration systems to an indigenous tribe, the Cañari, whose farming community and homes are nestled into the Andes Mountains. It is a tribe that has had little Western contact and predates the Incas.

The day began with a beautiful shared feast—each of the Cañari women spreading their colorful shawls side by side on the ground so community members could empty their baskets of farm-grown food. We ate, danced to an old man playing a homemade didgeridoo, then set off to demonstrate the water filters and enjoy a special treat—the community's sacred hot springs—just an "easy, twenty-five-minute hike" away.

It would have been a short and easy, twenty-five minutes if you lived at high altitude and regularly hiked up and down the Andes Mountains. The "quick" stroll turned out to be a ninety-minute hike down two thousand feet of very steep switchbacks on the edge of a cliff, in alternating ankle-deep mud and loose gravel, at altitude. I had been known to trip on a curb walking down the street, so I was terrified. An hour into our descent, when I first saw beneath the clouds enough to see the river far below us, I thought, *Oh, that can't possibly be our destination. I simply can't get there. God knows how I'll ever get back up.*

But I kept walking, determined to push through to the bottom of the mountain so I could share the clean water systems we'd brought. Though I momentarily lost a shoe in the thick mud, and was skidding on the gravel, I kept my eyes just a few feet ahead, focused only on the very next step.

Once we reached the river, we demonstrated the clean water systems to an amazed community of indigenous people, who were taking as many pictures and videos as we were. While we'd planned on heading to the hot springs, the elder of the community informed us that it was literally a spring with hot water flowing in the middle of the raging river. We were invited to wade out to the spring while holding hands to prevent being swept away, but we decided against it. It was not quite the leisurely soak in the hot springs we had imagined.

That same elder then told us that we needed to leave promptly or we wouldn't make it to the top of the mountain before dark. I could have sat on the bank of that river for an hour or more just to rest, but with dusk quickly approaching, we heeded the old Cañari man's warning and began our ascent.

I was exhausted, scared to be in slippery mud along a cliff, and about as close to needing help as I get. Looking up, as we set off, I steeled myself for the climb, ready to push through, though I had this sinking feeling that it was unlikely I could make it to the top before dark. With just one little bottle of water, I realized I wasn't going to have enough to drink. And if I were to find myself alone, I wouldn't be able to find my way out of the maze of small trails carved into the hillside.

There was one fitness trainer, Travis, who, during our previous days of travel, had shared that he was craving exercise. As we started our climb, he called out, offering to take anyone's pack that needed to lighten their load. When he looked at me with a gleam in his eyes, I thought of that white knight, smiled, and slowly peeled off my pack, holding it for a moment before acquiescing with a mix of gratitude and embarrassment.

Appreciating the new lightness of each step, I reflected on my swirl of emotions. The voice that said "You can do this Ms. Independent" was giving way to what felt like a slightly older and definitely wiser voice. As independent and powerful as I might be, I also needed to be aware of my own limitations and be willing to off-load some of the burden at times. A burden—that is what that backpack felt like to me. But to Travis, my burden was an opportunity, a welcomed challenge.

My situation at that moment made me flash back to the time I first hired a bookkeeper, relinquishing a job that I hated to someone who was actually fired up by numbers enough to make them her life's work. I began wondering what other burdens I was living with that could be simply off-loaded. Where else is this possible in my life?

Without my pack, I made it through the first hour of the climb, but I was increasingly becoming exhausted. My legs were shaking, and my chest was pounding. Unfortunately, we were just reaching the most treacherous stretch of the climb, where the trail was only a foot or so wide and the ankle-deep mud was slick.

I looked up at the narrow path and over the cliff and felt scared and unsteady. I wasn't sure how to safely make it through. In that moment, another man noticed my pause and, without a word, reached out his hand. A voice said, "I don't *need* help. I can do this." Yet I reached back, took his hand, and breathed a sigh of relief. We climbed in silence for the next forty minutes or so. He stayed with me, his calm, present, positive, reassuring hand leading me up along the cliffs.

Clasping his steady support, I picked up the pace and began, for brief moments, to take my eyes off the ground in front of me. I started noticing the exquisite clouds in the valley, the luscious green around us, and the slowing beat of my heart. I felt such connection with and trust for that man who was steadying my walk, and it looked like we just might make it to the top before nightfall.

When we hit firm ground, he left me with my thoughts to go assist the next group through the treacherous mud. As I relaxed more, now climbing on solid soil and a sidewalk-width pathway, I recognized that maybe asking whether or not I needed help wasn't the right question. There were times in my life when, if I had to, I could power through alone. But this day of hiking was reminding me to simply ask, what else is possible if I am willing to say yes to support?

Yes, maybe I could have made it up the muddy cliffs by myself. I'm not sure. What I do know is that the support allowed me to finish faster. And instead of being terrified and staring at the ground, I was calm and present and able to relish the views even as my legs were exhausted and shaking. The man who supported me on the climb—he and his wife are people I admire, people I wanted to connect with on the trip. That experience fused a bond between us that will last a lifetime.

While the trail widened, the climb didn't feel like it was ever going to end. The ascent was even harder, and a lot longer than any of us had anticipated. It was certainly longer than the little ten-ounce bottle of water I was carrying could last. Our small group found itself parched, scared, and out of water.

Just as a sense of panic was beginning to settle in, a few of the local Cañaris approached us with large jugs of water and the filters we had provided them a few hours earlier. While we sat there in the mud, exhausted and dehydrated, two local children filtered the water and filled our bottles. Our demo had worked. The children knew exactly how to use the filters, and now those filters were being used to save us on our climb. Sipping slowly as I watched the water flow into the next bottle, the line between giving and receiving felt fuzzy at best. I wondered about other ways that I served and where else this line between giving and receiving was no longer so clear.

I still tear up thinking of those children and their families, having made it home so quickly yet coming back down the mountain to take care of us with their gift. They provided us the sustenance we needed for our return.

We made it to the summit just as nightfall was coming—our final ascent guided by the lights already on in a few community homes. We said our goodbyes and climbed onto the bus.

As we bounced along the dirt road, my thoughts turned back to that white knight on that mural.

No, I don't need someone to save me. But what new possibilities are out there if I off-load some burdens, take an outstretched hand, or simply notice how deeply I am served by giving and receiving?

Maybe it isn't about need. I now choose to recognize and say yes to the white knights riding beside me.

MOTHER AFRICA

DESMOND NEYSMITH

I CLOSE my eyes, and I am on the plains of Africa. The scene is magnificent. I can sense Mother Earth. Her feminine essence is truly overwhelming.

I am here to connect.

I am here to love.

I am here as long as I choose.

I am here without regret or fear.

A Mind's Eye View

At first glance, I see very little. Then I open my eyes a little more, and I see a little more than before. Now I see trees. I see lots of browns. I see a lack of water in my field of view. To actually *see* the absence of something sends a shiver down my spine. The life force in this land is strong, and it has lived in this cycle for millennia. Green and then brown, and then green and then brown. Now it is brown. It's perfect. It's always perfect. I close my mind's eye.

The Sweet Smell of My Success

I can smell the African air. It's saccharin and fragrant with hints of distant decay, which all add to this sweet, delicious, pungent scent. I breathe this broth into my belly, and it feels as if I am inhaling the whole continent. The unique mixture of the odours is intoxicating—an atmospheric liquor that leaves me euphoric. The dust. It smells like . . . dust. It's more of an aroma, a taste almost, different to the dust in London. This dust has a temperature and a flavour, and it makes me feel like the salt of the earth. I inhale the slow breath of Mother Nature, and her stillness quietens my soul. Everything is slower now, stiller now, quieter now.

Taste the Vegan Fayre

The food I am consuming leaves me nourished. After eating the flora, I feel calmer. The plants move too, just like the ants and the birds, but they march to their own drum. The rhythm is a slower one. The beat of the flora is one that appeals to me. They are rooted to the spot, yet they are *always moving*.

The great baobabs reach their might through this rhythm. Stillness apparent. Movement actual.

How do I do less yet achieve more?

If I consume only the still, do I become more still myself?

Consume the speedy, become the speedy?

Consume the still, become the still?

My taste buds can detect this energy-laden air. What is it that makes me want to lap it up so? The hot air catches the back of my throat. I am salivating as I write, experiencing this great Mother Earth through every sense available to me.

Feel the Rhythm

On my skin, what am I feeling? Dry heat, bone dry, dusty feet. I sense an overall feeling of balm on my skin. I have been stung, and I have been bitten. I know not by what, and I have no conflict. It's just on point in the continuum of being bitten and being not bitten. I feel a spider on my leg, and I can embody it. It's all part of the fibre of the Universe. I move, as does the spider, as do the hairs on my leg as my hackles bristle. It all flows into one. Is this the drumbeat that we *all* march to?

A spider has eight legs, and I have two. A fish has fins, and a bird has wings. Of course, we all march differently. How could we not? Yet we all come from the same source. The tree has roots, and the ocean has waves, but they march to the same drum as I.

Mother Nature is the metronome of life.

I'm smiling.

The Sounds of the Universe

As I listen, I begin to name the sounds.

The whispered hum of the breeze through the leaves.

The melodic chatter of the birds calling to me.

The percussive rhythm of twigs breaking, snapping, crunching.

My own heartbeat and breath.

Alone, these strands are the individual tracks of life,

All exclusive to each other and equally unique.

I listen with a peripheral ear.

The strands bind and weave into a symphony.

They unite and become one sound.

I open my eyes.

I buy my ticket.

The time to visit Mother Africa has come.

FORGIVENESS OVERDUE

LENA BROUSSARD

OUR NEW home was a world apart from the charming Acadian house in the country, where I had spent the last four years with my maternal grandparents. After my grandmother's passing, my mother and I moved into a low-income housing subdivision referred to by the locals as the projects. We had no phone or air-conditioning, and our budget was tight. But that was no concern of mine. My mom had a special knack for making any place feel like home. I was well-fed and well-dressed, and our home was spotless. She was proud and hardworking and had every intention of providing the kind of home environment suitable for a nine-year-old little girl.

Unfortunately, my mother suffered from depression with suicidal tendencies. After a short while, she could no longer hide her attempts, and they became more frequent. During her dark times, she would send me away for the night, leaving me with a friend, whose apartment unit was close by. Too close. Close enough for me to hear the sirens barreling down our street, a rare occurrence in our sleepy little town, even for the projects. Only two buildings away, I would peek out of the bedroom window while everyone else slept, dread filling my young mind as I watched the lights in the distance draw nearer, only to come to a halt where I feared most—directly in front of my unit. I waited, holding my breath, watching, hoping, and praying that my mother would not be carried out on a stretcher. I spent some of those nights in the emergency room, waiting on news.

Months passed quickly as the hot, humid summer gave way to the holiday season. My dad came to visit for the first time in four years. We spent Christmas Eve with his side of the family. At the end of a great night, upon my return, my dad walked me to my front door to say goodnight. I saw a note, written in my mom's beautiful handwriting and taped to the outside of the door. I was instantly alarmed. I knew the note instructed my dad not to let me inside. I knew she wanted to send me away again. I knew what it meant. Worried and filled with anxiety, I burst through the door before he could stop me.

I saw blood, blood dripping off the handrails to the stairs and blood dripping from the bottom two steps. I was fixated for a moment but soon allowed my eyes to venture up the stairwell. There were bloody handprints on the wall outlining the path of someone stumbling down the stairs, and little pools of blood everywhere. Images of Sharon Tate flashed through my mind, and for a moment, I thought Charles Manson had been there. Horrified, and with tears that seemed to stream from my gut, I knew I had to find her. My dad tried to hold me back.

She had slit her throat and wrists. I don't remember the rest of that night.

Home from the hospital, incoherent on meds, and with bandages around her throat and wrists, my mother lay listless, sleeping on the couch. It was just the two of us. I watched her sleep as I wondered what to do next. *What if she didn't wake up?*

The sound of silence is deafening when you have so many questions and fears, and yet no one is near to help. I counted the black tiles beneath my feet. I counted all of them over and over again. We had no phone. Who would I call if we did? I looked at the back door, then the front door, and then at the tiles on the floor again. The awareness of my surroundings gave me a sense of control.

Too young to understand depression, I lost all trust in my mother's ability to cope with her problems. I was angry with what I perceived as her lack of respect for life and lack of love for those of us in it. She seemed willing to abandon all that was good because she was hurting.

I was angry that I was not enough to make her happy, as she had pretended to be when WE sang "You and Me Against the World." There was no longer any you and me. She was willing to leave me all alone, hurting and scared.

She recovered, but the suicide attempts continued. One late afternoon, locked out again, I peered through the kitchen window. There she stood with an ice pick held high and aimed at her chest. I started banging on the window, screaming. Just before she plunged the pick into her chest, she turned and saw me. Upset by the interruption, she started screaming at me, slurring and staggering. I refused to leave the window, and she finally gave up on the attempt. Worry was never-ending.

She grew very fond of painkillers, and they were her first choice of remedy during bouts of depression. It was difficult to tell the difference between overuse and overdose. At times, she slept for days. I woke myself up and got ready for school in the mornings, praying that she'd still be alive when I got home.

Years went by quickly. Eventually diagnosed with bipolar disorder, she was in and out of rehab for prescription-drug addiction and depression. When she was sober, she was beautiful. And I would have hope, hope that it would be forever lasting. But it wasn't. When she relapsed, she lied, said hurtful things, and was manipulative. I hated her. I missed her.

It has been a little over twelve years since her passing.

I recently realized that I was still angry. The awareness of my anger came about unexpectedly. While dealing with someone exhibiting many of the same manipulative behaviors as my mother, also due to addiction, emotions that had long been shelved resurfaced from deep inside of me. My feelings of frustration, anger, and lack of control seemed to steer me toward memories of my mom, memories that I had set aside long ago. Prior to this, I would have described myself as rather numb regarding our past and her actions. I would have said, "My mother had many wonderful attributes, but unfortunately, she had issues." And I would have left it at that. I had put my mother in a box with a label and I didn't like to talk about those difficult years. I certainly didn't want to appear as a victim.

After all this time, was I still harboring hurt and anger?

If I had to describe the essence of my mother's character, it would be fair to say that she always tried her best to look at situations from other people's perspectives. She wanted to understand where others were coming from instead of judging them. I simply can't stress that enough. I took that to heart and have lived my life trying to emulate what seemed so effortless for her. And yet ironically, I had never afforded her the same compassion and understanding.

The answer was yes, I was still angry. And it was time to let go. It was time for forgiveness and understanding, and time to allow the beauty of who she was to be a part of my life again. She had a tender heart. She was wise and profound, often keeping me in deep thought. Her passion for others and capacity for empathy was endless. Her friends remember her as someone who welcomed them with a cup of coffee, always ready to listen.

All this time, I strived to be just like her. I just didn't dare acknowledge it. Anger snuffed out my memories. It strangled the beautiful moments in my life, keeping them from surfacing and breathing life. I chose to forget the true beauty of my past and what makes me who I am today. Forgiveness helped me set aside the anger to see the whole picture, and I am reminded every day of the things that I loved about my mom.

THE WALK

LAURA DEWEY

I KNEW the plan but little else. Our group was to walk down to the river with our hosts, the Cañari, one of the oldest indigenous people in the Andes of Ecuador (and all of South America). At the river, we were to do a demo of the permanent clean water solution we'd brought with us to leave with the community.

Fairly quickly, I realized this was more than a typical walk. The mud was deep on the path, trodden by horses that had gone before us. I had two choices: put my foot in the mud in a place that looked to be only a few inches deep or balance on the narrow wet edge of the path, a foot or two above the mud. The edge was preferable but not always available.

This dance took a tremendous amount of attention. One false step, and *bam* (or *splat*), I was going down.

The person in front of me was struggling. She didn't have great balance and was hesitant as a result. Instead of having compassion, I thought, *Aren't I blessed to be so sure-footed.* As I recalled, it was a little snarkier than that. Basically, I was pretty high on myself, making myself better than her in my mind.

Bam! I slid as I leaped slippery rock to slippery rock. This sure-footed girl was on her butt. Hard. Hand scraped, startled, and pretty sore. *Hmmm, that was interesting*, I thought.

After slogging through for a seeming eternity, we left the canopy of vegetation and mud to enter a new phase of the walk—a grassy, steep decline on the side of the mountain.

My relief to be free of mud was brief as my rarely used downhill muscles began to sing. Down, down, down, the path zigzagging so we wouldn't slide straight to the bottom.

The bottom, where is it anyway? We were in the clouds, so I had no sense of where we were headed. Where is this river? How long *is* this walk?

By now our group had broken into pods of people with similar pace. My pod was cranking. We were doing great. I heard a yell from down below and asked someone in my pod what that was. I don't remember exactly what she said, but it was about the horses. I distinctly remembered saying, "Yeah, but the horses are doing better than we are."

Bam! I was on the ground again. This time with a leg twisted underneath me. Thankfully, I didn't fall full force or I am sure I would have broken something.

In that moment, it became crystal clear. The two times I fell, I was taken down by my own thoughts. Once when disparaging someone else, and the other when disparaging myself. I stood up and whispered to myself, "God, I get what you're telling me. I hear you."

We'd been at this steep decline for God knows how long. I was winded, and my muscles ached. Still there was no river in sight. Then it hit me. "I just realized. We're going to have to go back up this same way, aren't we?" I said to the leader of my pod.

"Yup," she said.

"Ugh."

Though relieved, I was unable to fully celebrate finally making it down to the river. The vision of being stranded in the dark, midclimb, left me totally preoccupied throughout the clean-water demonstration.

Needless to say, as soon as the demos were done, I was on the path, single-minded and a little obsessed. My survival instinct was in full force.

When I started, I was in a large pod of climbers—Cañari women in front of me, twentysomething Cañari men behind me, then my friend Simon, and an eight-year-old boy named Edison. This was hard, steep climbing, but the women (not young and in skirts, mind you) clasped their hands behind their backs and walked like they were skating uphill on ice.

When I had the breath, I spoke Spanish to Alfredo, the young man behind me, and thanked him for being there. I told him I felt safe because of his presence. After a short time, my climbing group had whittled to four—me, Alfredo, Edison, and Simon. Everyone else had left us in the dust.

It was clear that Alfredo stayed to take care of me, and Edison was there to take care of Simon. Was this an instruction from the community leader? Or did it just happen organically? I didn't know. What I did know was that Alfredo was my angel, and how he got there didn't matter.

At one point, I stopped for a swig of water and asked Alfredo to hold my pack for a second. He offered to carry it from that point on. It wasn't very heavy, but I nearly cried with gratitude. This girl that had a hard time asking for help was getting her ass kicked and every ounce helped.

The climb became absolutely grueling. At times I wondered if I could continue, but then I'd wonder, *What's the alternative?* So I kept going. I began to ask myself, *Can you just take one more step?* I probably asked this question a hundred times. Each time I decided, *Yes, I can take just one.*

My mind and body were struggling in one way, but in another way, I was high as a kite. My heart was beating hard, and my lungs were pumping. My legs were still working, and my mind was answering the call—*wow!* I felt so powerful and couldn't help but revel in the miracle of my body.

At one point, I was offered a horse, and I refused. I was invigorated, challenged, and determined to finish what I'd started (damn it!).

On the way down, I thought the mud was a hardship. On the way up, I was thrilled to see it. Seeing mud meant that only a quarter of the hike remained. Perspective.

Eventually, I heard chickens. *Chickens! That must mean we're back to the village.* Sure enough, it was not a mirage. Indeed, we had completed our journey.

It was a journey of my physical body but also of my mind and spirit. Of the three, my mind seemed to have the most difficulty. It was quite literally taking me down. After this humble realization, I allowed it to join the graceful flow of my body and spirit. They knew exactly what to do. All I had to do was get out of the way.

BLOOD MOON

ALFRED JACOBS

WHEN I'M outdoors at night, I always feel a sense of mystery. The dark night sky and the lights in the heavens set my imagination loose. I imagine what people thought before science, before the moon landing. I wonder, *Why does the moon disappear and turn red? Why is it so big? Is it getting closer? Is it on fire? What is happening?*

I live in a relatively quiet neighborhood, so I was looking forward to a peaceful evening. I dragged my comfy lawn chair to just the right spot in my yard, setting it up and wrapping myself in a soft blanket. I expected to be there for some time. I sat in meditation to quiet myself so I would be able to fully embrace the mystery of the lunar eclipse. Everything was perfectly in place so I could appreciate this celestial event.

The *blood moon prophecy* is a series of apocalyptic beliefs promoted by Christian ministers John Hagee and Mark Biltz. It states that four consecutive lunar eclipses, coinciding on a Jewish holiday, with six full moons in between and no intervening partial lunar eclipses (tetrad), is a sign of the end times as described in the Bible in Acts 2:20 and Revelation 6:12. On the night of September 27, when the tetrad was ending with a lunar eclipse, the sky was crystal clear in Orange, California.

As I sat in my chair patiently waiting for the big moment, my sacred space was invaded. My neighbors began a loud discussion about why the fish was overcooked or something else inane.

Didn't they realize I required stillness? I thought. Then I became aware of a barking dog somewhere nearby. Once I was focused on the distractions, they were everywhere. Cars and motorcycles were zooming up and down the street, and a siren was wailing in the distance. I was irritated.

I got angry and began to plot what actions I could take to control my environment. How could I deal with the neighbor, find the dog, and of course, stop the cars? In the meantime, the eclipse was unfolding, and I realized I'd forgotten why I was there in the first place. Instead, I was fantasizing about how to deal with the annoyances. Perhaps I could bang on the neighbors' door and tell them to shut up, shoot the dog, and since I already had the gun in my revenge scenario, I could go to the street and blast a couple of motorcycles from underneath their riders. That would probably get their attention.

When I realized how ludicrous my thinking was, I laughed at myself. But I was still annoyed.

At one point, I heard the message: "Alfred, the eclipse is happening at this moment, so you can either sit here and watch this miraculous event take place in the heavens, or you can remain pissed off and miss it altogether."

"I get it. I get it. I surrender."

I understood that this was a learning opportunity being presented to me. Could I just be here and spend time watching the eclipse? Could I release all this crazy mind chatter? Could I accept this moment just as it is?

I have this theory about how Spirit teaches me the things I need to know. A friend of mine refers to this theory as "The Two-by-Four of Life." When there is something I need to learn, the Universe whispers, "Hey, Alfred, here is something you need to learn." I can choose to listen or blow it off. If I ignore it, it will come back again. The message will become stronger: "Alfred, you haven't taken action yet, and your inaction is going to impede your learning." Again, I can choose to ignore this voice. But if I do, it will keep presenting itself over and over again, each time in a stronger way. Ultimately, it will whack me on the head with the metaphorical two-by-four.

Sure there was noise, but this is where I live. If I didn't want noise, I could have sought the serenity of the desert; but I chose to be here. I could make the best of it or go into the house, be annoyed, and never experience this rare event. I chose the first option, and I was able to let go of the noise. I'm so glad I did because the most amazing thing happened during the next ten or fifteen minutes. The dog stopped barking, the neighbors stopped yelling, the street traffic quieted, and all I did was let go of the annoyance. Oh, and then there was this "blood moon" thing.

I can't explain any of this, but it was my experience. I believe there are lessons from Spirit that come to me when I am ready to hear them. I have been aware of these mysterious whispers most of my life. I didn't understand their relevance for a long time. I think I do now. The whispers are my intuitive voice. The more I hear, the more synchronous and graceful my life becomes.

AWAKENING TO THE ANGEL WITHIN

KIRSTY HANLY

I WAS what I like to call an angel child. Others might have described me as being slightly clueless to the workings of everyday life. I was a dreamer—a bare foot child of the '70s, who ate more than my fair share of lentils and homemade yoghurt. I chalked on paving stones on hot summer days, and spent time with grown-ups who talked about rebirthing, homeopathy, baking whole wheat bread, and living past lives.

I arrived in this world reluctantly after a difficult birth, and from the earliest time, I could remember living with a feeling of gentle disbelief with what I was *in* in this world. I carried the strangest feeling of surprise, like I was a traveler who woke up in a mysterious foreign city they hadn't bought a ticket for. I just didn't get this life that I had landed into.

My parents were hippies, who, before I was born, had opted out of the old way of living, let go of attachment to possessions, and travelled to India overland for adventure and awakening. They were both the black sheep of their families, having left small for the promise of something different in London. These were people without a plan, who, one day in February 1975, found themselves with a beautiful baby girl.

Once I arrived, they were tethered to a different way of life by this child who had picked them. But the tether wasn't quite strong enough, and it soon became the journey of a stressed single mother. There was no family close by to offer support, or money to pay the bills. And there was me, and my cute, chubby half brother, who came along shortly thereafter. The three of us—a triumvirate of magic and struggle.

My brother's father was off doing his own life; and my father was off doing his own life too. They were men with a convenient story of a need for freedom. Coincidentally, they both thought freedom meant drugs and alcohol and the ability to do whatever they wanted to do, whenever they wanted to do it. It was a story that untethered their responsibility to us. Unfortunately, the little me had believed that if I just tried hard enough, my dad would come back home.

I was the angel child with her head in the stars, always with a sense of "What the hell is going on here?" I had already felt that life was strange, but had at least felt safe in the family unit. When the bomb hit, I was catapulted into a different reality.

Thoughts of my father leaving still make me cry, even though I have had a lot of therapeutic work around this. I have, however, come to understand that the emotions that I feel don't belong to me, but to the two adults who struggled to come to terms with how they felt and the mess they had created. They belong to the people who shouted and screamed at each other in front of me until I could stand no more and would lock myself in the bathroom to shut out their reality. And they belong to the two people who, when they weren't shouting, caused me to feel damaged, hurt, resentful, and so, so sad, because of their silent, negative energy. As a child, I would try to adapt myself to make our lives better. I would contort and breathe differently, and imagine that if I could just work out exactly what to do and exactly who to be, all would be well.

So the angel child went to school and made friends but felt lost. I just didn't get that environment at all. There were expectations. They wanted something of me. But what? I was all about trying to get things right after the bomb had hit at home. So I tried to be good and learn the things that were and weren't on the curriculum.

To fit in, I needed to know about TV shows and pop bands, go to Brownies, and take part in swimming competitions. Really? Dancing around a plastic toadstool in a fluorescently lit hall wasn't something I enjoyed or saw the point in, nor was swimming up and down in a bath of chemicals. I have memories of dancing bare foot around an actual toadstool in a field. Somehow, somewhere, I remembered swimming free. That was where the magic lay for me. If only I could find it again.

But I didn't find it. Instead, I learnt to forget who I was. I learnt to copy others. I assumed that everyone else got it, and I didn't. I now see that life is a big and crazy mystery to us all. It's just that some of us are more sensitive to the unruliness of it than others. Back then, living in this world felt like a big research project—me amongst the muggles.

I did really well at my project though. Or at least I got through school at age sixteen and had enough good exam results to please. It turned out that I was really good at learning a formula and retaining the information just long enough to apply it before I would crash and burn. I left school earlier than most, as I never did figure out why I was there.

I went on to one of the world's leading drama schools and was the first person in my year to get a job with a world-renowned producer.

I completed my degree and got a proper job, and it all looked pretty good on paper. But in order to do those things, I had to squash, squeeze, and contort that angel child into a box and bury her deep underground. On the deepest of unconscious levels, with all the wonderful skills that I had developed, I was able to lock her up and put her to sleep. I thought that I needed to do so in order to do life, and to prevent other people from dropping explosives that would blow up that life. I lived in continual fear and self-protection mode. It was exhausting.

Not at all surprising, I developed an eating disorder and a very suspect relationship with alcohol. And I spent one particular year living almost entirely on diet cola, coffee, and cigarettes. I was seriously codependent and chose unhealthy relationships with men. I would do, do, do, and mask, mask, mask. And then I would crash. I had a nervous breakdown and a serious illness—my mind and body were calling out for help. My parents were still pretty absent even when I needed them the most, but I carried on. I moved forward, grew up, got married, and had children.

Without realising it, I was growing into myself. Through the gift of watching my young children, I slowly became aware of a very quiet, distant memory showing me that there was another way to be. But I had no idea how to find the key to the long-forgotten box.

I am still not sure at what point I began to notice the stars begin to align—the moment when I allowed myself to connect to the truth of who I am and who I could be. But after slowly allowing myself to strip off the layers of protection I'd built, to reveal what had always been underneath, my perspective shifted. Then one dark November evening, I found myself standing in the rain, and at that moment, I allowed myself to connect to that magic that I remembered from long, long ago. In an instant, I had an epiphany that shook me awake — something that I could never un-know. It was then that I saw life for what it is. It was then that I realized the importance of allowing the angel child in me, the one who is in each one of us, to play free. The box was unlocked. I relaxed, and I breathed differently.

I'd like to say that life became super easy from that moment on. It didn't. I am human. But it did take on a lightness that I hadn't experienced before, and I became aware that I had choices. I could choose to stay awake or go back to sleep. I could allow a full expression of myself or retreat back to the fear. I have chosen to continue to take action towards living a life of feeling inspired and connected.

Today, I choose nurturing, acceptance, healing, freedom, and playfulness. My beautiful angel child is now celebrated and allowed to dance bare foot in the sand. She has been freed to grow up into a woman who can use what she knows to wake up each day and create a life full of inspiration and magic. She knows a very special secret—that we all have exactly what we need inside of ourselves if we will only let it free.

THE BALCONY GIRL

DILSHAD DAYANI

HOLDING MY masala chai, I gaze outside my kitchen window. The rain continues to pour. With the smell of rain in the air, I find myself at my chest of drawers, rummaging around. I pull out the red album; the family pictures and stories bring with them a wave of nostalgia. I'd give anything to be with her for just one moment, to hold her hand in mine and whisper a final farewell. All I am left with are photos— pictures that portray a legacy deeper than one could think possible.

Snuggling deeper into my rocking chair, I see her face as if it were frozen in time. She was seven years old when she was orphaned. Alone and with nowhere to go, she sought refuge from her older brother and his wife. With a heart of devotion and determination to add value to the lives of those around her, Dolly took on a responsibility that was larger than life, going beyond expectations.

Everyone knew her as Dolly. To me, she was my mom and my hero. They say the apple doesn't fall far from the tree. In my case, the apple grew wings and flew. She gave me wings. Dolly taught me that I could overcome any obstacle and achieve anything I set my mind to.

As a young girl, barely ten years old, my mom, without faltering or murmuring, became the caregiver of her brother's household. She fulfilled her duties with excellence and devoted herself to raising and nurturing her brother's children and her youngest sister.

One day, her life took an unexpected turn after a couple of relatives came for a visit. Enthralled by her kindness and etiquette, Dolly's uncle spoke with her brother, offering to adopt Dolly while leaving her sister with him. Having had his own children and grandchildren, adopting Dolly would delight his heart.

Suddenly, Dolly was living in a fairy tale, mesmerized by her fortuitous lifestyle. Though her uncle brought her into a life of luxury, Dolly missed her sister and brother. She decided to leave her uncle's palace to return to her brother's home.

How can I eat good food and live as a princess while my little sister labors throughout the day, tending to the household to feed herself? she thought.

She followed her heart, often saying, "The mind tries to negotiate and debate certain circumstances, but the heart conquers peace—that place of comfort—and tells you what is right for you."

The hours ticked by slowly. I can imagine her lifting her head to check the time. She had passions that were unusual for girls her age —a passion to learn, to grow, and to understand. Her secret in life was the attitude that nothing could stand in her way. And nothing gave her greater joy than the fragrance of paper and the feel of a pencil in her hand, which teleported her into another world, giving wings to her imagination and the courage to educate and empower herself. There were no restrictions and no rules to conform to.

With no way to further her education, Dolly worked her hardest for her brother's household to earn the freedom to seek her friend's help, and the help of their teachers. Each day, Dolly expectantly waited on the balcony of her home, her large brown eyes eagerly scanning the landscape for a glimpse that school was over. She waited for her friends to return home from school with feedback on her homework.

With a flourish, she would race to greet them, barely able to contain her excitement. Social etiquette would be expedited in her eagerness to know the day's lessons.

Dolly and her friends agreed that she would do her homework at home, and they would convince the teachers to check one extra book. As a girl who was unable to go to school herself, this was the only way she had to learn. She found opportunity in adversity.

This woman was my defender. When I pushed the limits, tested the boundaries, or dared to see how far I could go, Dolly was there. She cheered me on.

When my father did not understand me, she stood up for me. In the midst of an authoritarian culture, Dolly would defend me, her daughter. Through her quiet manner, she spurred me on to be more than I thought I could be.

Her life was her words. From her, I learned the heart of generosity. I know of no one else who delighted in giving away their treasured belongings to others who truly needed a helping hand. Her love was limitless, and her compassion stretched beyond borders. She was my Mother Teresa, my Princess Diana.

Holding my masala chai close to my heart, I sigh. For a moment, I am back in time—back in those moments when Dolly would share her dreams with me. If she lived in a different time, era, or perhaps even a different culture, she would travel the world. She would feast her eyes on everything the world had to share—its cuisines, sights, cultures, and worldviews. Other times, she would close her eyes and tell me how she would love to ride a motorbike and enjoy the high-speed thrill. She was very adventurous.

A smile touches my lips. Her courage transcended culture and generations. She is my inspiration, my history. As a mother, she understood that words were not as powerful as actions. But when she did speak, her words spoke volumes.

Amidst it all, Dolly kept on pushing limits. Then suddenly, she was gone. It was while I was lying in a hospital bed, recovering from a surgery, that she had flown away. A devoted wife, she passed away on her fiftieth wedding anniversary. But she is not truly gone. No, Dolly lives on.

Taking her story deep into my heart, I took on her mantle of devotion, perseverance, and dedication, devoting my life to empowering women to empower themselves. My life's mission is to encourage women of all ages to get an education and be proud of who they are.

THE FIRST ESCAPE

JOHN P. MORGAN

SHE WAS in the kitchen now. The pots were clinking. Once they came out, you knew she'd be in there for a while.

Diving for the floor, I brushed the side of my face along the soft carpet so that my eye could see beneath the door. The light was coming through the kitchen window and casting her shadow into the hallway. I was sure she was getting things ready. She wouldn't even notice.

Spinning up and around, I looked at the clock by my bed. The red numbers, the ones so much brighter at night, read 3:07.

He wouldn't be home for an hour. And she'll just be in there making something anyway. Some stuff I'd like, and some stuff they'd tell me I had to finish before getting up. She'd be so busy with that.

It was all too small in here, and the air was too still. It was also too quiet, but at least it made it so I could hear the clinking. Out there, there was so much space. The air was different and the sounds filled your ears. She'd never realize I was gone.

I climbed onto my bed and put my head against the window. I'd thought about it so many times. I knew it wasn't far. There was a clear space between the bushes where I could land without touching the flowers. She hated it when I walked around in there, but I was good at it. She didn't know how good I was. That's why she was always worried.

I'd hung from the tree and dropped to my feet so many times, almost every day, and that was much higher than this. This was easy. So why was I worried? Getting caught? Not really, because all she would do is put me back in here again. It wouldn't get any worse. I had all my records and my puzzles, and it wasn't so bad in here. But the air does go very still, and it wouldn't be like it is out there. If there were any day to be out there, it was today. The air was perfect, just the way I liked it. It was warm enough that I didn't need a jacket and cool enough that when I ran through the woods and my breath pumped, it would feel good on my throat.

I put my fingers onto the cool brass window lock and turned it slowly, watching the curved metal come free and feeling it lighten. Resting my chin on the wooden window frame, I breathed in the scent of pine. It smelled good. Lowering my chin, I put my teeth against the frame, sinking them into the soft wood. My forehead rested against the glass, and I looked out at the trees behind the houses across the street. Watching them sway, I imagined the sound the wind was making with them. I could hear my heartbeat too. Even though the cold was still on its way, my breath showed on the window around my nose. I could see it when looking down at the wood in my teeth.

Letting them sink down deeper, I wanted to bite straight through it. My jaw began to ache though, so I pulled away and watched the fog vanish from the glass. With the tip of my first finger, I inspected the marks my teeth had made in the wood. They'd never notice, but I would always remember, for years to come, every time I saw it.

With that, I lifted the window, slow and steady. The air came in and up the sleeves in my T-shirt, down my belly, and around my back. It smelled good, and the sounds were just like I'd imagined. With both my hands, I pulled the little locks on the screen and lifted it too.

Everything went so quickly now. I was done thinking.

Spinning myself around, I put my hands on the bed and stuck my sneakers out the window. Wiggling my legs, I pushed myself through until they were straight out there, and I had my hands on the wall inside. More sliding and I went from my belly to my chest. I liked my weight on the windowsill. I liked feeling all the ridges, where the screen and the window sat when they were shut. They were for stopping all the sounds and the smells from coming inside, and they felt good on my belly and on my chest too.

Bringing my hands to the edge, with a final shove, I let all my weight fall into my fingers. Looking over my shoulder, I could see the spot just below me. This was nothing. With that, I let go. And in a second, I was on the ground. I didn't fall or stumble. I just landed, and then I stood up. And I looked back. What struck me was how close the ground was, and how easy it was to get out here. I couldn't believe I had stayed locked up in there all that time They would have to think of something else.

Putting my hands in my pockets, I walked across the front lawn. The stick I'd found yesterday was still lying there. I'd forgotten about it. It was a good stick, so I picked it up. And with it came a bounce in my step. There was no bothering to look back. She was certainly still in the kitchen. There wasn't going to be anything to see.

In full sprint, I was crossing the street and headed for it. I watched the concrete turn from gray to black as I leapt onto the driveway. I watched the pavement end and the grass begin. I watched the green turn to dirt, and all the leaves and sticks begin to appear as I made my way into the woods and down the path. I listened as the sounds changed with the colors. I could hear the next ones coming before they came, and that pulled me faster toward them. So fast that it was just colors and sounds beneath me.

The deeper I got in there, the faster it felt like I was going. Everything was whizzing by, and the ground was sloping down and taking me with it, pulling me harder and harder. The more I got into it, the more it had me. I just kept going until I'd gone so far the air had become wetter and filled with wood. Looking back wasn't going to be a problem because the only thing behind me was also ahead of me— just trees everywhere and sticks, mostly rotten, but a few good ones probably, and lots of leaves of all sorts of colors and sounds. Of course, there was the path—the one I'd come down and the one that went on ahead of me.

They had never been out here, not even once. Not this far anyway. So I slowed my sprint to a jog and then a walk until things were quiet again, and then I turned around and looked back. I'd gone far enough.

Digging the toe of my foot through the leaves toward the dirt, I watched the still path. And I remembered all the times I'd sat on my floor, looking up at the window, and all the times I'd put my face against the glass. Now here I was standing with the trees and the sticks all around me, and with the wind on my face. The only thing to listen to was the leaves.

"DUTCHICAN"

CRICKETT KOCH

WHAT ARE you waiting for? This is what you've wanted your whole life! I told myself. I had entered the number but hadn't hit the green button on my phone. My stomach was up in my throat. It was ten minutes past the time I said I would call, and I was shaking nervously. With tears in my eyes and a lump in my throat, I pushed Send, knowing there was no turning back. As my phone began to ring, so many things were swirling through my head. After the second ring, I heard this soft little voice say hello. Silent for almost a second, I answered, "It's me."

"Well, hello me, it's Mom." I was so overwhelmed with emotion that I didn't even know how to respond.

I knew I was adopted from the time I was three years old. My parents told me even though, at that age, I didn't quite understand what it meant. But they knew—because of vindictive relatives who would have been evil enough to tell me before they did—that they needed to share that truth with me as soon as possible. My mother always told me that if I ever wanted to find my birth mother, she would do everything possible to help me. My dad, on the other hand, said, "Well, I'm your dad, so why would you want to find anyone else?" I assured him that nobody could take his place, but his words and the thought of seeing him cry made me put the idea of a search out of my head, though I thought about it briefly every now and again.

It wasn't until high school, after I'd met others who'd been adopted, that I began to think about it more. After high school, I seriously considered finding my birth mother because it became more and more relevant and important in my life. My friends were getting married and having children, and I had met the guy that I knew I would marry. But it was after I had my own children that the need to find and meet Donna, my birth mom, really hit home. The thought of giving up one of my own kids perplexed me, and I wondered about Donna's situation. How could she have given me up?

Once my father passed away in 1998, I knew it was time. My oldest was ten, and my baby was six. And I was getting older. I knew I wouldn't forgive myself if I didn't try to find her before she died. I felt I needed to find Donna for what I believed would be the completion of my life story.

I exhausted all my resources and was about to give up when I saw a show called *Three Wishes* on TV. It was a miracle that I even saw the show as it only had a three-episode run. While watching the show, I learned that it was the company Worldwide Trailers—located in White Settlement, Texas—that did the detective work needed to bring the lost family members together.

My goodness, I thought, *that is right around the corner from where I live in Garland.* I wrote their number down then tucked it away for a few more years.

One day, almost like it had been placed there by the hand of God, I opened a drawer, and there was the number. It was time for me to make the call. I did and was given a caseworker. During the process, I learned that the name on my birth certificate was Bandera, an Italian name, which made me wonder about my heritage. Come to find out, the name was not that of my biological father. It belonged to a close friend of my birth mom, who had helped her find an attorney to handle the private adoption for me and my parents. Donna had found out that my biological dad had lied to her. He turned out to be older than he'd told her and already had three kids.

Three months after I made the call, they found her. They found Donna. I remember driving to work the day I got the call from my caseworker. She said, "Are you sitting down?" What she said next was surreal, numbing, incredibly awesome, and shocking all at the same time. "We've found her, and she wants you to call her tonight." As I arrived at work and stepped out of the car, I don't think my feet actually hit the ground as I walked into the building. I went around the corner and into the door before exploding with emotion. My boss immediately told me to go home and not worry about working my shift—to just get prepared for my call. I had to figure out what I was going to say. With my birth mom in Oregon and me in Texas, the two-hour time difference would give me a long time to think.

I barely recalled the drive home. Once I got there, I spoke with my husband, telling him what had transpired. I called my adoptive mother and told her I was coming over with some news. When I got to her home, I sat her down and said, "Well, I found her. I found my birth mom."

My mom immediately freaked out, saying, "What does this mean? What does this mean?"

I said, "What do you mean 'what does it mean'?" She began rambling and crying and then asked what I was going to do. Extremely confused, I looked at her and said, "Mom, first of all, what did I just call you? Mom, right? And second of all, you told me from the beginning that if I ever needed your help in locating my birth mother that you would help me. Well, I found her, and I thought you would be happy."

The next thing out of her mouth kind of shocked me. She said, "Well, I lied because I didn't ever think that you'd find her." I left my mom's apartment kind of dazed, as I'm sure she was. About an hour later, my mom called. "I'm sorry for reacting the way I did. I've realized what this means to you, and I truly am happy for you."

After our initial conversation, my birth mom and I spoke for three hours, and it felt like we had known each other all our lives. We enjoyed discovering the many similarities we shared. She told me she had been concerned that I was going to call and cuss her out for leaving me and not raising me herself. I told her that thought never crossed my mind.

I learned that I had a half-sister, which made our reunion even more special.

Donna never knew if I was a boy or a girl but somehow gave my sister, who was born ten years after me, the same middle name I was given by my adoptive parents. She said she couldn't have gone through with the adoption if she had held or looked at me. She knew that giving me up for adoption had been the best thing for us both.

When it was time to fly to Oregon to meet my mom, a local TV news station in Dallas and their sister station in Eugene picked up my story, covering my journey from beginning to end. I landed at the airport to cameras and reporters and ended up on the six o'clock news that night. The plane had been delayed about an hour, but I was greeted by a crowd of strangers in the airport, who had learned why the news crew was there. The crowd included the Oregon Ducks.

As I came down the escalator, the lobby was filled with people. And as I hit the last step, a roar of cheers and applause erupted. My sister and my mom and I all ran together and hugged one another for the first time, crying and thanking God. As I looked around, I saw that there wasn't a dry eye in the house. Reporters were crying, strangers were crying, and the big, tough Oregon Ducks were crying. After the interview ended and the crowds began to dissipate, we looked at each other and smiled. We were together for the first time after almost fifty-one years.

As I embraced my mom, I realized how much I looked like her. She is full-blooded Dutch, and my biological father, whom she did not remain in contact with, was Mexican. I was a "Dutchican," as I like to call it. I've visited Oregon eight or nine times since that first meeting, and my sister has been to Texas to see me. I could not be happier. My story is now complete.

THE REVOLUTION WITHIN ME

MAI FAWAZ

GROWING UP as a female in a hypermasculine culture was challenging. I was taught that my femininity was shameful, that my voice and soft features were a sign of weakness, and that I had to hide my body because it was sexual, sinful, and provoking. At a young age, I lacked the right words to describe my experiences but understood that I was being discriminated against for something beyond my control.

I felt it when I was catcalled and harassed on the streets before I even hit puberty. I could see in the perpetrators' eyes how they saw my weakness and used it to terrorize me. When I walked home with my girlfriends, we would hold hands, huddle together, and speed walk in horror whenever we passed a group of male youngsters as they were the most dangerous. They found power in their unity. I felt it every time I would hear my sexuality being used as an insult. I felt it whenever I was in a crowded place, and men would try to brush themselves against my body. It was an everyday struggle that I had to endure in silence. Over time, the abuse began to feel like the norm.

Sometimes, I thought something was wrong with me, that I was somehow guilty for being born a female, and that being feminine meant being weak and humiliated.

Although I thought of myself as privileged because I was born to a well-off family, I was aware that I was not free of oppression. I lived in a prison of fear. I was afraid to walk alone on the streets, stay out late on my own, or even dress the way I wanted. Egypt is one of the most dangerous countries in the world to be a woman. I might have been financially privileged, but I was still at the lower end of the power pyramid. Certainly, things could've been worse for me if I had been born to a poor family. A poor female in Egypt is oppressed by both patriarchy and class.

In Egypt, the middle class is increasingly diminishing, and the upper class lives in a bubble behind walls of fancy compounds and social activities that are only available to those lucky few residing at the uppermost of the socioeconomic pyramid.

A year after I graduated from university, December 18, 2010, the Arab Spring happened. It started in Tunisia when Mohamed Bouazizi, a Tunisian street vendor, set himself on fire in protest of police harassment, humiliation, and the confiscation of his merchandise. Bouazizi sparked the revolution in Tunisia and, later on, a series of revolutions that spread through the entire Arab world in Tunisia, Yemen, Egypt, Syria, and Libya.

I watched in anticipation as things started to escalate in Egypt. The regime was violent with the people, but that didn't seem to affect the protests. People were tired of being abused in silence. They hadn't had a voice for thirty years.

I was tired of being silent too, so I joined the revolution. We called for bread, freedom, social justice, and human dignity, not so much to ask for. Maybe I had always had bread on the table, but I was still in search of my freedom. And I felt a deep connection to and much empathy for the people. Despite our social differences, appearances, and backgrounds, we were all suffering from oppression. During this time, I became aware of the oneness of our world.

January 25, 2011, was the first day of the Egyptian revolution. The eighteen days that followed were a surreal mix of reality and fantasy. Despite the violence used against the protestors by the regime, the solidarity of the people was a dream come true. The first time I joined the demonstrations was such an overwhelming experience. Being part of a massive movement of humanity awakened a mixture of contradictory feelings in me. I felt fear, excitement, and the unfamiliar feeling of contentment. It was as if I had finally found the missing pieces of the puzzle to my larger self.

All kinds of people were contributing to and participating in the protests—rich, poor, men, women, young, old, believers, nonbelievers, Christians, and Muslims. It was as if we were a family of millions. There was so much goodness, hope, courage, generosity, persistence, and strength. I was exposed to a whole new world I hadn't known existed.

It wasn't all flowers and sunshine though, and the brutality of the police left me traumatized with images I will never forget. Regardless, the warm spirit of the revolution healed me and brought me closer to the people as we shared our happiness and our sorrows. I didn't want to see so many people dying, but it wasn't the revolution causing the death and the chaos. The values of the revolution were loud and clear: freedom, social justice, and human dignity. The death and chaos were evoked by a system that refused to adhere to our values.

There were snipers on top of buildings, and protestors formed groups of volunteers to catch them, knowing the probability of being shot dead. Doctors built tents to offer free medical services for the injured, and Christians held hands and formed horizontal lines to protect Muslims while they prayed. It didn't matter if you were a man or a woman, rich or poor, the differences between people disappeared. The only thing that mattered was our shared humanity and our strong will to create a better Egypt for us all.

It was the power of compassion that held us together. Though the word "power" had always represented images of force and coercion, the revolution introduced to me a different type of power, a feminine power that was soft and gentle. I lost myself in the revolution, my background, my social status, and my negative experiences. I felt both like a nobody in the middle of millions of people and a somebody whose presence was important to the cause.

On February 11, 2011, Hosni Mubarak stepped down. It was one of the happiest days of my life. The people of Egypt were dancing in the streets, celebrating and hugging each other. I didn't know what was going to happen next, but it felt as if the whole country was being reborn. Individually, I too was being reborn and transformed.

I discovered who I am and saw myself and the world with new eyes. For the first time in my life, I saw the truth behind the core of my being. It was a paradox, full of contradictions, both feminine and masculine, kind and strong, vulnerable and powerful, and fearful but courageous. I was unlearning the lies about my sexuality that I had inherited. I let go of being a victim of the shame and fear. I found my idealistic side, a side of me that I'd always been ashamed to reveal because idealism has long been associated with impracticality, naivety, and foolishness. Before the revolution, I was never really interested in politics and maybe I never dreamed of a revolution. But I certainly dreamed of a more beautiful world, and my experience within the revolution seemed to validate the possibility of this promise.

Unfortunately, I had to wake up from my fantasy and realize that the day Mubarak stepped down from power was also the day my dream ended. Though the struggle for freedom wasn't over and the demonstrations continued, the people of Egypt were tossed around for three more years by different forces of power. We had to confront the old regime of Mubarak, a military council, and the Muslim Brotherhood. Nothing was changing. There were some noticeable changes on the streets after Mubarak stepped down, but the voice of the revolution wasn't as loud and clear as it had been. I continued to join the demonstrations, but things never felt the same again. The streets weren't safe, and the spirit of the January 25 Revolution was gone.

One day during protesting, I found myself in the middle of a mass sexual harassment. A few men circled me and separated me from my group. Being inside one of those circles felt like you were a piece of meat being groped at by hungry monsters. I started to scream hysterically when a man pulled my hair and began to drag me away. Someone from my group heard my screams and was able to go through the crowd and grab ahold of me. We held on to each other until we reached the nearest building, and the men were gone.

I went back home, and all the tragic events of my childhood flashed through my eyes. I found myself back at square one, feeling weak and disempowered. I felt a mixture of anger, sadness, and hopelessness. Other girls and women were being harassed too and often in much more brutal ways than what I had experienced. The attacks were all over the media. The more stories I heard, the angrier I got. I was angry that being a woman was somehow shameful. I was angry that it made me vulnerable. Once more, I was alone and detached, broken and shattered. I began to think about how when I had been younger, I thought my experiences were my problems. I was realizing that it was not about me and that the struggle for human dignity is every woman's problem. It is a social and a global problem.

I became aware of how privilege systems are built on the concept of separation. The politics of fear is the fuel used to drive the separation. Patriarchal men have a fear of women taking away their power, and the rich fear the poor will take away their wealth. And those in the majorities fear the dominance of the minorities. The problem with privilege systems is that they are invisible. They are hidden under cloaks of safety, such as men being over protective or the wealthy being conservative. Most of us accept these strategies as the price we have to pay for our "safety," and we fail to notice that the system that is built to "protect" us could be slowly killing us.

The revolution had freed me, yet here I was again, slowly killing myself because I was ashamed of my experiences and vulnerability. I was ashamed to share my story and instead was building walls of separation, trying to protect myself from the judgment of others. The only freedom I needed at that moment was freedom from my own oppressive self.

When I look back, I think about how powerful it felt during the revolution when people stood up for each other. The amount of energy and love I received during that time made me feel invincible. Every once in a while, I'm hit by reality, but the memories emerge from inside me and wipe all the pessimism away.

Everything seems to be the same on the outside. The right to freedom of speech and peaceful protest is restricted, and I don't feel safe walking the streets. Things didn't turn out the way I wanted, and it might take years to see real political and social change. But inside me, there is a festival of transformation.

My job is to stay true to everything I experienced during the days of the revolution and true to the promise of what is possible. Courage, kindness, and strength are the seeds of the future. I will keep them alive within me so when the time comes, they will burst forth and flower. They serve as a reminder and living proof that it's real. I've been there. I've seen it. I've lived it. The revolution is within me.

FULL CIRCLE

ANGELA CRISCUOLI

I WAS scared and unsteady, but she took my hand and kept me safe. Then I saw another, scared and unsteady, and suddenly, I wasn't scared or unsteady. And it was I who kept another safe.

Swimming has always been challenging for me. Maybe it has something to do with my grandfather's tragic death. While at the beach with his family one summer, a drowning man caught his attention. My grandfather jumped into the water and saved the man's life, drowning in his place. My grandfather's death, and the fact that I didn't know how to swim, didn't keep my family from having a pool in the backyard when I was growing up. We played Marco Polo and did underwater handstands, and I was able to dog-paddle my way through it all, summer after summer.

One of my neighborhood friends had a pool too. And on one particular day, we were playing in her pool when, all of a sudden, I lost my rhythm and couldn't keep my head above water. I experienced the classic drowning scenario: I was unable to regain control; my head kept going underwater then popping up; and I lost my breath as I gulped in the water. Fortunately, my friend's older sister noticed and pulled me out of the pool. I went home, but I don't think I ever said a word about it to my parents, or anyone else for that matter.

When I was in my mid to late twenties, the owner of the company I worked for had a place in the Catskills where we gathered annually for a two-day party that included tubing down the local river. It was my third year to attend the event. When I arrived, I noticed that the water level seemed high and the current was a little rough. With some trepidation, I got my raft and joined the rest of my group.

As we rode down the river, laughing and shouting, we encountered some small rapids, which made it difficult for us to control the direction of our tubes. The water became turbulent as we approached a fork in the river. My tube was forced down the left fork, while everyone else's tubes went right. I was alone. Ahead of me, I could see rocks and boulders in the river creating areas of dangerous rapids. Then suddenly, in one split second, my tube overturned and I was out.

I got caught in the rapids and was smacked against the rocks over and over again. The current pulled me underwater, and I was unable to find the strength to pull myself back up. I took in a lot of water, and was unable to breathe. At some point, I felt completely relaxed. I clearly remember thinking, *Okay, this is it. It's my time. I am fine. I am at peace.* Just as I had accepted my fate, I felt someone grab the back of my shirt and head. I was dragged towards the river bank and thrown onto shore, before the river carried my rescuer and his kayak away, never to be seen or heard from again. I was SAFE!

When I got home the next day, I found a number of messages on my answering machine from my mother asking me to call her. I did, and when she picked up the phone, I heard her say, in a fearful, shrill voice, "Angela, is that you? I dreamed you were drowning."

Almost thirty years later, though my fear of water was pretty well developed, I was intent on being around people who had similar interests as mine. So when I received an offer to go on a four-day river-rafting trip down the Klamath River with an organization that I follow and have great respect for, I really wanted to go. But my fear of water took over, and I declined the offer. On the last day and hour of registration, my desire to be around these people outweighed my fear, and I registered for the trip, turning my fear to excitement.

The day I arrived at the camp, I met the other rafters then set up my tent for the night. The next morning, after we packed our dry bags and prepared to get on the river, I found myself at the riverbank, wondering what the heck I was thinking.

What am I doing here? I thought. At that same moment, the organizer of the trip asked if there was anything anyone wanted to share with the group—anything anyone needed to feel supported. I was able to blurt out, "I am afraid of water and will need some support." The group acknowledged my fear and was fine with it. Nobody said, "Why did you come on a rafting trip?" Instead, they said things like "Good for you that you had the courage to be here. We will help you." With that, we put on our life jackets, found our rafts, and off we went.

On the third day of the trip, we took a small break from the river and traveled just a short distance downstream to go hiking. We learned that the hike entailed navigating a field of huge boulders, steep narrow paths through the woods, possible encounters with rattlesnakes, and two river crossings through freezing water. Eventually, we would end up at a magnificent waterfall.

I was thinking, *Holy cow! How am I going to do this?* But I was determined to see that waterfall. As we took off, one of my traveling companions, who saw me struggling on the boulders, took my hand, and said, "Don't worry, I'll stay with you." When we got to where the trail began, a woman in our group decided, after her own struggle to maneuver the boulders, that the hike up to the waterfall would be too challenging for her. She made the decision to rest and wait for our return. I was thinking I should do the same but chose to persevere.

The person holding my hand and keeping me safe never left my side.

She helped me climb the steep, narrow wooded path and encouraged me when I lost my breath as we plunged into the frigid, rapidly flowing river that crossed over the trail. And she told me she would take care of me when we had to swim across a section of the river that was so deep I couldn't touch the bottom. She was in front of me, saying "You can do it. It's okay. Don't worry!" as I dog-paddled my way around the rocks. And it went like that all the way to the magnificent waterfall—which was, as promised, a beautiful creation of God.

On the return hike, I was a bit more confident, but that special person stayed by my side and was always there when I lost my footing and faltered. With her as my angel, I made it back safely to the head of the trail. The adventure wasn't quite over though. We still had to navigate those giant boulders to make it back to our rafts.

As we headed out, I noticed the woman who had chosen not to join the hike just ahead of me. She was very unsteady on her feet. I saw her falter and almost fall. I could see the fear on her face, and without thinking, I let go of the hand of the person who had kept me safe. And somehow, on my own, I expertly navigated myself to the side of the woman who was struggling. I grabbed her hand and steadied her. Suddenly, it was me telling someone else who was frightened, "Don't worry. You can do it. I won't let you fall."

As we made it back to our rafts, I was celebrating my newfound freedom from fear.

HERE IS THE NEWS

SAM OBERNIK

IT HAS taken me an inordinate amount of time to actually string these fifteen hundred or so words together without a verse, chorus, bridge, middle eight, rhyme, or reprise as with the hundreds of songs I have written throughout my twenty-five years as a songwriter. Here, there are no supportive resting places that come with musical accompaniment, or punctuating gestural flourishes that are made through the expressive physicality that is the performance of a song. No energetic transaction between audience and player that magically occurs, augmenting a live improvisation of a song. Just this. Words, one after the other, committed to the page. Suddenly, I am a songwriter, yet no writer at all.

For me, it usually starts with a melody. I hum a sequence of notes that stick in my memory, then play a few chords on the guitar or piano to plot a starting point on the map that will be the journey of the song. What does the melody evoke in me? How do I feel? Where am I? Where would I like to be? Who is with me? What is missing? How do I want to feel? Mostly, I just allow myself to sing simple, intuitively phonetic but nonsensical sounds along to the melody and decide that the final crafted words *must* fit those specific sounds.

So, for example, the last song I wrote a few weeks ago began with the words "Here is the news." What does that mean? Why is it that those particular words are floating up for me? I won't be decided on answering these questions until I feel the entire song is complete, thus, allowing myself to take the same interpretive stance as any listener hearing the song for the first time. It is an invitation to myself and the listener to "make of this what you must."

Here is the news, making kings out of fools

And behold, holy soldiers

Got nothing, not nothing to lose.

So strike out and do something,

Or nothing will be everything that you want,

Like the hole in your head,

A poetic explosion in motion in figures of eight,

So get out of the bed that you made.

And I won a war on good credit and score,

I tease out the thorns from your rosy hoard.

But I'm bored of talking in circles and rings,

Searching through needles and pins.

Here is the news, I will read it to you,

I won't measure you by what you don't say.

Call me your toy, and eventually, I will break in your hand.

I will shake every silence you keep,

It's tireless and deafening to me,

But no man is an island.

And I've walked in your shoes,

I have whistled the tune

To the march of the hours,

I'm powerless, time travelling . . .

Here is the news, I will read it to you,

I'll undress every truth till it's naked.

So tell me a story of hope all vainglorious,

Battles you've fought with great wit and brute force,

I'm listening . . .

Throw me a line I can spin,

Let's dig a big hole and jump in.

Like fish in a barrel, we'll swim . . .

Here is the news, I will read it to you,

You can't measure me by what I don't say.

Here is the news, it's not my point of view,

I'm just explaining.

Here is the news, you can take it or lose it

Or break it.

Here is the news,

I can't promise you a happy ending.

At the start of the lyric-writing process, I followed a more obvious path from "Here is the news," i.e., the classic newsreader introduction to the events of the day, touching on what must have been uppermost in my mind at that moment, being daily acts of terrorism in the name of religious ideology—which makes no sense to me, but perfect sense to the business of delivering news content.

This turned quickly into something far more "normal" in human behavioural terms. "So strike out and do something" was inspired by a recent conversation with my twenty-two-year-old son, who talked about his sad realisation that for his generation, active political protest seemed to acceptably reside mainly within the filter bubble of social media—that the gravity of saying but not really doing anything was suddenly clarified for him as being worse than not thinking about it at all.

"So get out of the bed that you made." The course of lyrical intention changed here again, this time touching on something that flowed out of me like a natural spring. It suddenly became a meditation on my own presence as someone who not only plucks intuitive reason from the ether to apply through my voice to music, but also as someone who has created a relatively new supporting role for my own identity, being that of one who helps others find their own voices of reason and respective supporting roles in themselves.

Teaching what I most need to learn in these ways is the prevailing leveler. Once I consciously began to practice this tenet for life, my own mission took on a whole new purpose and impact. When someone writes to me in gratitude for having changed their life, be that through a song or a life-changing conversation, I mirror those thanks because they have changed mine too.

"I won a war on good credit and score" is an egotistical rant of self-justification. I rebelled, I fought, I fell, I loved, I learned, I grew, I created, I succeeded, I feared, I failed, and I survived.

"But I'm bored of talking in circles and rings" basically makes up part of the *why* for why I do what I do for a living.

"Searching through needles and pins" is like Don Quixote's needle in a haystack, years of therapy and intensive introspection—searching for something tiny, yet of great importance, hidden in something that is relatively enormous, left me numb, exposed, and standing off-balance. While I had found all these shiny, pointed objects of wisdom and insight, I had destroyed the chaotic structure of the haystack that provided protection, and creative distraction through the thrill of the search.

"I won't measure you by what you don't say." The space that is silence. Room to breathe, to grow thoughts. While the music is still playing, or as gravity works its magic in the space that holds any communication. Silence is the great clarifier. Like the chaos theory that's the butterfly effect of when the silence breaks, whatever comes out is of distinct consequence and needs to be heard—to be witnessed—because "No man is an island."

"Let's dig a big hole and jump in" is about the stories and the scripts that I dig a hole with every time I write a song, committing myself to the process. Whatever depths I am called to reach, I need to dig—to descend into the dark and the dirt without planning how I'm going to engineer my reemergence back to the stark light of reality.

Each one of my songs owns a part of me, of my story—given up willingly to set the tone of a performance. To invite reaction. To test the depth of feeling. To be released from the inaction of my own circular thoughts. My story can become your story. I invite you to jump in the hole with me; "like fish in a barrel, we'll swim." We don't have to touch or even notice each other—just swim around each other, experiencing what it feels like. Feeling the same, but different.

"I can't promise you a happy ending." This is the caveat of truth that resides in the voice of any imparted wisdom. It's a loving agreement we can perhaps all quietly make a pledge to maintain as we interact with each other with all our projections of feeling. I can only promise to stay true to myself, to this moment, and to whatever truth we want each other to know. A happy ending to anything is one reached through the love, pain, and lightness of being that brings us to any destination.

A song is never truly ended happily. There is always some element of the composition that the writer feels can be adjusted, deleted, or further explained. Like any recognisable ending to any life process, the trick is to leave it where it asks to be left. To take a step back and trust that we have done enough to let it live or die in its own permanence of having been.

Each song completed is a benchmark of distinction, a milestone for a new creative exposure of self, exploring what is known and what is possible. Every finished song teaches me something about myself that I have previously failed to notice otherwise. It sometimes feels akin to writing that difficult letter to someone, yet never sending it. And while many songs will be heard, their true message may not always be found out. Such is the beautiful license of subjectivity. Sometimes, the detail is not always in the detail but in the sum of a song's parts, unlocking feelings like a skeleton key. No one's door is safe, and beneath every door is a threshold.

FIFTY-THREE FEET DOWN, AND IT'S DARK!

RICK MILLER

IT WAS 10:00 p.m. when the Rio Rita pulled out of the Underwater Explorers Society on Grand Bahama Island. Our mission was to explore the old Hydro Lab site and search for, identify, and photograph as many marine life examples as we could. The team consisted of two diving legends, Lou Fead and Bahama's Ben Rose, and four of the top dive magazine writers. Oh yeah, and me—a rookie diver, trained in Texas lakes and rivers, with barely half a dive log full of experience.

The boat was leaving at 10:00 p.m., and this was my *first* night dive in the ocean—no big deal. Diving in low or no-visibility water is pretty common in Texas. So how much harder could it be?

An ocean reef comes alive at night. With pure-white light in crystal clear water, colors are saturated, sea fans and sponges open, and the really big fish come in to feed. With my heart beating rapidly due to a bad case of imposter syndrome (why am I diving with all these experts?) and a healthy case of fear of the dark, I listened intently as Lou gave us instructions: drop anchor and a dive line with beacon light into sixty feet of water, descend in pairs, explore for forty-seven minutes, return to surface, and debrief.

When we arrived at the target spot, surface swells were well above average, and it was decided we would exit the boat Navy SEAL– style with a back roll off the side of the boat. To add to my growing adrenaline rush, I was chosen to be the first to go overboard, grab the dive line, descend fifty-three feet, turn on my own personal dive light as a signal that all was secure, and wait for the rest of the team.

I looked down at the beacon light attached to the diver safety line below. And on signal, I grabbed my mask, tucked my head, pointed my toes, and rolled off the gunwale. It looks so easy in the movies. In reality, at night, it's like taking a ride in a commercial washing machine. Grabbing the line, remembering that the first rule of scuba diving is to keep breathing, I descended slowly toward the light at the end of the line.

On the surface, the boat moving with the swells caused the light to become a swinging pendulum. The closer I got to the light, the more rapidly it would swing. I now figured out why I was chosen to be the first to descend. I was the biggest and heaviest guy onboard. I was there to keep the light in place.

When I was about ten feet from the light, a rogue wave must have pushed the boat forward, freeing the anchor and allowing the downline with light and me to move rapidly through the water. I'd never considered underwater skiing to be a viable sport and would gladly give testimony that it was not fun, particularly in the dark.

As the line moved forward what seemed like hundreds of feet, the light smashed into a coral head. And there I was, fifty-three feet down in the ocean, not on target and in total darkness. At this point, several things came to mind: *I am alone. I am in the dark. I am in the ocean. I don't know where I am. I need to turn on my light.*

Instantly, a second wave of thoughts passed through my head: *I am in the ocean at night. The really big fish come in to feed at night. I am a Texas fisherman. Fishes are drawn to light. Really big fish come in to feed at night. Do not turn on your light.*

In my head, I saw a diagram:

Boat on top of water

Line hanging from boat

Me hanging on line Light shining from me

Me equals bait

No, I was not going to turn on light.

At this point, remembering to breathe was not a problem. I was consuming my air at an amazing rate. It was the second big rule in diving that snapped me out of my paralysis of analysis: never dive alone. Remembering that and the knowledge that six of the top divers in the world were just fifty feet away, waiting for a signal, made it easy to act. *Click.* On goes my light.

What I saw next, not more than ten feet away, caused me to gasp. It was the edge of a coral wall that was brilliant in color and definition. It looked like Walt Disney had taken his magic brush and painted a giant mural that was alive with color and movement. Coral that appeared to be a dull, faded purple in daylight was now transformed into reds, purples, and oranges.

The marine life was indeed larger, not miniature, aquarium-sized fish but supersized versions of what you see in the daytime—giant groupers, magnificent parrot fish, and plate-sized angelfish. My reverie was suddenly interrupted by the presence of my dive buddy, followed by the team. They circled me, communicated in diver sign language, asking if I was okay, and relayed the fact they were slow to respond because of conditions topside. Lou checked my air gauge and laughed, causing an explosion of bubbles, as he saw that in just a few short minutes, I had done some really heavy breathing.

We separated into pairs, collecting our information, enjoying the quietude, and cataloging specimens. After a bit, Lou signaled to us to gather round him in a circle and kneel on the sandy ocean floor. He then wrote on his marker board four words that chilled my soul: turn off your lights.

No, nada, nope, been there and done that. No way was I turning off my light. With a hard stare and a head nod, Lou looked at me with a look that said, "Trust me. Turn off your light." Reluctantly, I clicked my light off and waited for my eyes to adjust to the inky darkness of the depths.

It was there I saw something new. Through the gin-clear water, 251,550 miles and fifty-three feet away, was the moon. It looked so bright, so close, and so peaceful. At that moment, we collectively looked at each other with that look that comes from sharing a common experience—a look of knowing and a look of understanding.

In that circle, there was a peace and feeling that under that full Bahamian moon, we as humans could become one with nature and with one another. We swam together through that reef system, the only light coming from the moon and the bioluminescence of the ocean and its occupants. Arriving at our dive line and ascending safely to the surface with lights on, I felt I was leaving a place I knew I would often return—not just physically in different parts of the world, but also in my mind.

YOU ARE EITHER PREGNANT OR YOU'RE NOT

LIZ SCOTT

I MADE the most significant decision of my life one grey day in December 2009. Daylight was fading as I was trudging through the mud on a solitary walk when the answer to a life-changing question came through loud and clear. I paused to check if I had heard correctly. There wasn't an inner voice *telling* me the answer. It was more like a knowing. I suddenly knew without a doubt the answer to something that had been unclear for years. For the first time in a decade, there was a sense of certainty and peacefulness about my direction of travel.

It had been a bumpy, long-haul journey to become a mum, and I had reached the final fork in the road. Adoption had given me the choice of saying yes or no to parenthood. A young boy had come up for adoption, and my husband and I now needed to make a decision. My husband was going to support me whichever way we travelled. It was down to me. Should I take the fork in the road that headed towards motherhood? Or the one that took me away from ever becoming a mum? Either way, my life would never be the same.

When I married my husband, who had two wonderful children by a previous marriage, I always assumed we would start our own family with ease. But life had other plans. We ended up going down the road of IVF treatment, a journey that cruelly builds up hope before dashing it down again.

Was I ever pregnant? The answer should be easy. You're either pregnant or not. There is no half measure once you've conceived. However, what happens if your embryo is not inside you but in a hospital Petri dish? Are you pregnant then? Your potential child, your future, your ticket to fulfillment is just a cluster of cells, smaller than a pinhead. And it's slowly growing in a hospital laboratory several miles away. Would this count as being pregnant?

It was a question I grappled with when I went through my ten-year journey of IVF treatments. I tried so many therapies to help me on my journey. This included hypnotherapy, reflexology, counseling, meditation, and acupuncture. Each time I went through an IVF treatment, I "conceived." And an embryo, a potential child, started its life. However, the embryo never survived its journey to become a human being, and I never became a mum.

Our final step to becoming parents took us down the road of adoption. For two years, we spoke with a social worker and learnt about the reality of taking on a child. We were cautious. Were we up for this? What would it mean? What would it be like to parent a child that wasn't your own?

Then one day, the social worker sat down with us and showed us information on a six-year-old boy called Saul. For the first time in my life, I realised that becoming a parent was a reality. My husband and I looked at each other with a mixture of excitement and nervousness. In just a few months, Saul would become our son. Surely, raising a child was the most instinctive and rewarding path to take.

Saul, like all children in care, had experienced an impossibly tough start to childhood. Alcoholism and addiction were present in his home. His mum was very young, and his dad was absent.

It seemed so unfair to consider there were children who were neglected by their natural parents and taken away to keep them safe. Yet here we were, my husband and I, a loving and caring couple, who would have done anything to have our own children. But we couldn't conceive. Why didn't God, if there was a God, give the children to parents that could cope? Why did he allow children to be neglected? It just didn't seem right.

So here we were at the fork in the road. In two weeks' time, we were going to see Saul in his foster home for the first time. He would learn we were going to be his parents, and this would be the start of a careful transition as he eased himself away from his foster home. We were at the fork, which meant stepping towards saying yes to becoming parents, or no to living a child-free life.

An unexpected feeling descended on me when I heard about Saul. Here was a child who had been dealt such a rough hand in life, yet I wasn't sure I was the one to help him. I expected to feel an explosion of certainty about at last becoming a mum, and though I knew there would be nervousness at the unknown, the explosion never happened. The silence felt too loud.

We had two weeks to decide, and I knew that once we stepped onboard this final stage of the adoption process, there was no going back. It was the equivalent of pushing myself off the top of a helter-skelter. Once I let go at the top, it would be a whirlwind-spinning slide. My head was nearly bursting when I considered the pros and cons and the ifs and buts. I felt paralyzed and didn't know what to do.

The strangest thing happened at this point. Though it would seem that I should think and talk about the options in front of me, or talk with friends and think hard about what to do, a deeper wisdom took over. Rather than ask advice and churn over the options, I was in neutral. For several days, whenever I strayed into thinking about what to do, this wisdom soothed my mind.

I was on my walk that cold December day, not even thinking about whether I should say yes or no to taking Saul into our home, when the answer came to me. I still remember the rocky path, the mud, and the wet sludgy leaves. I was trying to keep my footing and make it back to the car before nightfall. As I paused to look ahead, the answer became clear. Saul wasn't meant to be our child. I realised it with a mixture of sadness, peace, and relief.

My journey to become a mum was over. The answer to adoption was no.

At the start of my journey to become a mum, I would never have imagined I would be sitting here today with such love and peace in my heart, as I reflect back on that time in my life. There were moments of sadness and what-if's. However, I was so glad I listened to my deeper wisdom. I allowed something within me to find the answer, and I trusted in that answer.

Saul was adopted by a loving couple. And although I have no way of knowing for sure, my sense says that he found the right family and has at last found the love in his life that he deserved to find.

THE AFFAIR

ELIZABETH WEST

THE DREAM was so real. It was 5:30 a.m. when I woke up, wondering if my husband was cheating on me. I tried to go back to sleep, but I just couldn't shake the uneasy feeling I had. As I lay there, paranoia began to creep into my mind as I wondered if there was some validity to my dream.

Unable to shake my uneasiness, I decided that 6:00 a.m. is a perfectly acceptable time to become the amateur detective I'd always wanted to be. I started searching my bedroom for anything that could give me some answers. My first thought was to check my husband's phone and computer, but my husband was out of town and had those two things with him. Desperate to ease my mind, I managed to find an old iPhone of his that hadn't been used in two and a half years. I located a charger and plugged it in.

Once it powered up, I looked at his emails, call logs, and texts. I couldn't find anything out of the ordinary. I started to feel a little calmer though I continued my search. I scrolled through a list of contacts and found an email address with his name on it that I had never seen him use. I went to the email provider's website and entered the address and one of his known passwords. Voila, I was in!

What I found next shook me to the very core of my being. There was an entire email history connecting my husband to an affair that had been going on for at least a year. Suddenly, I couldn't see, breathe, or function. I wanted to scream, cry, yell, and hit something; but all I could do was sit there, shaking uncontrollably. Worst of all, I couldn't even confront him because he was in a time zone three hours behind mine. I kept telling myself that I was still dreaming. I just needed to wake up.

But it was no longer just a dream, and I had so many thoughts and feelings running through me that they were starting to morph into one jumble of emotions that I would have to untangle. I was hurt, angry, sad, and sick to my stomach. I wanted to talk to him, smack the shit out of him, scream at him, and hold him. I was in total disbelief. After all, this was a man who despised *The Bridges of Madison County* because it promoted cheating.

At that moment, I couldn't imagine—as strong as everyone had always told me that I was—how I would make it through such a devastating betrayal. All my life, I had been very vocal about what I would do if anyone ever cheated on me. I just knew I would leave and never look back. Now that I'd found myself in that position, I wasn't even considering leaving my husband. Instead, I was bound and determined to find the answers as to why the affair happened, and do whatever I had to do to save my marriage.

I felt that in order to save my marriage, I needed to read each and every one of the emails to understand what had happened to cause my husband to reach out to someone else. I needed to understand the connection between him and his mistress, the how and why. I painstakingly went through every single word of every email. In hindsight, that may not have been the best idea that I have ever had!

I only read them once, but that was all I needed. They were burnt into my memory, and I couldn't get the images of what I had read out of my head.

I felt so alone. I had nobody to turn to. I didn't even have my husband, the offender, there to help me understand and work through the pain. I didn't want to turn to friends and have them speak ill of my husband, so I just kept everything to myself. I needed to sort through and make sense of it all, and I knew I needed to do so by myself. Out of desperation, I did reach out to my husband's mistress. I begged and pleaded with her to just help me make sense of what had happened. She took no responsibility for her part in the situation.

I was adamant that leaving was not an option for me. I loved my man, and I was determined to not only save my marriage, but have it thrive. I knew that healing my marriage would be hard, and it was. I needed my husband to be with me, but he was gone five months for work. We had to work on healing and repairing our marriage long-distance. We attempted couple's counseling on the weekends when he was home, but that didn't go well. The weekends were the only time we had together, and going to counseling was difficult to work into that short amount of time, so we nixed that. But we got to know each other again. We spent time together, just the two of us. And as a family, we discussed what happened many, many times. We read books about marriage and infidelity and figured out when, where, and why our marriage had broken down.

It has been almost three years since my discovery. That first year was extremely difficult. The highs and lows were unbelievable and could change at a minute's notice. Having to ride by the exit where the other woman lived, worrying about running into her at the grocery store, and even seeing Spanish moss on a tree would often trigger unwanted emotions, sending me over the edge. She had told my husband that she loved Spanish moss.

For a long time, I wondered if my husband was still in contact with her, whether in person or electronically. I also ruminated on what she had that I didn't. I compared myself to her constantly. I despised her and was envious of her, all at the same time. So many times during that first year, I thought that I wouldn't be able to get past all the hurt. I often second-guessed my decision to stay and work things out. I rationalized so many things in my head. I thought that if it had just been a one-night stand or just sex, it would have been easier to handle. But a full-blown emotional affair from a man that was never emotional with me crushed my soul. I felt empty inside most of the time. But for the world to see, I put on an Academy Award–winning performance.

The last two years have been much easier than that first year. That's not to say that I still haven't had triggers that have made me sad, angry, and hurt. But they happen less and less, and I'm better able to deal with them. I sought out individual counseling to work on me and the issues I've had with abandonment and not feeling loved—issues that stem from my childhood. I also started meditating and getting Reiki. And now I'm putting pen to paper as my final step toward healing.

Discovering this huge act of betrayal wasn't the end of my marriage, though it might have been easier to walk away. The pain will always be there, but it has definitely lessened over time. Forgiveness for myself and my husband was necessary for us to move forward, though I have not forgotten what happened. I think it's a pretty safe assumption that I will never forget. However, I can now look back and say that not only did I personally survive and thrive through it all, but my marriage did as well.

I do not wish the pain and betrayal I experienced on my worst enemy. But I don't subscribe to the school of thought, "Once a cheater, always a cheater." I believe good people can make mistakes. We are all human. And while I don't accept responsibility for the mistakes he made, I can see how my actions influenced what happened.

This life-changing event was the swift kick in the ass that my marriage needed. If the affair hadn't happened, my husband and I would have eventually divorced. We were both guilty of not putting the other first, not listening to the other, and essentially living like roommates. We worked and continue to work together so that this breakdown will never happen again. We laugh and genuinely love being with each other now. Our relationship is a complete 180 from where it was when he began his affair. We are each other's biggest cheerleader.

FATHERLESS CHILD

KHALIL COFFIELD

IN THE summer of 2003, I got a call from my biological father. He was coming to Dallas to pick me and my sister up to spend the summer with him and his family. I remembered feeling overwhelmed with excitement at the thought of seeing him for the very first time. For so long, I'd watched other fathers with their families and wondered what it would be like to have mine in my life. Maybe now I would no longer feel like a piece of me was missing.

The summer went by, and I waited. But my father never came. My eight-year-old brain decided he didn't care about me and that he didn't want anything to do with me. Though disappointed, I don't remember hating or blaming him for not showing up. Maybe I didn't want to feel the pain of his rejection. However, I knew one day our paths would cross.

It would be New Year's 2012, before I would have another opportunity to meet my father. My sister and I traveled on a bus to Midland, Texas, where he lived with his family. As we hopped on the bus, I was excited and nervous all at the same time. I was finally going to be able to say that I had met him. Assuming he was anticipating our arrival, I texted him, "We are on our way to Midland right now. We will be at Granny's house soon." He never replied.

When we arrived at the bus terminal, my grandmother, his mother, was standing there waiting to pick me and my sister up. It was our very first time meeting her, and I felt an instant love as I got off the bus and fell into her arms. I texted my father again, this time to let him know we'd made it to Midland and would be at his mom's house the whole week. I just knew that he would come by to see us.

Within a couple of days of arriving in Midland, I met my cousins, my half brother, Taveion, and some new friends. Taveion and I bonded instantly, as if we had known each other our whole lives. We were inseparable. One day, my brother and I were at a friend's house when he asked, "Have you seen or talked to our dad?" I told him I hadn't, though I had texted him to let him know we were at Granny's. Immediately, my brother picked up his phone and called our father.

When he answered, Taveion put my dad on speaker so I could hear everything that was said. "Hey, did you know that Khalil was in town?" My father replied, "No, I didn't know he was here." From the moment those words came out of his mouth, I sat in silence, the frustration building up inside me. I was so angry. Everything in me needed to be heard . . . needed to confront my bold-faced, liar father. I wanted him to feel my hurt and my anger. I texted him one more time.

"Man, I'm with Taveion right now, and I heard every damn thing you said. I was coming down here hoping to start the New Year by putting the past behind us. I texted you on Sunday to let you know Ariell and I were here, and now you're trying to say that you just found out yesterday? Bullshit! I cried my eyes out last night because I wanted to meet my dad, and I just knew we would see you, man. But those tears weren't for you. You don't deserve them. I have had so many people in my life that have shaped me into the young man I am today. It sucks that you couldn't know me, but I guess that's what they call life. You don't have to sit there and lie to my brother about anything, man. You don't ever have to worry about me or Ariell because you better believe I've got this, and she and I don't need you. Thanks for being my sperm donor."

Later that day, when I got back to my grandmother's house, she told me she had received a call from my dad, saying that I was being disrespectful. He told her about the message I'd sent him. She told me it was okay and that it was his fault for not coming to see us. She said, "Don't worry about your father. You have your family here, and that's all that matters. We will always be here."

I sent that message out of anger because everything in me wanted to build a relationship with my dad, and after being the one to make all the moves and put in all the effort, I once again felt like he didn't want to be a part of my life.

The night before Ariell and I departed for home, we received an unexpected visit from the man I call my father. He was a tall black man with a scruffy beard and glasses. He showed up at my grandmother's house with his family, and I never felt so out of place in my life. When I sent that final text, I thought that we would never meet, yet here he was. We didn't talk much, but my father did apologize for not being in our lives.

After meeting my father, I realized that I had already come a long way without having him in my life. It was freeing not to worry about him anymore and to realize how blessed I was to have so many other people in my life who cared about me. It was because of those people, many who weren't biologically related to me but chose to love me, that I would soon be the first in my family to graduate from college. It was because of them that I had been blessed with opportunities to travel and gain knowledge.

I am twenty-one years old now and live life without regret. I always forgive even when it's hard. I had to forgive my father because part of me knew that I couldn't put all the blame on him for his absence in my life. I also knew I had to forgive him so I could move on.

Because I knew the pain of not having my dad in my life, I wanted to fill that void in someone else's life, so I volunteered to be a big brother through the Big Brother program. I benefited from the program and knew it was my chance to give back. I now mentor a young boy named Elijah. And when I am with him, I see the same pain in him that I felt as a boy, wondering where my dad was, why he wasn't in my life, and if I would ever see him. As I spent this past Father's Day with Elijah, I had to confront his sadness, letting him know that everything would be okay. I had to tell him how I learned to live my life without my father.

It was so hard telling those words to an eight-year-old boy, "Your father may never be in your life." But as I said those words, I was also able to reassure Elijah that I would always be there for him. I would be there to see him grow up, supporting him along the way as he becomes the successful young man I know he will be. While I am still growing as a man myself, I know I have to make good choices as I have this little boy looking up to me. I know that I have already made a difference in Elijah's life, and he has definitely made a huge difference in mine.

SUPPORT FROM THE UNIVERSE

TESSA SHAFFER

WHEN I was twenty, I wasn't sure how the Universe worked. And ten years later, I am still learning. But it was then, in my twenties, when the Universe first started shouting at me. After leaving my bartending and waitressing jobs—jobs that had brought many characters into my life, including my now husband, I somehow landed a dream job. I traded in pouring shots and enduring karaoke nights for a steady job with benefits at a design company.

I loved being a part of a company that was so creative. Though I was an artist and a writer at heart, I didn't have much experience or the qualifications for a job with the company other than that of front desk girl. Luckily, they saw potential in me. I became "the gatekeeper" of the company, a name given to my position by another employee—I thought to make me feel better about my low position on the totem pole. But I quickly learned that the front desk role was the most important one of the business. I was the first to shake anyone's hand who entered. I faxed and filed all the important documents, and I saw how each department in the company worked and where each could work better. Within three years, I had moved up the company ladder through sales and management and then, in a twist of hard work and fate, became a part of the hiring team to find new gatekeepers for the company.

However, the downside to success in any career is what you trade for it. I paid for it with my health, time with my family, and my soul's purpose. The stress of managing employees and closing big deals was heavy, but the heaviest stress became the inner knowing that I wasn't doing what I was supposed to be doing. I had an aching that told me that I was out of alignment with my purpose, and the more I ignored this aching, the worse my health got.

Though an artist and a writer, in the five years that I had worked in a creative environment, I had let my own dreams and creative ideas fall to the wayside. I would drive home from a ten-hour day and ask myself or God, *What is this all for?* No one ever answered, but I knew there had to be something more.

I didn't know what I would do if I left my job, but I also didn't know what would happen to me if I stayed. One night I started crying in a confession to my husband that I just couldn't work the way I was with all the stress and the lack of purpose. He had been witness to my fading joy at the job I once loved. And our limited time together on the weekends had been replaced with my migraines and my scheduling of work for the week ahead.

I was so busy filling up my calendar that I ignored the need to fill up my heart.

My husband asked me what I might do for income if I quit. I thought I could always go back to bartending, but in that moment, I said, "Make jewelry?" I never even wore jewelry, but I had recently found joy in creating it for friends and family. He said, "Okay, let's buy you some professional jewelry tools." His faith in me was amazing. But I was still unsure—mostly about what other people would think. So many questions and fears came up, so I sat with the idea for months, creating a constant inner dialogue that said, *Is this a good idea? Will I be able to make this work?*

Driving to work one day, I was sick with stress. I thought, *I should just do it. I should just put in my resignation today.* But there was just no way. There were meetings scheduled and projects to see through. And despite my husband's support, I was worried what other people would say if I left a steady dream job to take a chance on something new. I was very much aware that I would be trading in my IRA for penniless hopes and wishes.

Just then, as I was talking myself out of the risk of a new beginning, the radio played the song, "Sometimes goodbye is a second chance." The lyrics were about leaving and about realizing that it doesn't matter what other people think. After the song ended, I said out loud, "Wow, was that a sign?" Then I flipped the station, and the song I landed on was none other than Ace of Base's "I Saw the Sign." I laughed. It was a good conversation with the Universe. I felt heard and supported, but I was still afraid to make the jump.

Later that week, I was in a store to find a gift for a friend when I picked up a book, revealing a misplaced book behind it. It was a children's craft book titled *Jewelry Making Made Easy*. I looked around and paused for a long time, thinking about the odds of picking up the first book and having that misplaced book behind it be about making jewelry. And then I remembered the songs earlier that week, and in my head, I said, *Okay, I think I got it. Thank you.*

The following week at work, the phones were ringing like crazy. It was chaotic and stressful, and I just thought to myself, *This stress just isn't me. This can't be my life anymore.* Moments later, I received a call from a potential client, inquiring about pricing and designs for his wife's new jewelry business. In my five years working at the company, we had never received any inquiries from a jewelry business. And this husband calling for his wife's jewelry business reminded me of my own husband's support to make the leap of faith. I jotted down a few notes from the caller, and when I hung up, a coworker asked what the call was about. I said without thinking, "Oh, it was just a message for me." I finally received the messages from the Universe, each one a bit louder than the previous one. I knew then that I was on the right track in my thinking, and that I would be supported in my career change.

A few weeks later, I started my own jewelry business from scratch, thankful for every step of business practice I had learned in those five years at my job. Working from my heart welcomed a new kind of success, as I now sell my designs through national distributors. Recreating my life allowed me to create my own schedule, and it opened the door for me to write again, fulfilling my soul's purpose and inspiring others to live theirs.

It's been five years now since I started trusting in the synchronicities of the Universe, and now I'm taking notes on how and when it is at work, and including those notes in my next book. I've learned that the Universe isn't selective. It speaks to everyone in time, but it's the brave who see the signs and choose to pay attention. There is risk, but there is also great reward in following your heart.

GLIMPSES OF GENIUS

JO HODSON

BEFORE I met him, I had played it safe. I played out my life so safely and quietly I'd barely made a dent. Spiritless conformity and tantrums in the company of those closest to me, these were the symptoms of what I now see as me not fitting into the life I had created or maybe the life that had been created on my behalf and one that I had blindly stepped into.

I was stuck in the world of pleasing people, not wanting to be seen as different or be the centre of attention. Playing outside the rules would change all that, and I shied away from it all. My innate curiosity was not yet strong enough to break through these barriers of society's control and expectation.

There may not have been one specific moment. Nothing that screamed at me. *This is it. This is what you have to do* now!" It was instead a creep of realisation. It was a steady enlightenment that there was another way to live. It was a realisation of just how small a life I had been living and how much that had dulled my soul.

As it neared Christmas 2012, that realisation reached a crescendo. I was working as an architect. From the outside, my career looked great. It had glamour and prestige, and the company had won numerous awards. And it was in a studio set in a beautiful location in the middle of the countryside.

But inside, my soul was dying.

This wasn't my life's calling. This wasn't my path to the fulfillment that I yearned for. I felt this deeply, yet I didn't know what path was. How could I leave the safe life that I knew until I had something else ready to step into?

I had stalled for years in the lead up to that moment, often working sixty-hour weeks with little mental capacity to ponder an alternative life. It all seemed so far beyond my reach. I didn't know anything else. It would be a waste of my university education to leave this career path now. Friends were moving up the career ladder, settling down, buying houses, and having babies. I sensed pity in their eyes as I battled with the fundamentals of my own life.

With these thoughts and feelings causing chaos in my mind, I struggled to reach out to others, even those closest to me. I felt their own fears and limiting beliefs reflected back to me twofold, and it made my situation seem even worse and more deeply overwhelming.

But *everything* changed when I met the *boy*.

It is said that people come into our lives for a reason, and I truly believe this to be the case. At twenty-eight, I was plodding through life, living up to society's expectation, and seeking external validation for every move I made. I played by the rules and never coloured outside of the lines. The yearning inside to be something more was just a seedling, and I didn't water it.

I don't have Asperger's syndrome, but for a year, I was in a relationship with a guy who did. This was at times an incredibly difficult and tumultuous journey, but one that I now look back on as a defining period of my life. Within weeks, he had literally shattered all my illusions and turned my perception of life and everything I thought I knew on its head. As he let me into his world, I was, for the first time, able to see my own for what it truly was.

His life was black and white—a series of carefully calculated opportunities. There was nothing so important in his life that he would not have been prepared to walk away from, if he had needed to start over.

My life was a series of balancing blocks and shades of grey. Procrastinating, I never quite reached where it was I felt I wanted to be. I would get distracted and frustrated and succumb to self-doubt and the mediocre.

In living with the boy, I saw firsthand both the pain and the glory in the extremes. An extract from my journal, written as the New Year rolled round just three months into our relationship, summed up so beautifully what I felt and the powerful conflict I would soon face in so many areas of my life.

Because you are amazing, you are not easy. If you were easy you wouldn't be amazing.

I had written him that line, amongst many other heartfelt words, on lots of coloured paper notelets that I had folded up and placed in a glass Kilner jar. Those words spoke volumes. Those words had opened up so many questions for me, for us.

Living in his world was intense. It was like diving into a dark pool and not being able to touch the bottom or even have a sense of how far I'd need to swim to reach the edge to hold on and take a breather.

One lunchtime, I was making pancakes for dessert. I'd made this particular recipe before, and he was excited when I mentioned I was making it again. Everything was going well until at the last moment, I remembered I'd forgotten to put a little sugar in the batter. It wouldn't have made much difference, so I casually mentioned it as I served them onto a big plate in front of him.

In a split second, all hell broke loose.

I froze, bewildered.

He couldn't handle the sudden change in expectation he felt was being demanded of him. It was a situation he had no control over.

He launched the plate full of pancakes hard at the dining room wall.

There was anger, resentment, disappointment, and guilt on both sides of the table.

In that moment and the hours that followed, as we talked openly, he taught me the power of acceptance. For the first time, I also became aware of the distinction between accepting and understanding. It was one of the most difficult but important lessons I've ever learnt. There was no way I could ever have understood the quirks and intricacies of his world, but I learned to embrace and accept them. And in turn, he learnt to accept my experience of the world even though he could never understand that either.

In accepting the way things are, it does not mean I condone or give in. Instead, in shifting and removing the anger from a situation, I create space to act from my heart and not my head, which in turn gives rise to compassion and empathy not just for others, but also for myself.

Learning to accept myself, as I grow and evolve and succeed and fail, continues to be a huge focus of my onward journey.

After a year with the boy, it all ended. He had shown me all I needed to know and gifted me the tools for my psychological toolkit. Now it was time to step up and apply them on my own.

When he was in full flow, life with the boy had been nothing short of amazing. He believed in me so deeply, that in those moments, I believed in myself too. I was terrified of walking away and losing all that he had ignited inside me.

So much had shifted inside me over that last year. And without him there to challenge me at every corner, I wasn't sure that I wouldn't fall back into the patterns and routines of my previous ordinary and superficial life. Though I was surrounded by people who loved me and wanted the best for me, they unknowingly prioritized my safety and kept me small.

They couldn't see what I could now see.

One month after I walked away from my life with the boy, I quit my career in architecture, quit my nine-to-five routine, and launched myself into the unknown with no backup plan or any inclination of how my life would unfold from that point forward. Was I ready? Or was I simply too scared of falling back into my old habits such that this felt like my only option?

I now live my life on my own terms, whatever that may mean from moment to moment. I am learning to honour my failures and celebrate my successes—open-hearted and open-minded. In accepting myself, I am freed from the burden of seeking external validation.

Now and again, I catch myself in those quiet moments—the pauses in my day, reflecting back to that time in my life. As I do, I observe glimpses of his genius within the depths of my own soul. Each time, I open my heart a little bit wider and appreciate his less ordinary life. It is the catalyst for me stepping into my own.

EVERY DAY WE RAN

MATTHEW THOMAS

I WAS twenty-two years old at the time and had only been in Ashland, Oregon, for about two years. An injured back and interest in the mechanics of the human body led me to attend a talk by Dr. Erin Pollinger at the Hidden Springs Wellness Center. The center was a beautiful sanctuary nestled between the major streets of Ashland and surrounded by commercial buildings. It was a peaceful retreat landscaped by fresh foliage and a small pond sheltered under the arms of a young willow tree. That day's talk was to be on "Network Spinal Analysis."

I was instantly drawn to Erin. Her knowledge of the body was extensive, and she was generous with her time. I knew I wanted to work with her, and somehow, I would make that happen. After her talk, I approached her and spoke of my interest, and also of my financially meager situation. At the time, my job afforded me to just barely pay for rent, food, and other minor expenses.

Erin proposed a trade of services. She had recently bought two black lab and collie mixed puppies named Misa and Lucy. Being both a mother and the owner of her own business, she was having trouble making sure they got the proper exercise that they needed. The agreement was that if I walked them every day, she would give me a spinal adjustment every week. I thought this was a good step in the right direction. It wasn't the direct study that I had wanted, but I did need the adjustments. And I could learn from our sessions by observing what she did and asking her key questions. Plus, walking the dogs would be good exercise.

As it turned out, walking the dogs became my real training. This trade of services would require me to commit myself to a daily activity without fail. Commitment like this had always been very challenging for me. I rarely finished what I started, and it was common practice for me to play leapfrog with my interests and hobbies. I was not very good at routine, and my record of missed school days and work days had always pushed the limits of what was acceptable. Now I had committed myself to an inconvenient and daily routine that would take a good portion of my time to fulfill.

Erin lived about a mile and a half from me, and I had only a bike for transportation and not even that some days. Our agreement was that I would get to her house and then use her car to drive the puppies into the mountains, where I would run them on the trails for about an hour. True to my character, within the first two weeks, I tried to get out of it. I was too sick or the bike broke or work kept me late—I don't remember what excuse I used, but it worked. Unfortunately, it came with a guilty conscience.

I had expected Erin to just brush it off with a "No problem" and a "See ya tomorrow." Instead, I was to learn that Erin had a great deal of integrity about her commitments, and she expected the same of me. She didn't scold or lecture me. She only talked to me about the importance of sticking to our agreement.

Her words came to me at a time when my integrity about completing what I said I would do was already being challenged in multiple ways.

I knew that I would get out of things if I could, most of the time.

Naturally, I also wanted to be seen as reliable and responsible, so I had learned to measure a balance between how much I could miss, what excuse to use, and when. I had become pretty good at it, but I knew that none of it would stand up against Erin, even if it did work in other areas of my life.

I had reached some sort of emotional tipping point, and Erin had pushed me the rest of the way. I made a distinctly important decision shortly after I ducked out of my responsibility with the puppies. It was a decision that I didn't believe had much more weight or integrity to it than many of my other decisions, but it stuck all the same. I decided that I was not going to miss another day walking the puppies no matter what. No matter how hard it got and no matter the conditions—the weather, lack of transportation, broken down, or sick —I would still show up. And this was to become my most important integrity test.

The coming days, months, and even the full year and a half that I ran those puppies. I never missed a single day. In that time, I had transportation challenges, an injured ankle, days of snow, days of rain, and days where the sun had already gone down. But the worst was the poison ivy. I knew how to avoid it, but the puppies would run off the path to explore and then race back to me and get me covered in the stuff. In the entire time that I ran them, there was only a handful of weeks where I didn't have poison ivy on some part of my body.

Traveling in the mountains with those puppies became a time of reflection, meditation, exercise, learning, or whatever I needed it to be on any given day. Some days were just pure frustration and me wanting to get it over with. It was stunning to me that I had the gift of being able to escape it all, and run through the mountains with such loving, joyous puppies every day, yet it was still a struggle for me to want to do it. It would always have been easier to just stay home and watch movies, play video games, sleep, or whatever else, especially after a long day at work. But to get up and do something so rich with experience that it touched my very soul with the purity of nature—I never got why that was such a challenge.

Being with those puppies are some of the moments in my life that I treasure the most. My integrity back then has become an anchor for my integrity today. I wish I knew exactly what made that shift possible. I do know that the day I decided to be committed, I meant it right through to my core, though I had tried plenty of times before only to fail on other commitments. I think it was not so important what I felt that day or on any of the days that would follow. Instead, what mattered was the choice I made each day. I chose to be in those mountains no matter what I felt or what excuse my mind might conjure up as to why that day was the exception.

Every day we ran from hot asphalt to cool waterfall. We ran from mountain rock to forest soil. We cut streams, crossed log bridges, and traversed fields of flowers. Every day we ran.

BIRTH AS I KNOW IT

ANNE FERRIER CROOK

I WAS floating on my back in the ocean, wondering how in the world I got there. I lay still, allowing the buoyancy of the water to support me as the waves gently rocked me back and forth. Looking up at the blue sky, I felt so raw—terrified. I had this gnawing feeling in my stomach prompting me to bolt and start making other plans. I was afraid of being left behind.

Instead, I allowed the fear to pass and simply wash over me.

I had just packed up my life in Colorado, putting everything in storage so I could be closer to family for the first time in twenty years. I was thirty-eight years old, and it seemed like a great opportunity to make some changes. Parts of my life in Colorado had come to a close, including a part-time job and a relationship.

Living as a mountain girl in Colorado, I was used to pushing and striving toward that next step. Going through life with "I can do it!" as my shield, I was fiercely determined. My athletic nature had served me well, creating a strong sense of courage and resilience.

Yet this fierce determination took a huge toll on my health, and I ultimately broke down from stress as a result. This led to a life on an antidepressant, and it became my new shield.

Now here I was in Hawaii, free from the antidepressant but feeling so overwhelmed by the emotions coming to the surface. My body was sending me a message—a cry to let go and open up to transformation. Somehow, I found the courage to listen. Breathing in and out, I looked my fear straight in the eye without blinking. I began surrendering to the wisdom of a voice that would become the biggest game changer of my life: my inner healer.

As I lay there in the ocean, I thought about how my sister and her two young children had just left the Hawaiian Islands that morning and taken off for Nashville. It made sense for her to leave. After all, she was fresh out of a divorce, a newly single mom, and could no longer support two small children on her own. Yes, she had warned me not to move there for them given her life could shift at any moment.

As my childhood fears surfaced, I thought, *How did I wind up here in the middle of nowhere? I just moved here for god's sake.* I wanted to support my sister through her divorce and spend quality time with my niece and nephew, and now they were all gone. I tried to make sense of the perceived abandonment. I gave myself permission to feel it *all*. Little did I know that my deeper purpose on Maui was beginning to express itself. I was surrounded by it—water.

As a certified birth doula, I assisted in hundreds of births, witnessing the magic of this life-changing transition in people's lives. Yet I did not fully understand the impact birth had on my own life until I was in Hawaii, surrounded by the ocean. I began to see my life events differently. The deep spiritual significance of water became apparent to me, and I realized that water is a divine life source for my health.

My fear began to soften, and I could see that I was brought to this island for a special reason—beyond my family.

Floating in the ocean that morning ended up being my first step toward trusting in the process. I soon discovered that certain things were beyond my control and that, when I let go, beautiful gifts organically showed up in my life. Before that moment, I had no idea what it meant when island locals referred to my new surroundings as Mother Maui; nor could I grasp that I was indeed giving birth to a new part of myself—a more graceful and feminine part, guided gently yet powerfully by Maui's sacred waters.

I began connecting with water in profound ways. I started noticing its buoyancy to support me while floating on my back, which literally translated into a new awareness that "life has my back." I was no longer meant to live with that outdated shield "I can do it!" all on my own.

I realized that my passion for birth was my passion for healing and transformation, and that our health weaves together a beautiful dance between life cycles where healing and aliveness come together.

As the ocean waves gently rocked me back and forth, my awareness continued to shift. The fluid movement of water taught me that healing is not linear. It dances to its own rhythm. So rather than resisting my struggles, I began to embrace them, allowing the deeper message to open me and expand.

I finally put down my shield and stopped fighting. It required a whole new level of courage I had not known before, one that went beyond my athletic strengths and fierce determination. It was speaking a brand-new language, telling me to let go and surrender to my higher power.

I lay there, floating, listening, and connecting to the natural world.

I realized my breakdown in health had been my *breakthrough* toward emotional healing and transformation. The struggle of chronic stress and developing a thyroid condition had become my path forward. *My gift.* I saw how the contractions in childbirth paralleled the contractions in my life, which became the fertile ground from which to grow.

Falling in love with Maui's waterfalls, immersing myself in nature, and learning about the healing properties of negative ions, I connected deeper with my purpose. Enjoying moments of pure bliss, I was like a kid coming alive again. Shifting my awareness and recognizing the healing power of water, I watched my own divinely orchestrated birth. I now understood my doula work on a much deeper level. I could see how it brought me full circle back to my own health. Rather than striving and pushing through life changes, I discovered a gentler approach of allowing and creating more room inside for greater freedom.

The healing power of water had a message for me, and it was during this unique juncture in my life that I received its beautiful gift. The ocean became my divine medium. It brought me a deeper understanding of *birth*. I came to understand that birth goes way beyond the labor and delivery room. It reaches far and wide into the colorful tapestries of our lives. It is the integration of body, mind, and spirit, moving us to let go and expand into our wholeness.

Floating in the ocean became the sacred pathway toward my own awakening, sending a message of safety and guiding me to my true self.

Taking refuge in this newfound wisdom, I have become more fluid in my body. I feel more. I trust more. I receive more. And I am connected with my deeper purpose to live it boldly in the world, awakening to the magic of birth.

Right before my departure from Hawaii, I returned to the ocean to write about my discoveries when I noticed dolphins in the distance. I swam out into the bay and approached them gently while floating on my back, allowing space if they chose to grace me with their presence. Soon, about twenty dolphins surrounded me as rays of sunlight beamed through the ocean. I could hear their sounds underwater, and it felt like I was getting filled with love and affirmation right before my departure.

It was a magical moment.

My lessons in Hawaii continue to propel me forward to shine my light out into the world and to choose love over fear. It is my new formula for *thriving*.

THE DREAM OF DREAMS

MAUREEN HUNTLEY

THE ELEVATOR is translucent. It slowly begins to glide upward with ease, each floor disappearing into the next and so on. I grip the handles of the wheelchair tightly, holding on for dear life. It is heavy, black, worn, and old. I have never really seen her in a wheelchair before. But here we are, ascending upward to some unknown place, for I, the dutiful daughter, do what I'm told with love. Nora Mary, rather Mary, as she preferred to be called, is my mother.

Slowing down to a stop, there is a silence. I have the urge to ask like a child would, "Are we there yet?" knowing full well that we had arrived. It is the very top of the building. The elevator opens. The most magnificent glass atrium—big, beautiful, and clear—is revealed.

As I push the wheelchair forward, I'm struck with awe as to the majestic beauty of this place. Colored lights zing in prism fashion as though there are thousands of stars holding this space.

There is now an urgency to move along. In the distance, across this grand open area, is a large boardroom. It is massive and translucent.

The door opens, and we slowly enter the room. Looking up, I see that all the seats have been taken, except the empty one that is directly in front of my mother. She leans forward, putting her hands on the back of the chair as she tries to pull up her frail body. The wheelchair pushes back as she does so.

I feel uneasy, not knowing why we're here. I look to my mom's right and see that it is her brother, John, who is seated next to this empty chair. At her left is Martha, her sister, standing at attention, ever so ready to help her into her seat.

Mom was the youngest of twelve. All her siblings are at the table, yet they are all deceased. They beckon her to join them. I look back at John, saying, "No! No, not now!" He looks confused. I put my hand on top of Mom's hand to stop her, and I move the chair back. She doesn't give in to me. Martha looks at me disapprovingly, as she often did in life, as I try to stop Mom from doing what she believes she must.

"NO!" I scream. "Please, not now. I'm not ready." Martha shakes her head. "No!"

"Please, please, give me two more years with her. Please?"

Slowly, Martha looks at me. Her eyes are full of sorrow, maybe because she thinks I'm ignorant to the ways of the Universe or maybe, just for now, she's losing this battle.

"Soon," Martha decrees.

I nod, but I don't want to think about the word "soon." Hurriedly, I pry Mom's hands off the back of the chair and push it in. She steps backward, ready to sit into the wheelchair. I order her to walk.

"No, walk. You must walk."

She obeys my demand. It's hard for her as she struggles to do so.

We leave, heading back to the elevator. My beautiful mother keeps looking back as I keep pulling her forward.

I wake up, sweating, and realize it was only a dream.

My busy day begins. It is the morning of February 2, 2009. I get up as usual, get the older kids ready and off to school, make beds, start laundry, and then send the youngest to school.

When I get back home, I call my good friend Rhonda. I just need a friend. She's my reality check friend. Truthfully, there are times that I really don't want to hear her version of reality, but the dread lingered. My parents didn't answer my phone calls, and I so needed a friend check-in.

As we sit with coffee in hand at my kitchen table, I tell her the dream. It was, after all, only a dream.

The phone rings. It's Dad. Though 833 miles away from me, I still felt responsible for my parents' well-being, a carryover from my childhood to nurse and take care of everyone.

He sounds exhausted and is barely audible. His voice cracks as he tells me that his beautiful bride, as he called my mother, had a massive heart attack during the night. The doctors believe that it is nothing short of a miracle that she survived.

You never really realize how wonderful your friends are until you hit a wall, slide down it, and they pick you up, dust you off, and set you in a direction of clarity. How Rhonda did it that day, I'll never know. How I did it, God alone knows.

I sat on that flight to Chicago, replaying my dream over and over again in my head. The realization of what I dreamt set in. It was not just a dream. *Did I create this?* I wondered. *What if I only had two more years with her?*

Standing there in the O'Hare Airport cab line, it was cold, really cold. I remembered why I had moved away. A ten-minute wait and a forty-five-minute cab ride, then I'm deposited at the front doors of Evanston Hospital. It was now late afternoon and hours since I had known Mom's prognosis.

Dragging my luggage behind me, I get to the reception area. There, seated at the long desk, was a very proper woman in her fifties wearing her conservative suburban outfit and speaking in a very paced manner. "Can I help you?"

I blurted out my mother's name, hoping she was still there. I meant to ask what room she was in, but my mind kept going to the fact that she might not be there, and nobody let me know. I tried not to go there with my thoughts.

"Yes, a room, a room number, and a pass." I hurry over to the elevator and stalled at the up button, thinking, *I just want to go back to normal because I know in my heart of hearts, my days of normal are over for now.*

As the elevator goes up and up, the vision of the dream comes back again, but nothing here is translucent. This is not the beautiful, light-filled, prism-like space I had dreamt about.

The doors open on the top floor. It's cold, dull, and dark. And I am full of fear. There, in front of me, is the nurse's station. I burst into tears. A motherly middle-aged woman—who looks exhausted herself—smiles knowingly at me.

"Just go down the hall to the right."

Mom would always say "Take a deep breath." So there I am, just doing my best to breathe.

As I get to the doorway of her room, I peek in, and she sees me. Running over to her, I hold her and gently kiss her head. Then I sob out the words: "I love you, Mom. You're my hero."

Slowly she nods and grasps my hand. With her other arm around my neck, pulling me close, she quietly and deliberately speaks in her Irish brogue, "Maureen, Maureen, I thought I was a goner. But there you were."

Six days before my beautiful mother passed away, I had a dream. Mariah, my eighteen-year-old daughter, was on my right, and Mom was on my left.

"Mariah, look at you. I just finished nursing you, and I did a good job." She beams with joy.

"I just finished nursing you, Mom, and I didn't do a very good job."

She smiles reluctantly. "You did a great job. But I'm tired, and I'm done."

Slowly I nod. "Yes."

My beautiful mother passed away peacefully on January 16, 2011, two and a half weeks shy of the two-year time period I begged my Aunt Martha for in my dream of dreams. She kept her word, and I kept mine.

I am eternally grateful for those two bartered years. They went so fast, yet we packed a lifetime into them. Family secrets were exposed, puzzles solved, tales told, and more life expansion happened in that time than in all the years of my life up to that point.

It needed to happen. I helped make it happen. I'll own that.

"JUST LIKE MY DAD"

TRAY WITHERSPOON

AROUND 1977, when I was in second grade, I was put into the hospital with viral meningitis. It was the first time I remember seeing my dad. I'd never seen a picture of him and wouldn't have recognized his voice from the few conversations we'd had on the phone. So when he walked into my hospital room, I asked my mom, "Who is that man?"

I don't exactly remember when I started to feel bad about not having my dad in my life, but the painful memories go back pretty far. My mother often reminded me, my older sister, and my younger brother that "he left us for another woman."

Eventually, we ended up living in a house with my divorced grandmother and an aunt who was also single. My grandmother raised me for most of my younger years until my sister and I were able to fend for ourselves. We were then left unattended while my mother worked nights as a nurse.

My grandmother, a very bitter woman, would make me work like a dog before my mom moved us to our own place in 1978. I remember hot summers in the panhandle of Texas when my grandmother had me hoeing cotton alongside her. As a young boy, I never understood why she treated me so bad. And if tried to stand up for myself or made her or my mom mad, they would always say, "You're just like your dad." That phrase stuck with me for many years.

I guess that was when I started to blame my dad for my life. I knew that the other kids my age did not have to work like I did. They were able to play sports and do other "kid stuff" I wasn't allowed to do. When I would ask, I was told "We can't afford it" by both my grandmother and my mother, in the same breath, blaming my dad for not sending enough child support.

At the age of eight, my uncle became the light in my dark young world. He had a huge positive influence on my life. That summer, Uncle Reydon made sure to pick me up every day for the local Vacation Bible School, where I gave my life to Christ. That started a wonderful journey for me, where love and forgiveness could reach the hurt inside me. My uncle became more than an uncle. He is my friend and brother today.

In 1980, we moved to Weatherford, Texas, where I finished school and made a lot of good friends. In 1991, after I'd left then returned to Weatherford, I ran into a girl I knew from high school while getting gas. I stood outside her car window, asking how things were going— just the normal catching up. I knew she had been married and had a daughter, whom I could see snuggled up and sleeping in her car seat. She was so adorable with those two little ponytails on her head. After a brief conversation, I came to understand Rachelle was no longer in a relationship, so I asked her out.

We dated for six months or so, and I fell in love with both her and her daughter, Brittany. I asked Rachelle if she would marry me and let me be a part of her and Brittany's lives. She said yes, and my life as a father began.

Not having my dad in my life instilled in me a desire to always be there for my children. I was passionate about being a great dad and knew I would be there to teach my kids the most basic things about life—something I had not gotten from either my dad or my mother.

Weeks after I was married, we found out Rachelle was pregnant with our honeymoon baby. It wasn't expected, but again, I was excited. Eight months earlier, I had been single; now I was married with a two-year-old daughter and a son on the way. Life couldn't have been better.

Jacob was born in October of 1992, and Christian, my youngest daughter, followed in 1995. Being immersed in fatherhood with my three kids was truly one of the happiest times of my life. I changed diapers, did laundry, cooked, and even learned to fix hair, making ponytails and dog ears for the girls. I was very involved in the everyday events of my children's lives, and I loved it.

Almost every night, I would pray with my kids, tell them Bible stories, and read to them using different funny voices. One of our favorite books was a book of poetry called *Where the Sidewalk Ends* by Shel Silverstein. Each one of the kids had a favorite poem from the book they insisted I read every day. I read my favorites as well. Reading those poems was one of my most cherished memories from that time. Life wasn't perfect, and I made some mistakes, but my desire to be the best father I could be only grew with time.

In 2001, my world came crashing down around me; and though I tried, I couldn't fix it. My wife of nine years wanted a divorce. Crying, begging, and pleading had failed. My marriage was over. I was not going to make her sell the house or move as I wanted to keep my kids' lives as stable as possible. So I packed what clothes I had and a few other things into my little truck then went back into the house and tearfully begged my wife one more time, saying, "I don't want this. Please, don't make me go."

My children were crying along with me. Burned into my memory was a picture of those three babies I loved so much, saying, "Daddy, don't leave." I was devastated. It was the most difficult thing I have ever been through. The next six to seven months were incredibly difficult, to say the least. As much as I wanted to run away and not face the divorce or the new man living in my house, I worked hard to put my kids first. I continued to face my pain by going to the house to pick them up. I couldn't have made it through those days without God's help.

I have continued to be a part of my children's lives. I have watched them grow into amazing young adults who are loving and kind. I have great relationships with all three of them. We talk frequently and spend time together when we can. There have been many times my children have expressed their love for me and thanked me for consistently being in their lives. They know I love them and that I never gave up on them. I wasn't "just like my dad."

I HAD TO BE ME

SUE REVELL

I HAD imagined this day many times. Indeed, I had walked this path on many occasions in recent years. But I never dreamed that on this particular walk on this particular day, I would be singing and singing loudly.

Surely, no one sings as they leave their final negotiation meeting ahead of redundancy.

But as I walked back down that path, negotiations concluded, I sang. The words that seemed to be sung not by my voice but by my heart were lyrics from a famous song that I had only been introduced to the previous year, *I Gotta Be Me*, from the musical *Golden Rainbow*.

> Whether I'm right, or whether I'm wrong, whether I find a place in this world or never belong, I gotta be me. What else can I be but what I am?

> That far-away prize, a world of success, is waiting for me if I heed the call. I won't settle down, won't settle for less, as long as there's a chance that I can have it all.

As I first heard those words played one Saturday morning, I had no idea how pivotal they would become in my life. Or did I?

The path I was following as I sang that afternoon marked the end of a journey that had begun some two years previously. I had been invited to a meeting at work to discuss my future. My strategy in meetings, where I have a sense of uncertainty as to what might unfold, is to listen carefully and give nothing away. Oh, and make copious notes.

It was good to have a pen and paper to focus on that afternoon because it was, at best, a carelessly conducted discussion. Finding myself discussing the potential end of my twenty-seven-year National Health Service career with people who hadn't even taken the time to find out what that career had involved was tough. And the fact that someone in a position to bring about the end of this stage of my career could miss that I had been a nurse for fifteen or so of those years was simply unfathomable to me.

I had left home in 1985 to start my nurse training. We talk a lot about journeys these days, but the journey up the motorway that day really did mark the first day of the rest of my life. I learned so much in those three years of training—so much about nursing and medicine, so much about people, and so much about myself. And when I thought the journey was over—that I'd arrived—I soon realised I had only just begun.

The twenty-seven intervening years that led me into that office that first afternoon had been incredible. It was not all perfect, of course. But I had influenced and made a difference in more lives than I could ever have dreamed. As my career developed, I had worked with some amazingly talented people and had some incredible opportunities and jobs, both as a nurse and later as a senior manager and leader.

And now I was being presented with another opportunity, albeit one that hadn't consciously featured on my horizon. Part of me was deeply wounded. I was so close to that coveted thirty-year service milestone.

Yet a little piece of me, the part that was very soon to start to grow beyond recognition, knew that here was a gift—the opportunity to do something completely different with the next half of my career.

But it didn't feel like it was time. Whatever time would feel like, this wasn't it. I wasn't ready. There were things I needed to create space for and put in place in order to set up my future as well as possible.

I gave very little away as I left that first meeting. Whilst I felt numb, I was far enough along my personal development training to know that it was up to me how I *wanted* to feel. I had a choice. Yes, I needed time to hurt and to lick my wounds, but the choice of how to react or respond was mine. No one could take that away from me. Not giving any immediate reaction in that meeting meant that I had created the space to choose my eventual response, to choose to be in control, and to choose how I wanted to *be*.

I knew I wanted my apparent and, indeed, eventual departure to be on my terms. I had witnessed too many others in this position who had lost themselves in frustration, sadness, hurt, and pain. I had colleagues who had lost their sense of self, their self-esteem, their self-respect, and their self-worth.

I resolved there and then that this would not be me. I would do my absolute best to be the consummate professional and to be the best version of me that I could be in this situation until the end. I knew that it wouldn't always be easy, and it wasn't. I made sure I had great support mechanisms in place to give me the best chance of success.

I set my intentions. I knew the timescale I needed that would work best for me. I couldn't have dreamed at the beginning that I would negotiate the perfect end date, but I had resolved to always behave in a way that increased the possibility of making that happen. I resolved to continue to work hard and to always behave like an adult even when a tantrum would have been justified. I chose to be constructive and to be honest about my needs while not making the situation any more difficult for those on the other side of the table. I chose to see them as simply doing their job.

I had heard of people leaving relationships elegantly. I think they call it leaving well. That was how I wanted to leave this contractual relationship—elegantly and with my self-respect intact.

Looking back, I still find it hard to believe that I really did do it my way. The approach that I took helped me to create exactly the right amount of time that I needed to get the practical things in place that I felt I would need to survive in a whole new world. I undertook five different jobs in that time. Oh, the irony, given the definition of redundancy. I was grateful to have an excellent and hugely experienced mentor outside of the organisation, who helped me to keep a very broad perspective on seizing opportunities that would help me in my new future. I worked hard, embraced complex and challenging roles, and applied myself professionally. Those roles weren't necessarily complementary to each other, which didn't always make life easy, but some of them were surprisingly complementary to what I do now and simply enhanced my skills further, preparing me for my new world. You might even think it was meant to be.

I gained new qualifications and built new networks not just locally, but also worldwide. I created a deep personal understanding of how coming from a place of choice could help me develop my resourcefulness and resilience. I not only created the time I needed, I created space in my head and my heart in which to adapt to a whole new way of life. I created space to become an even better version of me—the me that would go on to help others become the best version of themselves too.

The song I sang was right. It still is.

I had to be me, and I was.

FREEDOM

JO DIRNBAUER

THERE I was. The decision was made, and there was no turning back. The best shortcut to our destination, West Berlin, was the ferry from Gedser, Denmark, to Warnemünde, East Germany.

It sounds easy, *but* the first sign that created a crawling fear within me was the fact that this huge ferry had only six passengers. It was an old ghostlike ship, hauling railroad cars and only three motor cars—ours being a brand-new yellow Karmann Ghia. Upon arrival to shore, we drove our car down the ramp off the ship, only to be halted by a uniformed, stern-faced East German soldier. Why weren't the other two cars stopped? In an instant, I felt fear prickle all over my body.

Unknown to us at that moment, we were being detained because our West German license plate was not recognized as legal. No humor in this situation. We were ordered to remove the plate and, right then and there, purchase and install an East German plate. Tension was high. I was shaking inside. When done, we were ordered to put our camera out of sight and not to use it.

We were to be tracked by East German soldiers in watchtowers along our five-hour journey. There was no map. We were to just follow the trees that had white-painted circles around their trunks and look for signs that say Transit Berlin. No stops allowed.

By now I realized my freedom was gone. It had been snatched the moment we touched East German soil. *Poof*. You can't touch freedom, but when it is taken away, you miss the feel and the smell of it. Panic set in. What if our car ran out of gas? Or, God forbid, breaks down? My heart rate was high. We saw only one abandoned station, and that had chain-wrapped pumps.

Where were all the people? We passed just one family, and they stared at our bright, new car. A packed police car passed us, but cars were rarely seen. And those that were on the road were very, very old. Where were the window boxes adorned with beautiful flowers? It was mid-July. Everything was so drab, so barren, and so quiet. The few faces of those I saw in small villages were grim. Where were the stores? There were none. Stillness. The car ride was bumpy due to the cobblestone roads. Many things like this made me feel I had time-traveled backward. When passing a small road crew replacing cobblestones by hand, I noted that they were all women. That was a surprise. Contrasted in nearby fields were modern pieces of farm machinery—old with the new.

As we got closer to Berlin, we noticed more military encampments and manned watchtowers hidden behind tall fences. A large convoy of soldiers passed us by, but we all convened at the railroad crossing as an old coal-fed locomotive hauling shiny, new Russian tanks chugged by. I had a fear of eye contact with the soldiers, first when they passed us, and then while we endured the long wait for the train to go by. It was dark when we reached the border checkpoint. We submitted our passports and were told to get out of the car. All our luggage was searched. I was scared. There was no talking. We did everything they told us to do as they barked orders. A huge dipstick-looking thing was put into our gas tank to check if we were carrying another person in a false compartment. In my mind, this was hard to compute. When we were finally allowed to proceed, we saw, up on a hill, machine guns pointed at us as we drove away into West Berlin. Freedom at last! Or so I thought.

Daylight brought the realization of a modern, bustling city with very little trace of WWII. Then I saw *the wall* at the Brandenburg Gate. It seemed everywhere we went, the wall was there. Numerical signs on the Russian side tallied the deaths of those who tried to escape. At Checkpoint Charlie, a temporary wooden structure was put up by the Allies. Gawkers like me with cameras were taking pictures of the new revolving concrete tubing being put in place atop the wall to curb any grip of an escapee. *Imagine that.* I guess the barbed wire had not kept desperate escapees from trying to go over the wall. What I saw and felt that day, I will never forget.

As I looked over into East Berlin, I could see no sign of freedom or smell any freedom in the air, enormous contrasts between the East and the West. Their checkpoint on the other side from Checkpoint Charlie was a concrete tower, housing guards and machine guns. It was very scary. Yes, restlessness was building inside of me. I wanted out. I felt the oppression of all those guns and soldiers facing West Berlin. So it was no surprise that we cut our stay short. We still had jitters and were always afraid we'd make the wrong move.

"You are leaving the American sector and entering Soviet territory." More intimidation. Our license plate had to be replaced again, the car was thoroughly searched, and our dual passport was held and huddled over. *What if they keep it?* I thought. *What if? What if?* We had no rights where we were. *Was that really my heartbeat?*

Two hours later, we were driving on the poorly maintained Soviet autobahn. This time, the road was bumpy because of grass coming up through the cracked cement. There were no cars, and the road was in the middle of nowhere. There was no freedom of travel for the occupied East Germans. Again, we did not dare stop the car.

Finally, there was a quick, calm border check into West Germany. I was overwhelmed with emotion. When freedom is taken away, everything changes. You are confined (do not take pictures, do not stray off the road, do not stop), and certain actions can mean danger and restraint from the occupier (rolling tube put atop the wall, windows cemented shut). There was such power in the hands of those that held our passports, and intimidation was all over the place. Here I am now, thinking about freedom, and my heart is racing—just like it did back on those two, life-changing, hot July days of 1969.

Did this terrifying and eye-opening experience change me? You betcha. I no longer take my freedom or opportunities for granted. When I see a magnificent field of Texas bluebonnets, I can stop on the side of the road and take pictures. Manned watchtowers? There are none. There are no barren shelves in the grocery stores where I choose to shop, and I get to pick what I want to buy.

There are a multitude of cars, big, small, new, and old on smooth-paved highways. Gas stations are everywhere with pumps that are full. Checkpoints crossing over into another state do not exist. And now, when I see barbed wire, it is being used purposefully on farms, for ranch fencing, and around prisons. There are no stares with grim faces. And, I am never scared when talking to people in uniform. There is no fear of arrest and I can move around freely.

I realize simple everyday things can be taken for granted, so each day, I take notice of all the freedoms around me. I find it a great exercise for living my life.

MOVING PAST DEATH

ERIC SPRINKLE

I REMEMBERED it was just two days before Christmas when I lost my wife of seventeen years.

An adorable, petite redhead, she was sitting on the couch, drinking coffee, that last morning as I ran out to buy some last-minute presents. I told her I loved her, gave her a quick kiss, and dashed off, promising that I only had one more gift (seriously, cutie, just one more) to get for her.

I returned to a warm home, smelling like cinnamon candles, and oh, so quiet. Laying the bags down in the kitchen, I crept through the house, trying not to disturb whatever she was busily working at. Or sleeping maybe? The bedroom was empty. I continued on through the rooms, waiting to stumble across her, head down, headphones on, Christmas music playing, and covered in wrapping paper.

At approximately 4:08 p.m. that afternoon, I called 911 to inform the operator that I had in fact found my wife's body, curled up in our bathtub, nonresponsive, and no longer breathing.

Christmas, New Year's, and the better part of the next three months passed by in a blur.

Months later, I established a pattern of burying myself in a busy season of summer work that at least kept my head occupied. Still, any time thoughts would intrude, they always carried with them the question, *When summer is over and life slows down again, what then?*

Autumn had always been our time for vacations, birthdays, and anniversaries. And now I was looking forward to a season seemingly designed to remind me just how completely alone I was. What would I do on her birthday in September? Or over our anniversary in October? What would Thanksgiving be like? Or I shuddered to even think, Christmas?

And so I asked our wonderful Heavenly Father if he would please, please give me something or anything else to do or somewhere else to go, just for this first year alone. Anywhere, but here. *Oh, please, dear God, please.*

The email arrived just three weeks later. It was from a friend who worked for United Airlines and had lost her own spouse a few years before. She asked how I was doing, wanted to know that I was eating, and wondered if I was in a place where I might make use of her employee travel benefit, allowing me to fly anywhere United flies for little or nothing at all.

Amazing.

That autumn, I lost myself in the narrow passageways of Venice, the high mountains of Slovenia, the tight river canyons in Croatia, and for a single afternoon, a small village on a crystal clear mountain lake with a church built atop the tiny island at its middle. The locals said that anyone who rowed out to the island and rang the church's bell would be granted a wish. I had only one.

As the days cooled across Europe, I flew back west, out across the Pacific. Exploring jungle trails leading back to hidden beaches and quiet waterfalls was followed by wandering the bright, crowded streets of Tokyo and Hong Kong.

Each location was remote and exotic enough to not remind me of an empty house sitting back in Colorado, waiting for my return. I wondered though, *Is any of this even helping, or am I just putting off the inevitable?*

I wrapped up my travels with three months in New Zealand, soaking in the scenery and experiences of "Middle Earth." I summited volcanoes, hiked mountain passes, and paddled warm green rivers through steep leafy canyons. The day I left, I sat at the airport in Auckland and watched the rain pouring down outside. New zealand was sad to see me leaving; I was too.

It had been a great trip filled with fun people, unexpected turns, and amazing place after amazing place. I was always moving on to the next thing—never stopping, never slowing down, never feeling comfortable, and never feeling at home.

But that was the whole point, wasn't it? Avoiding home by traveling around the world? I found a journal entry where I actually wrote:

> In what has become a pattern for this trip, once I start to feel comfortable in a place, I immediately leave it for somewhere else . . .
>
> — HONG KONG, CHINA, NOV. 3RD

I flew on to Sydney, Australia, and thought about where to go next. I'd circled the globe over the last nine months, and it seemed like it was finally time to go back. But what then? Wouldn't I just be right back where I'd started, only nine months later?

Maybe my travels had just been one long excuse to take off from my life for a while? To resist the "new normal" waiting for me by fleeing halfway around the globe. Maybe the folks that told me to stay home, cry my eyes out, and just get used to it (shudder) were right?

And there I sat in the Customs House Library, just off the wharf in Sydney, trying to make sense of it all.

And then I saw a book.

I recognized the author immediately. He'd written a book on survival I'd read years before, filled with thoughtful examples of how our brains actively process decisions, especially bad ones. This new book dealt with the same ideas but was now directed at people who had *survived* an event and, specifically, how they had moved on.

He mentioned a time-honored trick for moving past trauma, recognized by cultures around the globe—travel. He noted one of the attributes of travel that most helps us process dramatic change was the feeling of "being lost." How it allowed your brain to switch gears from a passive mode, processing everyday life, to actively readjusting into new patterns of daily living.

When processing pain, he concluded, the more lost you're feeling, the better. Seriously?

Could it be that I wasn't dodging life this whole time? That maybe the last nine months hadn't been my "checking out" on moving past my wife's death. Maybe, just maybe, my loving Heavenly Father had a plan for me the entire time. A plan to heal. A plan to restore. A plan to move me past this tragedy and drop me back into life, where I would be free, happy, and ready to live again.

I put the book away, stepped out into the sunshine, and looked across the iconic harbor with a sense of something new. It was a feeling I'd forgotten completely in my travels. It was faint, no doubt, but it was there. It was hope.

The next day, I stepped on to one of the longer commercial flights in existence—fourteen hours—and settled back, processing this new knowledge. Two days later, after a quick stop in LA, I was looking out the cabin window, down across the mountains of Colorado once again.

An hour later, as we touched down and taxied to the gate, the flight attendant made the usual announcement I'd now heard dozens of times, "If you're connecting to another flight this evening, we thank you for flying . . ." But this time, as she finished, her comments seemed directed specifically at me. "And if you happen to live in Colorado Springs," she finished, "we'd like to be the very first to say WELCOME HOME."

Smiling and teary-eyed, I stepped off the plane.

It was good to be home.

A LOUD WAKE-UP CALL

ANA CARAGEA

THE LANDING was smooth. It was a good flight after all, and the weather was not as bad as the captain had expected. We knew we still had ten to fifteen minutes until the plane came to a complete stop, even more until all the passengers were off the plane, but we were ready to be home. I was tired after the night flight and was already dreaming about my bed and pillow.

A sudden outburst from my colleague next to me brought me back to reality. I had no idea what was wrong, but she seemed shocked and upset. I noticed she was reading something on her phone when she started crying. *What was happening?*

"A plane crashed. A plane. One of our planes! Gone!"

I grabbed her phone, trying to make sense of what she was saying. Yes, the authorities were confirming the crash. It happened only a few hundred kilometers away from where we had just flown in that morning.

"What? It's not possible. It's an error. They don't know."

Immediately, my thoughts went to the people on that flight, and I started looking at our schedules to see who was on board as the operating crew.

No! It's not possible! Not real! My colleague just spoke with one of the crew members a few hours ago. It's a bad dream, and I just want to wake up from it. This is not happening.

The plane stopped. We had reached our final parking position, and it was safe to stand up. I hugged my colleague while tears poured down our cheeks. The flight wasn't over yet though. We still had passengers on board, and we had to assist them as they disembarked. We still had to smile. *How am I going to be able to smile when I know that my friends are no longer with us?* I thought.

I was scared. I was angry. I was shocked. *"No. It's not real."*

I don't know how we got everyone off the plane, but we did. And I don't recall when we collected our stuff to go back to the airport. I do remember the chills that I got once we reached the customs clearance and heard the prayers over the loudspeakers. *"Damn. It's real."*

I immediately started calling my family. No one was answering as it was only 6:00 a.m. They were all still sleeping. The first to answer was my husband, and I started crying while sharing with him what had happened. I wanted to quit my job; I didn't want to do it anymore. I didn't want to fly again, but when you have a loan and bills to cover, quitting is not an option.

That first day, I stayed in a state of shock. I was numb but trying to hold on to my sanity. I didn't know what to do or how to react. *Should I scream? Should I swear? Should I punch something?* It all felt like a very, very bad dream.

About a year prior to the crash, our company started a support project so we would be prepared for this type of situation. I had volunteered to be one of the supporters. I never ever, in my wildest dreams, thought or imagined that I would be called for duty. Then the crash happened, and I was assigned a shift that first day.

Everyone who was available rushed in to help. We were a family after all. We cared for each other. And now seven of us were gone forever.

I thought I was handling it okay until I got to work, where the flowers and the coloured Post-its full of messages were. But I wanted to make myself useful somehow and wanted to be present for others, to help. And then I realized that I, too, needed help. How could I give when I needed to receive?

All my life, I have been a learner, trying to grasp different concepts and situations that, perhaps someday, would prove useful. I am grateful, even now, for all the growth that happened in my life before that day. It paid off.

I believe that everything happens for a reason, but I couldn't understand the reason for the crash. *Why had it happened? Why now? Why with those people? Why? Why?* The more I tried to make sense of it all, the harder it was to cope. I tried to focus on my breath, but the air was so hard to take in.

As I became aware that I was the one in charge of my thinking and the one attributing meaning to the events in my life, I made a choice to attach an empowering meaning to what happened. The accident was a wake-up call for me. Life is short, and I didn't need to stay in a job that I no longer loved. It was time—time for something different, even if it scared me. The alternative was a life of feeling drained and miserable.

I did not lose my sanity throughout all the confusion. I am truly grateful for that. I did not lose my life, though I will always be aware that any one of us could have been assigned to that flight that day.

I did not lose my hope. I was given a second chance at life, with a newly opened mind and heart. I have become more in touch with what is important for me as a powerful and creative human being.

I lost two close friends and five amazing colleagues that day. I have since woken up from living life on autopilot—from my default future. For that, I will always be grateful.

Thank you for reading my story and for allowing me to honour my lost friends.

This is for Javi and Alex. I hope you have bright and strong wings. Love.

RAFAEL

KRISTINA AMELONG

I DO not want to tell this story as there is too much pain. Yet I know some stories must be told. Told in cycles, like the flow of water, in order to birth new stories. This story begins with me walking my dogs one September day in 2015, in Wisconsin.

My golden retriever puppy, Toby, is thirsty. I am looking for the creek the dogs drank from in the spring, the last time we were in these woods. We are making our way on a blacktop bike path along the meadow. Blue-green dragonflies hover, zip, and circle above a field of ragweed and yellowing fall grass. The dogs' tails run deep in the grass while their noses sniff the ground for rabbits.

With my iPhone, I capture the dragonfly's dance. I capture our meanderings through the field of flowers and stalks. I even capture occasional drops of sweat dripping off the dogs' tongues.

Then *bing!* A notice from Facebook. I ignore it, merging again with photographing, with the wind moving through the grass, with the dogs' path, and with my memory of a creek. Then I see a giant oak tree. I walk to its trunk, perching my iPhone against its bark and facing the lenses toward the blue sky of fall and the dying leaves, rich with their own circulatory systems. Satisfied with taking photos, I tuck my phone into my back pocket to focus on finding the creek and on my walking meditation.

Then the *bing* repeats.

I reach into my back pocket for my iPhone as the dogs and I stop moving. The dogs' tongues hang out as they make a circle around me. I open Facebook on my iPhone.

I read, "Jeanine posted in your Ecuador June 2015 group." I tap this notice to read the post. There are three words. "Rafa is dead."

I read the words again. "Rafa is dead."

I don't know a Rafa, I decide, tucking my phone back in my pocket and looking up to see a bicyclist rapidly approaching in the distance. The intrusion ruins my mental decision to return to my walking meditation, and instead, I am left returning to scanning what I decide I know about Jeanine.

Jeanine went to Liberia with some of the other folks from my Ecuador trip. Before Ebola.

Jeanine must know Rafa from Liberia. Jeanine must be letting only a few of our twenty-six mutual friends from our Ecuador June 2015 Facebook group know of Rafa's death. *I am not one of those people who know a Rafa*, I decide again as I remember the dogs and the bike.

"Sit," I yell out even before I pay attention to the three dogs' locations, imagining Sheeta chasing the biker down the blacktop. As I look down, I see all three dogs still at my feet, still panting with the heat of the early fall day and still attentive to my every move as the biker swooshes past us. The dogs do not move a muscle. I take a few deep breaths, noticing my increasing agitation.

With the bicyclist past, I snap my fingers, and the dogs and I move again to find our spring creek. Yet only a few steps later, I am thinking about how I met Rafael Bejerano Rangel in the beginning of

June, only three months earlier, in the colonial city of Quito, Ecuador.

I place him in time and space, and then it is as if he is in front of me. I see and feel Rafael walking through the door to our Quito hotel, with his didgeridoo hanging along the length of his entire tall body. His clothes are different—matching pants and top, both bright Christmas-red cotton. His wet black hair sticks to his head. He radiates warmth. I feel it across the room, even through the gathering crowd. A deep love begins to consume my body. Rafael was a shaman, a beautiful man, a soul mate.

Once we were all assembled in Quito, we were bused from our hotel to the airport, where we flew to the concrete town of Coca, which borders the massive Amazon River. We then eagerly swarmed onto three small boats that traversed, for nearly three hours, the petroleum-plant-laden river.

Rafael was in another boat. I never saw him. But once we arrived at the muddy village, we participated in the greeting ceremonies, where the young shaman, Rafael, danced a soul's tribute to the indigenous people there. It was a coming together of healers from around the world. We all then trek through the jungle under sheets of rain. Raul, one of the locals, painted stripes on Jeanine's and the rest of our faces with a wild redberry.

Later, as the others returned to their rooms, I decided to catch up on some work email. I found my way to the Yasuni Lodge's one location where I could connect to the Internet. I weaved working with listening to the jungle's raindrops. I was surprised at how quiet the forest felt. Meditation and work turned to worry about the lack of animal sounds in this Amazon rain forest.

Leaving worry, my attention traveled to the footsteps I noticed when my orange juice glass began vibrating in concentric circles atop the wooden table made from the forest. I looked up and saw Rafael smiling at me.

"Can I join you?" he asked.

Turns out, Rafael, who had grown up in Mexico, had also lived in the United States, in Wisconsin, on the same farm I had lived on years later when my partner and I tried our hands at a raw-milk goat farm.

"It's where I first began playing the didgeridoo," Rafael said.

I don't know what it is, but there is something about death. It always takes me by surprise. As I watch myself ponder if "Rafa" is Rafael, I begin to reflect on the death of my thirteen-year-old brother, who died thirty-four years prior. For so many years before my brother, Jay, died, he told his friends and family of his recurring dream of his untimely death. Yet we still weren't prepared.

I am not prepared for Rafael to be dead, though I knew it was him all along. I watch myself. I keep walking, running, and riding the wave of the moment. My body is moving with the camera across the yellow fields, looking for an invisible creek for the dogs to quench their thirst, wishing a dragonfly would slow down so I could capture its brilliance on video.

Thirty minutes later, we are leaving the field, the creek that is no longer there, and the dragonflies. I toss the puppy into the car through the window then open the rear door for the black-and-white border collie and the toy poodle to jump in. I slam the back door as the three of them lie down along the length of the back seat. Getting in the car, I push the electronic button to begin the engine. I am suddenly very glad we are all going now, leaving to pick up Rayna from her therapy appointment.

Picking up Rayna from her appointment, I find myself sitting on the steps, talking to Lucas, Rayna's innovative brain coach. I pull out my phone, not remembering anything I had been thinking about for the past hour. Lucas says something about Rayna hanging upside down on the rings today, something about her vestibular system. Yet I notice I am not really listening to his words. I usually hang on to everything that is said since he is our current best hope for healing my daughter's brain.

Instead, I am listening to the sounds of a didgeridoo playing to the sounds of red—to the sounds of Rafael being dead. I look at Lucas, and I say it aloud, "Rafael is dead."

BALI

OLIVER GRAY

SEPTEMBER 2014 marked the ten-year anniversary of my corporate well-being company.

I love my business. I'm passionate about everything I do. I feel really grateful for the life I have. So why do I think something is missing?

I often feel that the London way of life is not for me. But my business, friends, and family are all here. So this is where I will stay, I guess.

"Darling, please, you need to come visit me. You will love it."

I'm Skyping with my Romanian friend Oana, who has been living in Bali since 2011. And once again, she wants me to visit her. In the past, I had always said no. Today is different. I just finished my morning meditation, and my instinct says, *It's time to go to Bali.*

I was buzzing with excitement. I could feel in every cell of my body that it was time for an adventure. I had to go. I booked my flight for October and set the plan to stay a month. I told my team, who I run my business with, that I would be off to Bali and Skyped a surprised

Oana to tell her the good news. Finally, I'd get to see my friend in her magical new home in Ubud, Bali.

Oana's Balinese taxi driver friend Wayan collected me from the airport. I truly wish everyone could meet Wayan. This guy has a smile that lights up the world. Wayan has lived in Ubud all his life, so Ubud must be a pretty special place if he is so happy. An hour later, we arrived at a beautiful small house.

Oana greeted me with a hug and said, "Darling, welcome to your new home."

The gorgeous house she had arranged for me consisted of one room with a big four-poster bed. The weather is always warm in Ubud, so the bathroom and kitchen are outside. In front of the house is a beautiful garden with wild flowers and plants like I've never seen, big and bursting with colour. It's as if nature is shouting, "Look how healthy and happy I am!"

Over the next three weeks, I experienced the magic of Ubud, the amazing nature, the colours, the smells, the vibrant energy, and best of all, the people.

There are five main groups of people in Ubud.

The first are the Balinese. They are the most loving people I've ever met. They follow a beautiful type of Hindu religion, where each day, they give thanks to their gods for everything they have in their life. The Balinese have an incredible energy, love, and gratitude for life.

Then there are the holidaymakers and backpackers, who are drawn to Ubud, mainly for the famous monkey forest.

The third group are the yoga lovers, drawn to Ubud by The Yoga Barn, a massive yoga centre built out in the jungle with five yoga studios.

The fourth group, who sometimes overlap with the yoga lovers, are the hippie New Agers. These are expats who have made Ubud their new home. They will tell you that Ubud has a powerful spiritual energy. It's something I cannot explain but felt strongly.

The final group are the digital entrepreneurs, who work out of an amazing coworking space in the middle of the rice fields called Hubud.

I have made some great friends and business connections at Hubud. And thanks to my love of yoga, I spent most days at Yoga Barn, practicing yoga and making some special friends there too. It really amazed me how these friendships felt so effortless. I found myself connecting with so many like-minded people, who shared the same passion for life that I do.

Besides these friendships, I really cherished the simple daily smiles and greetings I shared with the Balinese, something that's so rare to experience in London.

It was the start of week four, and I'd now met most of Oana's closest Ubud friends. There was Christie, the mad English girl, who acted fifteen, looked thirty, and was actually forty-two years old. And there was Claudia, the smart New York marketing expert, who was born in London. I met Matt, the English web designer, and Grazina, the Lithuanian soul-searcher.

One evening we were all having dinner, and Oana said to me, "You seem to love Ubud. Maybe you should live here."

I replied, "I'd love to, but you know, my business is in London. It's not possible." As soon as I said "It's not possible," I thought, *When the hell have I ever said it's not possible?*

"Actually, maybe I could. I can work from Ubud. I'd just need to check that the team I run my business with are okay with it."

The next morning, after my meditation, I was buzzing with excitement. My inner voice was screaming, *You have to come back to Ubud!*

After a magical month, I went back to London. I shared my feelings with the team, "I've been running the business from London for ten years now, and although I love the business and love working with you all, I just feel so alive in Ubud. Would you mind if I go back and do my work from Bali for a while? We will text and email daily, and we can all Skype at least a couple of times a week."

The team were nothing short of amazing. They were 100 percent behind me.

I spent the next four months preparing to return to Bali in February 2015. I decided I'd give it a go for three months to see how I felt, then return to London to see how my team was doing.

Bali had a great effect on me. Over the past couple of years in London, I had felt like a flower slowly wilting. In Bali, surrounded by nature, the sun, and amazing people, I came alive again. I felt like a flower bursting with new life and energy.

After three magical months, I returned to London. My friends wanted to know all about Bali, and one question that kept coming up was "You look so happy, but how is your business?" The amazing thing was that during my time in Bali, my business had the best three months it had ever had.

Again, I had the chat with the team. I asked, "How do you feel about me living and working from Bali?" Once again, they were amazing and said, "If you are happy, we are happy." They did make one request—that I return to London every three to four months.

So they were okay, and the business was doing great. And I was the happiest I'd ever been. After six weeks back in London, I returned to Bali for a further four months.

Back in Ubud, I needed to find a new house to live in as my previous one was taken. In addition to running my London business from Bali, I'd set a goal to write my second book during this four-month trip. I had the whole framework for the book planned out. I just needed to write it.

My first ten days in Ubud did not go as well as my previous three months. I had intense jetlag, and my book was not flowing out of me like the first book had. And every property I viewed screamed at me, "This is not the place for you!" I was filled with a sense of frustration. I really wanted to find a house I could feel comfortable in, start writing my book, and enjoy the Balinese lifestyle. I kept reminding myself that I just needed to keep trusting my inner voice.

With that said, I started to question what was going on. I had lunch with my new best friend, Chelsea, an Australian web designer who was living and working from Bali.

"Okay, Chelsea. I've not slept much the last seven days, my book is not flowing, and I've now seen twenty-five properties, and every one I walk into feels wrong."

Chelsea replied, "Well, Oliver, maybe you are not meant to be in Ubud. Why don't we go to Canggu for the weekend? It's an hour from here on the motorbike, and we can chill out by the sea. And you can come back next week and house-hunt some more."

I took Chelsea's great advice, and we went to chill in a hotel overlooking the sea. I had the most amazing sleep ever. After a relaxing weekend, I listened to my inner voice. It was saying that I should stay in Canggu for a while, until I felt ready to return to Ubud. So that's what I did.

My book started to flow. I was sleeping well, and after a week, I felt ready to go back to Ubud to see my friends and find a house. I met up with Chelsea to house-hunt. Again, it was the same story. Every house I saw, my instinct said no. I was filled with a sense of unease and a knowing that I was not meant to be there.

"Oliver, what is wrong with this one?" Chelsea said in despair. I had no idea, but all I could say was that my gut was saying no. I explained to Chelsea that over the past eight years, I had only gone against my inner voice once, and it was a disaster.

After another two days and twelve more properties that didn't feel right, I decided to go back to Canggu. After a couple of days back, I knew that was where I was supposed to stay to finish my book.

I challenged my instinct as if it were a person. *Really? Are you sure? My book will take at least two months to complete the first draft, and all my friends are in Ubud. I don't know anyone here, and people aren't as open and friendly as they are in Ubud.* My gut replied loud and clear that I needed to stay in Canggu. As always, I followed my instinct and decided to stay to finish the book.

The first draft of the book took two months. I met very few people in Canggu but would visit friends in Ubud on weekends. The day I finished the book, my instinct said it was time to return to Ubud. I arranged to view some houses that day.

The first one I saw was perfect.

It was time to be back in Ubud.

THE PIT

LORRAINE FLAHERTY

THE SKY was dark, grey, and gloomy with huge rain-filled clouds that covered the moon. It looked as miserable outside as I felt. I curled up in bed in my old room at my parent's house, where old posters still lined the walls and piles of my old books filled the shelves. I could hear my parents in the room below—their voices raised. I was pretty certain they were rowing about me. I felt guilty for being there and ashamed, as if I'd let them down. But I'd had no choice but to go home with my tail between my legs. I had nowhere else to go. My plans had fallen apart. The contract on the home I was buying with my boyfriend had fallen though. The boyfriend was gone. The job I had forced myself to stay in so I could get a mortgage was no longer needed. It was gone.

I'd returned not so much the prodigal daughter as the fallen one. Whilst it had seemed to the outside world that my life was unfolding perfectly, the reality was somewhat different, and the so-called comforts of home were now of no comfort at all. No one wants to be thirty and living with their parents, especially when their disappointment felt almost palpable.

Unable to stand the looks on their faces, I escaped to my room and buried myself in my bed as deeply as I could go. I fell into a deep dark pit with no way of escaping. I was free-falling into a space that was so raw and so full of pain, that I just wanted it to stop. I wanted it to end. I really didn't want to live as I'd had enough. So I allowed myself to be swallowed up by it—wholeheartedly. I dived in as deep as I could go.

Occasionally, my mother appeared, mild concern turning to worry, then fear, and then abject horror as I refused to eat or drink or surface from beneath the covers day after day. "Leave me alone," I mumbled. "I don't want anything. I just need to be alone."

And I was.

I no longer cared whether I lived or died. And things that used to seem important, like hunger or thirst or how I looked, really weren't anymore. Yet all the while I lie there not caring and willing it to be over, there was this little spark—this part of me that did want to live. I knew I had things to do—something that would create meaning out of the chaos of my life and explain why I had endured the pain I had been through. I needed to do something to make sense of the life I had, thus far, been living and the choices I had made, especially those regarding the people in my life.

In my cocoon, I began to take a deeper look at my life and realised I had based my entire self-worth on what others thought of me. I had, it seemed, chosen to make myself needed, clearly reflecting a deep need that existed within me and one that I was completely unaware of.

I had become the go-to person when people were in trouble or in pain, something I had learnt to do as a child when I had been witness to my parents' early struggles. I became the agony aunt, the good listener, or the one to help shoulder the load. It didn't matter that the advice I gave was often not as warmly received as I might have liked or that after the event, on some occasions, I found myself on the receiving end of some very deep resentment from those to whom I spoke. I still put myself out there. I thought I was being a good person. And perhaps, I thought that by taking care of others, it made me a worthy human being.

I was wrong.

In the end, all that happened was that I became exhausted and depleted. And I struggled to maintain relationships of my own because there was very little left of me at the end of each day. I see now that deep down, I had hoped that if I gave enough to others, that one day it would come back to me. But it didn't.

It couldn't as I had never learnt how to take care of me or accept help. I was too focused on fixing the external world around me. When my heart got broken, it was nobody's fault. The relationship just wasn't meant to be. But as I stumbled through the heartache, the walls I'd created around me collapsed. When I needed support from those I thought were my friends, it wasn't there. The space was empty. I was alone. I had done a great job convincing people I was invincible. But I wasn't.

And that was when I fell into the pit.

I knew, as I fell, that it had to be done. I knew this was a pivotal time and that things had to change. I wasn't sure how, but I knew I had no choice.

As I began to emerge from my dalliance with death, I made a commitment to quit as the unofficial agony aunt. I also knew I had to let go of some bad habits, like drinking and partying too much and allowing people into my life—people who drained me. I was going to have to start over with an entire revision of my life. It would be tough, but the alternative was far worse. It was better to be alone than be with the wrong tribe, doing the wrong things in the wrong ways.

It was a baptism of fire, and the pit was unrelenting. But as I waded through the darkness, I started to feel something lifting. It was as though a heavy weight was being removed. I felt like a snake shedding its skin or a phoenix rising from the ashes. There was a freedom in it—a space in my mind that I had never known. There was a curiosity and a yearning to rejoin the world once again—only differently this time.

It had to be different.

I emerged from my pit, bruised and shaken, but I felt new and transformed. My old life, my old self, was dead now.

I had calls to make—difficult calls.

Resigning from my old life wasn't easy, but it had to be done. I found a room in a big house, and I moved in. I kept to myself, and I managed to find some peace. I was more alone than I had ever been, but it felt different. This time, my aloneness was my strength. And in that aloneness, I began to find me—the real me—not the me I had once thought myself to be. I was not the fixer or the martyr. Instead, I found my warrior—the part of me who was not afraid to go into battle and fight for what was right for the world and for me. I vowed to find my path, my true purpose. And that was exactly what I did.

In that darkness and despair, I found a simple truth: without honour and love for self, we are on a path that can only lead to suffering. I learnt that I was not responsible for the lives or the happiness of those around me. I was only responsible for me, and that meant taking care of my needs and generating my own happiness first. I learnt that all happiness comes from within, and when there were shadows deep inside, they needed to be acknowledged. I learnt that pain could not be hidden away and expected to fade and that pain is not to be feared because when we face our deepest fears, we grow stronger, and then we can fly.

Hindsight is a wonderful thing. I know now that buying that flat would have set me on the wrong course. My relationship, as lovely as it was, was not sustainable as we were on very different paths. It was a tough lesson, but I realised that sometimes, just loving someone isn't enough.

Letting go of the job was the best move I ever made, and letting go of people made room for new ones to come in—people who gave as good as they got and valued themselves and me in equal measure.

I also realised that my parents hadn't been disappointed. That was my projection. They had just been worried and had struggled to know what was best for me, just as they had done my entire life. The most important thing I learnt was that people have all the answers they need inside of them, not outside. They just need to know where to look and take the time to go there.

It is said that the darkest time is before the dawn, and it is true. I feel nothing but gratitude now for all who played a part in my life thus far and for all my experiences, including the pit—especially the pit. After all, it led me to my motto.

Life gives you everything you need. You may not know you need it when you get it, but it will always become apparent later.

OVERCOMING SHYNESS

CINDY FREY

AS A child, I was extremely shy. I was afraid to talk to anyone except one uncle and my immediate family. I knew I was different from other children but didn't know why. I lived paralyzed in a world of fear, unable to make friends.

During my early years at a Catholic school, I built emotional and physical walls to protect myself from other students. At recess, I stood in a corner every day, while the other girls played jump rope. They would ask me to join, but I always said, "No, thank you." I was too scared of making a fool of myself. Since I wasn't participating, they asked me to watch their purses while they played.

As I got older, I slowly started making friends, especially with the other shy girls or the ones considered "outcasts" by our peers. After transferring to a public school, I continued to connect more with others, but I was still too shy to ask questions in front of the class.

In sixth grade, my teacher tried a technique to help me and another student overcome our shyness. One day after class, she said to us, "I want you both to take turns yelling down the hallway. I'll be at the other end, and I want to hear you." My classmate and I looked at each other, not sure what to think, but we did as we were told. I thought her request was silly.

How can yelling bring me out of my shyness? I thought.

Throughout junior high and high school, I developed close friendships with a small group of people. However, my shyness in the classroom was still there. My first job during my senior year of high school was as a receptionist for the county school system. I was let go after a few weeks because I was not able to interact well with our customers or the rest of the office staff. I was embarrassed by the dismissal. After that, I obtained a job as a secretarial assistant, where I felt "safe" interacting with only the office staff. That job had a more relaxed feel to it than the first one and was less stressful for a newbie like me.

I avoided talking in front of groups as much as I could until I started college, about fifteen years after high school. I had no choice but to speak then since most college classes required presentations. In my final semester, I was required to give a presentation on a database design project. My first assumption was that I would be giving the presentation in front of about two hundred people, consisting of faculty, students, friends, and family. It turned out to be a small classroom with less than twenty people in attendance. Boy, was I relieved.

Most of my working career was in tech support for two state agencies. I realized then that I enjoyed helping people and did well with one-on-one teaching. After I retired from state service, I knew I needed a part-time job to supplement my pension. While looking, I came across an ad for an instructor on craigslist. The job posting was for a nonprofit agency, teaching basic computer skills to disadvantaged adults. I accepted the position. I then had to face teaching a whole group of people at once. Even though it had been several decades since my early childhood fears, I still believed myself to be a shy introvert.

How am I going to be able to teach a whole class of students? I thought.

My first class was small—only about nine students—but it was one of the most difficult classes I had ever taught. I arrived early that first night of class to prepare the room. As the students started arriving, I made sure to welcome them individually. When it was time to start class, all eyes were focused on me. As soon as I started talking, my hands shook and my voice quivered. It took about a week of teaching before I started to feel comfortable. It was a ten-week class that met four evenings a week, so my students and I got to know each other very well. I think having that first class be a difficult one helped me to be on my toes and keep the focus on the students' expectations rather than on my own fears.

As an instructor, I was also required to teach professional development. This encompassed a topic that was related to the regular instruction, like résumé writing, interviewing skills, finance, stress management, or presentation skills. When it was time for the PowerPoint assignment, the students had to create a presentation and deliver it in front of the class. To encourage them and calm their fears, I told them how difficult it was for me to be in front of people. It was then I realized how far I'd come.

The name of the program I taught was called the Empower Program. I liked that *empower* stood for "power from within," so I started using that word a lot in my classroom to help encourage a sense of confidence within the students. In turn, I think it helped me to rise above the uncertain feelings I had.

As a teacher, I had to be able to project my voice, so I worked hard to do so. I have always been soft-spoken, so it was a forced practice for me. It turned out to be a confidence builder. Maybe my sixth-grade teacher knew what she was doing when she made me yell down that hallway.

About a year into teaching, I was reflecting on where and who I was in my life. Suddenly, I had an epiphany: I was no longer the shy girl that I had been growing up. Holding on to that belief for so many years made me believe I was too shy to do or try new things. At that moment, I was able to release the subconscious thought that I was shy. It was no longer a part of me.

WHEN I STOPPED LIVING FOR TOMORROW

SABRINA SANTOS

AW, THE grace of being human. I have always thought myself to be someone who had an enormous amount of time to do whatever I wanted and who could accomplish anything while never actually taking immediate action or acknowledging the fact that tomorrow is not guaranteed.

I had a few missed calls from my mother on Friday the ninth of November 2011, but my phone's battery went flat, and I only managed to get in touch with her on Sunday morning. It's funny when you call your parents and you hear *that* voice and you immediately know something is terribly wrong. My mum picked up the phone, and I asked her about the Christmas presents. "What should I buy for the family?" I was super excited to go home for Christmas, but her voice told me something wasn't right. She said, "Don't worry about any presents. Your dad needs to talk to you about something that has happened."

I knew, at that point, someone had died. It was in her voice; death was in her voice. I got this crazy, shaky feeling in my head, wondering who it was. I felt pure panic as my brain automatically started a checklist, noting that Mum was still alive. I was talking to her. And it wasn't Dad as he wanted to talk to me to tell me who passed away. Then Dad picked up the phone and said, "I have very sad news to tell you. Your brother is dead." I froze. His words didn't seem real.

No, it can't be real! My brother is supposed to have lunch with me on my arrival in Brazil this week. No, it can't be real. I am coming home to have Christmas with him and the whole family. I told myself, *No, it can't be real. He is too young to die!* I screamed. I cried. My mum came back on the phone and said, "Please try to stay calm. Stop screaming and ask him to help you calm down."

So I sat on the red couch of my flat's living room in South London, and I called for him with my heart, my tears, and my thoughts. I said, "Brother, if you are anywhere in the Universe, I need your help. I'm here all alone, away from everyone. Please help me calm down."

At that moment, I felt this light golden mist cover me. The panic stopped and the pain lessened, though the tears continued rolling down my face. I felt my brother's presence with me, and it told me he was fine. He was fine, and I didn't need to fear or suffer anymore.

Later that day, I spoke with my mum so I could jump on a plane to go to the funeral. But once again, I was caught by surprise. They'd already had the service. My brother had passed on Friday, and even though I only found out about his passing on Sunday, it was already too late to say goodbye. Well, at least I thought I would get a chance to see him one last time.

He was murdered at work, shot dead at thirty-six years old. With so much life in him, it was a total shock to have him gone so early. But it was one of the most important moments of my life. My brother's death changed my perspective about so many things.

First, I realised there is no guarantee of tomorrow. Life is indeed precious, and people can be taken away at any time. So what is the point in living for the future? What is the point in gathering all this money to one day start living if I might not even get the chance to see the future? My brother never waited to live. He did the things he loved every day, and he died doing what he loved. For that, I will always admire him. He gave me a gift, not only with his presence and visits after his passing, but also, my brother showed me how to live life. He taught me that I needed to stop and rethink the fake life I was living. Until my brother's death, I didn't even know myself, and I was living only for others.

At the time of my brother's death, I was twenty-eight years old and was preparing to step into a managing director's role. I was working towards having shares in a marketing firm in London, stressed out of my head focusing on sales, and worried about how to make enough money to retire early. I had absolutely no clue who I was as a person, living instead as a "thing" in a monetary system that meant nothing to me. I was totally absorbed in what society considered being successful. I was drinking myself into distraction from what really mattered in life, and I had forgotten all my dreams. I had forgotten to live a life that mattered. I didn't even know what that meant. I was just existing.

I now understood that life is fragile and precious. I had to change. On that Sunday afternoon, the eleventh of December 2011, I realised I was only living for the future without even thinking that I might not have one.

It was a very sad Christmas at home in Brazil that year. It was hard to see the whole family in pieces—so broken. It took me a long time to put my own pieces back together, but the pain became more bearable with time. It wasn't because losing my brother hurt less, it was because the changes that were inspired by that event are now part of me. I came to learn that my brother wasn't really gone. He would always be around, watching over me.

My brother's unexpected death triggered part of my spiritual awakening and, most importantly, my human awakening to live life for today. I learned to be brave and courageous, and to live in the now —to accept life as it is, precious and short.

THROUGH THE VALLEY

HOPE HUGHES

I SAT in a room off to the side of the courtroom, waiting to see the judge. My palms were sweaty, and I was shaking. As I fought back tears, I felt like my heart would pound out of my chest. "Keep it together, Hope. Do *not* start crying in front of all of these people."

Finally, my name was called, and I walked in and stood before the judge. So many thoughts swirled through my mind. *How did this happen to me? What could I have done differently? I feel so humiliated.*

The judge asked me whether I had ever filed for bankruptcy before.

"No."

He looked over my paperwork and commented, "I see you had a significant decrease in income." That was an understatement. At that time, I was making about 55 percent less than I had been making as a lawyer at a big law firm. On the bright side, I was doing better than a few months before that when I was working as a document reviewer, making less than 25 percent of my previous salary.

When I opened my mouth to respond, I lost it, and the tears began to pour down my face. Gasping for air between sobs, and with a quivering voice, I said, "Yes, your honor, I was laid off from my job." I then wondered how many other people burst into tears in bankruptcy court. Some others there, who had also filed for bankruptcy, seemed not to be affected at all. Maybe they were just better at hiding their emotions. I could usually mask mine pretty well in professional settings, but not that day. There was some primal emotion associated with what I considered to be an abysmal failure on my part that just would not be contained. I felt I had not only let myself down, but my family as well.

So how did I go from earning six figures a year to becoming bankrupt? The answer is not so simple. It was a question I'd been asking myself since being laid off in July 2012, was still asking on the day I stood in bankruptcy court in early 2014, and continued to ask for a couple of years after that.

Working for a big law firm requires total dedication to that firm. I started out with that type of dedication because I was solely motivated by my desire to make a lot of money. However, that all changed on February 18, 2011, when God came into my life in a powerful way. At that point, my dedication shifted to knowing him. I knew in my heart that God had more planned for me than putting my trust in a job and doing whatever it took to keep that job, but I really did not have a clue what that was supposed to look like in my day-to-day life.

Foolishly, I started saying, even to my supervisor, "This job is not my source. God is my source." It is a true statement that you will have what you say—good or bad—because the partners soon made it clear that my job would no longer be my source. I didn't understand that God does use people, whether as employers, customers, or benefactors, to supply needed resources. My failure to recognize that fact was one reason I lost that job. It was almost like Eve in the Garden of Eden—I was deceived.

At the time, I believed it must not have been God's will for me to remain at that firm, but still I wondered, *Now what are you going to do?*

As panic arose inside me, I kept a calm exterior to family and friends. Inwardly, I asked, *God, where are you?* I received no response, just deafening, anxiety-producing silence. Months went by with no new job opportunities. Eventually, my savings was depleted, and I started using credit cards just to survive.

When I finally landed a permanent job, as I mentioned earlier, my salary was about 55 percent less than what I had received at the big law firm. With a family to support, a mortgage, more than $100,000 in student loan debt, and now tens of thousands of dollars in credit card debt, the new job just wasn't providing the finances for me to pay living expenses and make the monthly student loan and credit card payments. So in December 2013, I started the process to file for bankruptcy. The evening that I turned in the paperwork to my bankruptcy attorney, my blood pressure spiked so high I nearly passed out and had to go to an emergency room.

How far I've fallen, I thought. *I started out practicing bankruptcy law, and now I'm filing for bankruptcy.*

As I was going through these hard times, it seemed to me that I was better off before I became a Christian. But then I would remind myself of how angry, hateful, and miserable I was before. Still, I wanted to know why God allowed these bad things to happen to me.

It took nearly four years for me to realize that God didn't take my job from me. It was not his will for me to become bankrupt. My actions caused me to be one of those laid off. Believing that it was up to me to fix my lack of finances, by using credit cards, led to my bankruptcy. The years of lack that followed resulted from me being engulfed in fear. In short, I did not truly trust God to take care of me.

In November of 2016, I gave up trying to figure out everything on my own and trying to make things happen the way I thought they should. I was so exhausted from toiling, toiling, toiling, and getting nowhere. So I surrendered. It took more than four years for me to realize that God had already provided everything I needed. I thought

I had been putting my trust in him all those years, but I had not. I had been trusting in credit cards, whatever job I had, the partners at those jobs, whatever better paying job I was pursuing, and how much money I had in my bank account—anything and everything but God. When I took all my fears and worries and gave them to God, he took over, and the struggle ended. All the fear and anxiety left. God then gave me a vision of what I am to do with my life.

So my lightning-fast mind finally caught on, *Wow, God, you really mean what you say in your Word. If I trust you, you will give me the life I've always dreamed of. I am humbled and excited about our journey together. Thank you for holding my hand through it all and never letting go.*

NONNEGOTIABLE

WENDY ANTHONY

I KNEW I had to make a change. I'd known it for years and had made sincere efforts to do so, but I always quit—not right at the start, but eventually. My reasons always seemed credible, and they were strong enough to derail any little progress I'd made, causing me to feel guilt and disappointment. They were enough to make me believe that because I'd failed, there was no point in staying the course. And so week after week, month after month, and year after year, I gave up on my well-intentioned goal to lose weight.

The truth is I'd never been a heavy person. My whole adult life, I was an effortless size 2. I didn't really pay much attention to what I ate, and I didn't have to, as I loved running, biking, and dancing. But in 2005, I started taking medication for a health issue, and weight gain was the primary side effect. I packed on the pounds bit by bit, and in a few short years, my frame—which had been a slender 120 pounds —was carrying 195 pounds of unhealthy weight.

I had made so many excuses for my weight gain that I was in denial of what had caused it. It couldn't be my fault. After all, it was only because of my medicine that I had gained the weight in the first place, right? At first, yes, my medication was the catalyst; but I'd made it a scapegoat. I had thrown my hands up in defeat and developed deplorable eating habits. I had failed to accept responsibility for the fried, processed, and sugary foods that had become the staples of my diet. I ate mindlessly, with no regard for my health. I pulled into drive-through windows more than once a day because I was "too busy" to cook, and I believed that eating healthy would be too expensive. I drank soda with every meal, and I'd become sedentary and lazy. I justified my weight gain, explained it away, and accepted it as my inevitable normal.

On April 18, 2014, that life became unacceptable. I had to go back home to Trinidad for a funeral due to the sudden and tragic death of a loved one. For the duration of my stay, I was excruciatingly self-conscious and hesitant about visiting old friends and family. Comments about my weight from well-intentioned, but equally insensitive friends fed my insecurities. I was uncomfortable in my own skin. But these feelings weren't new. They had plagued my life for years now and were familiar and cruel companions that dictated everything I did and didn't do.

I'd fallen away from doing all the things I loved and held dear. I avoided going dancing—something I had looked forward to every weekend—because I felt so unattractive. I dreaded shopping for clothes because not only was it disappointing to have to try on larger sizes than the ones that fit only months before, seeing myself in a full-length mirror was daunting. And my choices were limited, forcing me to buy certain styles merely because the styles I really wanted didn't come in my size, making me feel even less attractive. Instead of dressing like I wanted to, I was dressing to cover up everything I disliked about my body.

I *wanted* to lose weight, and I tried over and over again. I ordered workout DVDs, bought weight-loss cookbooks, and even bought a journal to document my progress. Every single time, I started out excited and focused, saw progress after a few weeks, and even had friends mention that they could tell I was losing weight. But I was never able to stick with it. If I felt that I'd messed up my diet or missed too many workouts, I berated myself for falling off the wagon. My next logical summation was to abort the process entirely.

For years, my modus operandi was to start a weight-loss and workout program then abandon it. Each abandonment brought shame, guilt, self-hatred, and doubt. Each time I decided to try again, I'd beat myself up with the question, "Where would I be today if I'd stuck with it the last time? How much weight would I have lost by now? How healthy would I be today?" It was a cycle that I couldn't seem to break, and I was at a loss at how to.

On April 18, 2014, I was back in my Tulsa apartment, thinking about the life I wanted. I thought about how active and athletic I'd always been, and I wanted that person back. I could keep going as I was day after day, which would take no effort whatsoever. I would never run a marathon, complete a triathlon, or dance like I wanted to again. I'd soon be diagnosed with diabetes, high blood pressure, high cholesterol, and heart disease. That was guaranteed. But at least it would be easy. Or one day, I could run a marathon, complete a triathlon, and dance to my heart's content. I could be fit, athletic, energetic, and strong. But that would take a lot of hard work. But that *is* the life I wanted, and so I made my choice.

I went to my bathroom and looked at myself in the mirror. I saw someone who deserved to be the best she could be simply because she was worth it. I wanted it so badly for her. I didn't want 2015 to arrive with her wondering what could have been if she'd stuck with what she started in 2014.

In that moment, the simplicity of what I had to do became clearer than it had ever been, and a sobering and quieting reality hit. No one was going to lose this weight for me. No one was going to eat healthy for me. No one was going to work out for me. It was up to me and no one else. It was *I* who had to change, and I had to change now!

I wrote out my weight-loss goal and deadline: sixty pounds in six months. My plan was to work out three days a week and completely change my eating habits. I didn't know where to start, but I had a little information about how to eat healthy from all my previously failed attempts. I knew that sugary, fried, and processed foods had been my undoing, so I started with a short list of healthy foods I loved and went grocery shopping.

I needed a place to work out, and my apartment complex had a small on-site gym with some treadmills. In my running days, I'd always run outdoors, so this would be new for me. But I had to do something. I downloaded an app onto my phone that would train me to run 5K, running just three days a week. That was doable. I honestly had no idea how this would go. All I knew for certain was that if I didn't change, nothing ever would.

That first morning, my alarm clock went off at 4:30 a.m. I wanted to turn it off and disappear back under my warm blanket. But I didn't. I got dressed, walked across the dark parking lot and into the gym, and finally figured out how to turn on the treadmill. I started walking slowly—very slowly. Five minutes later, I started my first sixty-second run of the workout. My new life had begun. And what an adventure it has been.

Every challenging workout and every single choice to eat a healthy meal required that I keep my goals in clear focus, regardless of my emotions, setbacks, or circumstances at the time. I made my daily decisions nonnegotiable so when I wanted to quit during a sprint, I told myself that stopping before I was finished was not an option. When I ate an unhealthy meal due to lack of proper meal planning, I kindly reminded myself that it was okay and that I would make my next meal a healthy one. Achieving my goals required that I become a disciplined, sober-minded person who lived life deliberately instead of allowing life to dictate how I should live.

On December 31, I weighed myself to see how I'd ended my year. I was down fifty pounds. I've now lost a total of sixty pounds and am stronger and healthier than I've been my entire life. All I wanted was to lose weight, but the process transformed my goals and desires as much as it transformed my body. I began this path with the knowledge that it was entirely up to me to make the difference I wanted, and that awareness hasn't failed me.

9:23

LUCILE KNIGHT

8:36 p.m.

HIS RIGHT hand is on that little lower part of my back, where it always feels quite neutral, yet very intimate and protective at the same time. It looks like nothing, like a random place. But for me tonight, it is everything. It is me being taken care of by someone, being respected, and being appreciated.

With John, there are no games. There is only the pleasure of each other's company. The simplicity and self-evidence of it all is making me feel so at peace with the world, an emotion I haven't had the pleasure to encounter for what seems to be an eternity.

He is resting it there. And in his left hand, a pint of Guinness is warming up, almost finished. We have been in the Hope for about an hour, and I need to leave. The pub is filling up slowly, not bad for a Tuesday evening in early December. I guess everyone is keen to get out of work. The run-up to Christmas always does wonders for any bar within a mile-radius of offices.

People's voices merge into one, a cloud of hushed noises that surround and protect us like cotton wool. There are people minding their own business, and others with their noses in their glasses, not wanting to be asked any questions as they try to work out the logic of their lives. I finish my glass of Chablis and mumble something about having to go. I say that just for form. We both know we will not spend the evening together. But sometimes one has to do just that, state the obvious.

There are so many things we cannot state—the facts of his crumbling marriage; the status of my screwed-up, toxic relationship; and the details of our days in the same office. Why do the hours always disappear so fast when we're together, so fast that we seldom feel the need to hang on to niceties and clichés? For now, we're living with it, like badly stuck plaster. And we're doing just fine. Neither of us can deal with any more or any less. I don't know if this situation is helping our individual stories, but I know we both hold on to it because that immediate good feeling is what we need right now— short-term gratification.

He helps my coat onto my shoulders with the gentle way he normally does things. He then opens the door. The biting wind of winter engulfs itself into the opening, immediately waking me up to the reality of where I am going next—home—dissolving instantly the warmth I'd felt by being in this pub with John. Someone has just turned this colour movie into black-and-white.

We kiss, now completely used to the affair-shaped elephant in the room. And it feels so right, natural, easy, and effortless. It has only been three weeks, but I have already made my peace with what I am doing. We never mention what "we" are. We just enjoy it, and I think he must have found a way of coping with it too, as he's never raised the topic and never asked the dreaded question, where is it all going?

9:12 p.m.

A cab ride takes me home too quickly, and as I climb up the stairs leading to our apartment, a knot finds its usual place in my stomach. Hello, old friend. My limbs ache. It has been a long day. I'm sure my body is feeling the brunt of what my brain is working so hard to hide and push away. Guilt is a vicious one. One minute you think you have dealt with it, and then it comes back and bites you with a renewed viciousness.

The flat is empty. Mark must be out. I have no idea where he is or when he will be back. We don't talk much these days. I turn a couple of lights on, undress myself, and let the shower run its hot steam on my tired shoulders. Another day to wash off, sleep, and repeat. I am not my best friend at the moment, but I have gotten used to it. Familiarity with the worst feelings is what makes you accept them and keeps you from questioning them.

There is a knock on the door. "Hey, I'm back."

Mark peaks his head in. "When did you come home?" he asks.

"About an hour ago or so," I lie in a breath.

"All right," he leaves and shuts the door. And he comes back in a couple of minutes later.

"I was home an hour ago." Silence. "You weren't here."

So this is it? Am I going to keep on lying? We are both here, watching me like a deer in the headlights, clueless and exposed, nanoseconds before the full-frontal impact.

This situation is so ridiculous as we both know I have lied. We both know why, and neither of us can hide the fact that this cohabitation is now an utterly sad joke. He has tricked me by leaving the flat, coming back, and pretending he was just arriving from work. That's it. This whole disaster of a relationship has turned into a game of truth or dare.

Will you dare lie again and come up with excuses to keep us ongoing? Or will you tell the truth and face the only way forward —separation?

He has played his last turn by leaving and coming home to expose me. Now it is my turn. Will I pull another scared-as-shit rabbit out of our broken hat of tricks?

I am so tired—tired of lying and tired of telling myself that we can work through this and that we can and will go back to happier days— the ones when we wore our drugs-tinted glasses and everything looked pink, fuzzy, sexy, and felt like rock and roll.

9:23 p.m.

My hair is dripping lukewarm water on my shoulders. I am still in the bath, and he is still in the doorway of our bathroom. I look up, a stillness now filling my head.

"I don't want to try anymore. I'm not going to."

No more tricks. I am all played out. And with these words, the knot in my stomach goes. For the first time, I have picked truth.

TINY BITS OF COURAGE

BRAD FINKELDEI

I WAS walking my dog, Gabby, this past year and was just about home when I noticed a guy pushing his bike. He had several packages under his arms and two backpacks. Something wasn't quite right about the situation. Then I noticed the Amazon tape around one of the boxes.

That triggered my memory. *Oh, my order of little rubber chickens is supposed to arrive today. F—— ya!* I pulled out my phone and checked. The Amazon delivery had just been dropped off.

I rushed home only to see an empty front porch. No box. Immediately, I thought, *That guy stole my rubber chickens. I have to chase him down and get them back.*

I grabbed Gabby and ran down the street, intent on catching the guy with the bike. My heart was pumping, and I could feel the adrenaline flooding my body. I was scared but ran after the thief anyway, determined to get my chickens back. I didn't give much thought to what I would do once I caught the guy.

Let me back up here for a second. Why would anyone chase down a thief for itty-bitty rubber chickens? Well, just a few years ago, I didn't have the confidence to even think about doing something like that.

See, I was stuck behind a computer all day, working a corporate job I had come to hate. And all I wanted to do was travel the world and feel like I was making a difference. But I wasn't confident enough to take the risk to try something outside my comfort zone.

I had tried but never could seem to take the leap of faith necessary to change my life. I would say things to myself, like "Being a system administrator is safe, and the pay is awesome. Who in their right mind would risk the safety of a high-paying job for the unknown?"

Then I watched a documentary, *The Happy Movie*. It was a film about the science behind happiness. It opened my eyes to what was truly important in life. I really wanted to change my life, so I decided to reach out to a life coach.

In my conversation with the coach, she pointed out that I was using a big paycheck to compensate for my lack of confidence. She said, "You're buying things in order to get people to like you. You're pulling your confidence from a paycheck instead of from within yourself." What she said STUCK. It was the aha moment I needed, and I knew I had to take action.

So I drew the proverbial line in the sand and gave myself three months to leave the corporate world. I was going to go after my dream of freedom and owning my own business.

Then on June 21, 2013, I was walking Gabby and had a crazy thought. What if I get fired? That might make things happen a little faster, right?

Coincidentally, when I went to work that morning, I got laid off. I had to explain to my boss why I was smiling when he fired me. I left work excited to begin my new life but also a little scared, as I was leaving a life of security for the unknown.

Since that moment, I have been stepping into bigger and bigger levels of confidence as I do things I have never done before. I completely rehabbed my mother's basement without knowing what I was doing, while sleeping on her floor for nine months. I wrote and published my first book, and I gave a speech at an international conference in Ecuador.

It was while I was in Ecuador that I met and got to know Rafael, a shaman from Mexico.

Here's where the rubber chicken comes in. See, Rafael carried around a big rubber chicken everywhere he went. He also kept itty-bitty rubber chickens on him, passing one out to everyone he met. He used the chickens to remind people not to be "chickenshits," or to be "courageous chickens." He wanted to encourage people to do those things that scared them so they could live up to their potential. Rafael was an inspiring human being who loved helping others become the best they could be.

Shortly after I met Rafael, he went on vacation with family and friends to Egypt. They'd stopped in the desert to have a picnic when they were shot at from an Egyptian military helicopter. Supposedly, they were mistaken for terrorists. Rafael was killed.

After Rafael's death, I decided to carry on his message of handing out the little rubber chickens. I, too, wanted to remind people to step into their fear so they could overcome those things in their lives that might be holding them back.

But I couldn't do it without the box of little rubber chickens I'd ordered. That lousy guy on the bike had stolen my gift to the world. I had to get it back.

So I ran until I caught up with the thief and yelled, "Hey, you! What are you doing?" He was still walking his bike down the street, trying to play it cool.

In my deepest, bravest voice, I yelled even louder, "What are you doing with all those packages? I think one of those is mine!" In the most matter-of-fact way, he responded, "No, they aren't."

"May I look?" Sure enough, there was my package.

Excited to have successfully gained possession of my box of chickens, I tore into it only to find just *one* little rubber chicken. Just one. Not a bucket full of them—JUST ONE!

I thought to myself, *I was robbed twice! Once by the Amazon reseller and now by this jerk with the bike. WTF!*

I collected myself, tried to remain calm, and said, "You just stole a ridiculous little rubber chicken from my porch. What's going on in your life that you're taking random packages off people's porches?" I really wanted to know.

He was a young guy in his mid-twenties, and looked almost clean enough to not be homeless. As he talked, I really listened to him. He told me that four people in his life had recently died, he and his mother were both strung out on drugs, and he had recently become homeless. I heard him, and in that moment, my frustration shifted to compassion. That's a lot to happen to one person. I could totally understand why he had turned to stealing. I reached into my wallet and gave him six dollars. It was all I had on me. He thanked me, and I took my chicken and headed home.

Before I left though, I implored this young man to return everything he had taken. I gave him my information and told him I'd be willing to help him if he decided he wanted it. We parted ways, and I wished him luck. I left, still a little nervous but with a sense of making a difference. I thought, *Maybe this was the whole purpose of you ordering those chickens—to have that one conversation.*

That's what being a courageous chicken feels like to me.

MY RIDE HOME

JESSY CONFLON

10, 9, 8, 7, 6 . . . "Talk to me . . ."

5, 4 . . . "What's wrong? Come on, it's almost midnight . . ." 3, 2 . . . "It really doesn't matter that much. Come on . . ."

"HAPPY NEW YEAR!" shouted everyone around me. It was loud, so loud, and the ceiling lights were flashing in my eyes causing me feelings of confusion, anxiety, and discomfort. I never really liked crowded night clubs. But how could I dare complain about finally setting foot in the Adot, that famous place where I was told that girls would just throw themselves at you as long as you looked cool, high, and drunk enough. Arriving there, I was both impressed and frightened. I felt utterly out of place. But wasn't it extremely silly of me not to see the beauty of this place, the opportunities that would be served to me on a silver platter, and the luck that I had to be there with the Adot master?

Well, I must admit that I couldn't embrace the excitement, pride, and joy of being there. But I was up for trying, trying to have a good time and believing that this time, partying could be different. It could be fun—full of laughter and dancing. And it was a great opportunity to meet new and interesting people.

So here we were, dancing and laughing. *This is going well,* I told myself. It was genuinely okay, although my anxiety was growing nearly as much as the number of drinks ordered. Struggling to catch up with her, I was still only halfway through my first mojito. And I was fighting with my mind—a mind that wanted to be right and prove that this was not going as well as I thought. I could already observe a slow change of behaviour in her, and as much as I wanted to ignore it, it was happening.

Things were still somewhat okay, when some silly drunk boys dancing around us accidentally bumped into me a couple of times. *Oh well, it is New Year's eve, and we are on a dance floor in a crowded nightclub. How can I expect not to get accidentally bumped into?* I thought.

In a matter of seconds, that benign incident turned into an astronomical drama. *But wait, how did this happen? What had I missed? It couldn't possibly be that big of a deal. After all, I wasn't hurt, was I?*

As I checked my arms and shoulders, looking for some sort of injury that would justify the breakout, her voice was getting louder. The tension around us was flying at the speed of light, magically creating this massive empty gap, leaving us and the two boys separated from the crowd. Things were getting heated, and we were in a jammed club. How silly of me to be in there when I am very well aware of my fear of crowds.

At that moment, the long-built hope I had brought with me all the way from London to LA had instantly vanished. *What should I do? Stop this? Yes, that is the right thing to do. I should prevent a physical fight from happening,* I thought. In a desperate attempt to bring calm back and get the party started again, I turned to her with my most beautiful and charming smile, convinced that my panic was totally hidden and that my apparent nonchalance could manipulate anyone into thinking that I was chilled and relaxed. I was, after all, dancing and laughing. I was hoping to get her attention away from my so-called assailants and reverse it back to me. This strategy had worked in the past, so why not tonight? *It's gotta work again tonight. It is New Year's Eve. Come on!* I thought.

Well, not that night. It didn't work. The anger was already far too deep, and far too strong.

Seemingly coming from a divine gesture, two giant men came out of nowhere and not-so-gently separated all three protagonists of the outburst. My two "assailants" were asked to move away from us, and they did so with no further trouble. Shortly after, the crowd around us dissipated. We were back to normal. *Ahhhhh, what a relief. We avoided the worst,* I thought.

In a matter of seconds, I jumped from being the innocent victim who needed protection, to being an ungrateful individual, shaming her by making her seem drunk and out of control. Dark . . . her look and eyes were so dark as she turned, looked at me, and started cursing badly. *Shit, the anger is here. You found it, so run.* I thought.

I was now guilty of not trusting that she was protecting me and of treating her as an unreasonable and violent drunk. *Umm . . . was I?* Rewinding what happened in my head, I was questioning whether or not I actually did what I was being accused of. *Well, if she said so, I must have done it, right?*

Having anxiety, discomfort, and fear of another alcohol-induced breakout; anticipating drama; observing the incident escalate; trying to create a diversion; and finally, celebrating deep inside that trouble had been avoided, I definitely was guilty of *not* sharing her vision of this fantastic place or her version of danger.

I was only observing the incident from a sober, but admittedly judgmental point of view. *I bow down. Guilty as charged,* I tell myself.

Here we are again. 10, 9, 8, 7, 6 . . . 5, 4 . . . 3, 2 . . . "HAPPY NEW YEAR!"

The place was loud. Everybody around us was celebrating, dancing, laughing, and enjoying the party. But I could not help feeling completely isolated. I was screaming inside and begging someone, anyone for a way out. I was convinced that my only way out was to find a way to make this impossible story work somehow. My perception of life, of my life, and of what I deserved was so clouded.

I finally emerged from my deep state of confusion, emptiness, and panic, only to realise that I was by myself on the dance floor. *What do I do? What do I feel?* Unsure, I automatically started chasing— chasing hope, chasing the end of those never-ending conflicts, chasing peace, chasing the illusion of happiness, chasing an urge for normalcy and tranquility, and ultimately, I was chasing my ride home.

As I found her, I was immediately reminded of the sound of someone cursing. I was reminded of the looks on the faces of people around us witnessing such a scene, and seeing shame, pity, outrage, and shock on their faces. They were all staring at me. I was not sure how I felt. Shame? Yes. I definitely felt shame. At that moment, all I wished for was to disappear.

It was only the seventeenth minute of 2015. *It was going to be my year, remember?* I thought. *So why am I already feeling this pain again?* As I tried to escape this circle of shame by turning my back and leaving, strong arms wrapped around my neck, squeezing, pulling, and holding me back. I couldn't move. It hurt. All I could smell was this strong breath of alcohol again. People were now running towards me and somehow managed to take me away from the pain.

But wait, they were separating me from my ride home. Helpless, I ran away, trying to get out of that place. I was completely lost and hopeless, not sure where to go. All I could think was *It happened again.*

Could I keep denying the obvious? What about my hope for and faith in this relationship? *Have I definitely lost my ride home?* I thought. I ran, ran so fast away from that place, unsure of where I was running to. Where was I supposed to go? I didn't even have an address to get back to.

Not again! Six months had passed, and I was back in the exact same position—vulnerable, hurt, scared, and heartbroken. Enough! I had tested my limits enough.

My ride home was defined by the illusion that a single individual determined the direction of the rest of my life. Could I accept that another person's opinions and actions would dictate what I must do, feel, think, and say from now on? For some reason, I had awarded the status of "home" to her, and no matter how wrong things felt in my mind, body, and soul, all I seemed to focus on was going home.

Was it home that this ride was actually taking me to? I had felt so far away from home; so far away from myself; and so far away from my values, beliefs, and lifestyle for so long. I missed me.

That day was January 1, 2015. I promised myself that exactly one year later, I would be spending the New Year with my transformed and reborn self.

LIMITLESS OPPORTUNITY IN THE LAND OF OPPORTUNITY

JACOB MELAARD

"WELCOME TO Southwest Florida! How are ya?"

A short man in a suit welcomed us with a big smile on his face. He started chatting instantly and was asking all kinds of questions with an accent that I didn't understand, so I smiled and sheepishly nodded.

My girlfriend and I had just collected our luggage, and he was our contact at the airport. He was going to drive us to our new home.

It was a hot, pleasant afternoon at a small airport in Florida. I was exhausted, having just come off a sixteen-hour flight from Holland to Southwest Florida airport in Fort Myers. It was an emotional day, having said goodbye to family and friends, knowing it would be a while before I would see them again. Tears were shed and hugs were given. And many times, a final wave was waved as I walked through the passport control into my new and unknown future.

Having lived a rather sheltered life in a small village in the southwest of Holland, this was something different. This was new, and holy smokes, this was flipping scary. It was my first time being on another continent. Although being away from home wasn't completely new to me, this was different—more permanent and more real.

It was only three months earlier that we had entertained the idea of going overseas to get some kind of work experience. We never really took it seriously, and now it was becoming reality.

Resigned from my job, house up for sale, and only a few hundred guilders (this was pre-Euro) in the bank, this was going to be something completely new. I was a person driven by certainty back then. I always had money in the bank; a pension plan at twenty-five; a mortgage with all kinds of safety options for the future; and a clear vision for my career, relationships, and the upcoming forty years of my life.

Being raised in a small, sheltered community, this was a really big step and one that would change me forever. I didn't know that back then because all I felt was fear and a little excitement.

The fear was around being able to make it on my own, about standing on my own two feet, and about growing into an adult without the protection of my parents and friends. Without the familiar environments and knowing my way around, the great unknown was what scared me the most.

As we walked out of airport arrivals, the air engulfed me like a warm blanket. The sights, the smells, and the sounds—it was beautiful. Everything seemed so big—from the size of lunch served at the Atlanta airport during our layover, to the people, the cars, the buildings, and the roads.

The man in the suit was still talking. His name was Jim, and he could help us and show us all sorts of things. At least that was what I understood from what he was saying.

"This is your ride," he said proudly as we stopped our luggage trolley next to a huge Lincoln town car, one of those big luxury cars you see in the movies.

This was all so unreal to me. Growing up, I was told to fit in and just be normal because that is crazy enough. This experience definitely felt crazy.

Reminded of my youth, another childhood phrase came to mind: *Als je voor een dubbeltje geboren bent word je nooit een kwartje.* In English, this translates to "When you are born a penny, you will never become a quarter."

It was something that was said to me many times when I was growing up, and I believed it was true. This experience definitely felt like a million bucks, so you might imagine the impact all this had on me.

It shook the faulty foundations of my self-worth, self-belief, and self-confidence. All of a sudden, I realised that those words were not true for me. They were just passed on to me, and I had believed them. Until the present day, there is still some residue of those words in my head. They are not strong anymore and have no to little impact on me. And I like to think they act as a reminder to not believe everything I am told or think.

Sitting in the car, life felt so good. It felt abundant. And I still couldn't believe what was happening to us.

I sat in the back, and Jim got behind the wheel. Then something rather extraordinary happened. Jim asked me where I was from and why I was here in Florida. In that moment, I realised, as strange as this may seem, that I now needed to communicate in a different language. I couldn't get by with just a few words. I needed to step up and "own" the English language that I had practiced while in school a few years ago. A huge wave of fearlessness and confidence came over me as I started to listen and also respond to what he was asking and telling me.

It was surreal. I felt like a new person—a person with confidence and strength. I used to be the invisible one. I was quiet and shy to those who didn't know me and definitely not someone who would just be talking out of the blue to strangers in a foreign language. Speaking a different language made me feel like a different person.

It was a metaphorical embrace of life. I became fearless, not afraid to make a mistake anymore or to say things wrong. That's not to say I am never scared or doubt anything because I do. It's just that I no longer spend my time in a place of fear. I act and step forward in growth or stay in safety but I don't live in fear.

In that moment, I embraced life and all that was coming my way and have been living that way ever since. The moment I started that conversation in English, it never stopped.

These days, I like to think I am confident and that I inspire others with my passion—that of inspiring people to feel good.

English has remained the main language in which I speak as I never returned to Holland to live.

This experience fueled my desire for exploration, travel, and living life on my terms. Since that day, I have lived in eight countries on three continents, and have met incredible people along the way.

In that moment, when I started talking to Jim, my entire life changed.

CROSSING BRIDGES, CREATING RAINBOWS

ESTHER AUSTIN

IT WAS in 2013 when I finally faced and brought peace to one of my longest-standing demons. This was the year my mother was diagnosed with colon cancer. And I, along with my younger sister, became her carers. I wasn't prepared for all of it—the nurturing, the caring, the intimate interactions. Not with her.

On a daily basis, I was put in a position where touch became an important interaction between me and my mother. During this time, our initial, static conversations grew into either respectful and reminiscent ones, or comfortable periods of silence where an understanding of who we were individually, as mother and daughter, grew.

Even in the more vocal moments of frustration and weariness, when my mother was in pain and her body no longer had the will to understand its place in this world, I refrained from responding. When she would become intoxicated with pain, a pain that spoke its own language through bitterness and judgement, I just listened, as

I was beginning to understand this woman and the experience she was going through.

I'd barely hugged my mother during my lifetime prior to this, and the thought of touching her filled me with repulsion. So when she mentioned several times the pain in her body, especially in her head, I knew I could help ease it by conducting an Indian head massage. Unfortunately, that meant I would have to touch her. I needed to go into my quiet place to reflect and think about this. I had to prepare myself, my emotions. I had to really think about what it would mean for me to touch her. I knew if it were going to happen, it was up to me. My mother would not ask for a massage.

So one day, I plucked up the courage and asked her if she wanted a session. The first time I asked, she rejected my offer with a curt no. Initially, my relief was enormous. Still, something inside begged me to keep trying as I struggled to come to terms with the role I had to play.

Then one day, my mother agreed. She would have a massage.

I watched her get up from the sofa, hesitancy and tiredness in her movement. As she walked, I noticed the limp in her right hip and leg seemed more pronounced. She smiled briefly as she slowly and painfully lowered herself onto the chair I was using for the massage, our eyes fleetingly catching.

There was an intrepid silence and anticipation between us, neither one knowing what to expect nor how we would feel in such close proximity to each other. I stood still, briefly wondering what it was going to be like to touch her. I stared down at her head, noting the sparseness of her blend of black and grey and watching the beads of sweat mingle in between.

Was she nervous? How much pain was she in? I wanted to ask questions, yet I held back as I felt she needed only silence and touch at that moment in time.

I put my hands on her shoulders and asked her to inhale three times before I commenced the session. I felt her tension through my fingertips. I counted with her as she inhaled and exhaled, her shoulders fluttering up and down, slow and strong, yet tired and weary. I then put my hands on her head, which was clammy and cool, and initially felt some resistance.

Was this mine or hers? I wondered, a little apprehensively.

I didn't recognise this closeness, and I didn't like it. Yet the more I reminded myself that this was not about me, the more the repulsion of touching her began to abate. Eventually, I fell into a meditative massage, focused only on delivering a calming experience rather than emoting that I was massaging my mother.

The more I massaged her, the more I was able to get a sense of who my mother was. In the silence, the language of connectivity through touch became very revealing and potent. Her breathing became deeper and more peaceful as her head drooped. She looked like a child who had played all day and was now totally spent. There was a slight tightening in her shoulders, suggesting weariness. I sensed she was trying to protect herself from what life was now throwing at her and wondering what the next phase of her life would be.

My mother had already lost her husband fifteen years prior, and in 2007, she lost a child to breast cancer. I knew she had never really gotten over either loss. Now she was confronting this battle between the physical and spiritual, seeking to experience peace amidst the seeming chaos and pain.

As these thoughts ran through my head, they got me questioning, *What is my mother thinking? How is she experiencing my touch? Is she enjoying it? What is she feeling about her life and the changes she's faced since being diagnosed with this illness? Is she afraid of dying? Is there sadness about possibly leaving her children and grandchildren behind?* I am sure she was wondering how I was feeling too.

With each massage movement, I felt my mother become more relaxed and malleable, melting her away into a world where she could reminisce and experience respite from her pain. Her sighs became slow and deep and more rhythmical with her breathing.

When I held her head against my stomach to end the massage with a facial, there was softness. She was totally relaxed now.

I felt a flood of warmth and compassion as I glided my hands over her face, feeling the contours of the structured carvings of high cheekbones, which had always given my mother a regal look. I noted the black spots on her face, which accentuated a youthfulness she had always carried. She was eighty-four years old, yet most people took her for sixty. With her head resting on my stomach, I was able to study her features, all the while hoping she would not open her eyes and catch me. I think I was scared that she would see the curiosity and a semblance of emotion in my heart for her—things I could never expose.

I came to the end of the massage and my mother slowly opened her eyes, pausing briefly to allow herself to readjust. Her skin held a healthy sheen. I asked her how she felt. She smiled coyly, as if by the mere fact that she had allowed herself to be pampered, she had done something unusual and was still adjusting to this new feel. She said she felt much better. Still, I sensed a tiredness in her smile—one that had been there for a very, very long time.

I no longer felt the repulsion I'd experienced earlier when I first started caring for my mother. I felt a sense of freedom in knowing I had finally accomplished something I never thought I could do. I had found my reservoir of compassion and had dipped into it in order to get closer to my mother. I still didn't expect us to have a cuddly, lovey-dovey relationship, but there was definitely a respectful understanding of each other now.

I slept well that night because I knew I had crossed another bridge in my life—one that would impact and influence me on many levels. Something pivotal had shifted inside of me. I had gotten rid of a lot of my emotional "stuff" during my interaction with my mother, and I now felt so much lighter and freer. I no longer felt I was being held hostage by my past and the criticism I had experienced as a child. It had taken a long time to reach this place.

I knew that I could now be me—totally and unapologetically me. And with this new discovery of freedom came a sense of adventure and spontaneity in and for my life. It was fantastic how happy and content I finally felt. I felt like Dorothy from *The Wizard of Oz* because after all her travels and adventures, she realised that there was no place like home. Indeed, there certainly is no place like home.

WALKING MY WAY BACK TO ME

MANDY MARSHALL

I WAS forty-nine, living in a beautiful place and crying in the shower each morning. I didn't give a damn that the Caribbean was outside. Inside, there were no blue skies, balmy days, rum cocktails, or bikini-clad bodies on white sand. It was dark and joyless, and life seemed so utterly pointless.

Then I heard it. That whisper. So soft, so silent, calling, calling!

I nearly missed it. But it was there again every day, growing louder and louder. My name was being spoken along with El Camino de Santiago. I listened to every whisper—the tormenting and teasing. Then one day it settled over me, warm and soothing. I allowed myself to trust it.

"All roads lead to Santiago" is what the ancient pilgrims believed.

My road began in London, at the Confraternity of Saint James. I knew nothing of the route, the reason, the history, the distance, the hardship, the joy, the packing list, the friendships, the where, the how, or the what.

I called on a very special man in my life, David, for his knowledge, guidance, insight, and wisdom, which he shared with me in wonderful detail—all from his own experience of having walked the Camino years earlier. It was David who directed me to the Confraternity of Saint James as a starting point.

It was at the confraternity meeting that I collected my scallop, a map, and much more advice. It was also there that I met Tina, a fellow pilgrim, ready to walk her way to Santiago. We agreed to travel together from London to Saint-Jean-Pied-de-Port, the starting point, in France. Our chosen route was from El Camino Frances to Santiago de Compostela in Northern Spain. I was thrilled to have a companion as enchanting, as modest, and as caring as Tina.

I bought a beautiful pair of boots, hauled my backpack out of the attic, and was good to go. I was excited. I had been attending to guests as an international hotelier for so many years I had forgotten how to be a friend, a true friend, having conversation that came from a place of love, not a dutiful smile.

Leaving Saint-Jean in the early hours of that first day marked the beginning of many lessons to be learnt. The first was the backpacker rule: less is more. When you have to carry your backpack for more than fifteen miles each day, you learn to understand the importance of needing less to survive. This sense of freedom is liberating.

Tina and I began our pilgrimage together—a hand to hold as we climbed the Pyrenees through blinding snow and confronted vertigo-inducing heights. We hugged trees, laughed at the joy of saying thank you to the majestic pines as they towered above us, and edged our way down, down, down into Roncesvalles. After a much-needed two days to adjust to our boots, we bought a pair of walking sticks. We then joined in saying prayers for all pilgrims at the monastery and wished each other "Buen Camino," a farewell. Then we each began our individual journeys towards Santiago.

Each day, as pilgrims passed me, they enquired if I needed companionship or wanted to share their reason for being on this path. I wished them well and hoped that they would move off quickly. I needed this time to myself. I wanted to absorb the world around me, to have no one to please, to feel the sun on my face, to hear the clickety-clack of my walking sticks, and to let my mind wander wherever it wished.

The solitude was magnificent, bringing me closer to a stillness within. My thoughts were settling, comfortable, slow, and clear. I wandered aimlessly along dusty paths, through verdant forests, and across barren land that gave way to rolling hills, where the grass was a greener shade of green and the rapeseed flowers were more yellow than the sun. Passing through medieval villages, there was often no more than a church and a few houses. I would buy some fresh fruit, cheese, and a baguette as the locals all wished me a "Buen Camino." Endless days were spent walking through the stunning Spanish countryside. It was as if I was wandering through a Monet.

People cared, as reflected in the many acts of kindness I witnessed as I passed through villages and towns. Leaving a city at dawn, a local stopped me as I was walking the wrong way. I saw food and sweets left at doors and on windowsills with notices telling pilgrims to help themselves. Volunteers ran many of the albergues.

I walked alongside many pilgrims from all over the world, listening and talking. Many were guarded at first, eventually opening up. Some shared festering pain of loss, failure, love, fear, shame, and addiction. We discussed things beyond our realm of understanding and wondered where we saw our futures. We revealed wounds, exposed our darkest secrets, and laid bare our reasons for walking the *Camino*.

I too was sharing my experiences, sharing my photographs on social media, engaging with others as I attempted to share the magnificence of this experience, and trying to capture the wonders of what I saw as I walked mile after mile, mostly alone. I fell in love with the light of the world as it danced and teased as I attempted to capture each magical moment in a photograph.

And then the loneliness set in, deep and sharp like a knife slicing through to my very core. I gasped at the speed with which it came out of nowhere. Suddenly, I yearned for friendship, companionship, and someone to walk and witness this experience with.

We are sensitive creatures, us humans. We need to connect, be loved, be seen, and be heard. Yet all the while, we remain cool, aloof, and delicately vulnerable. I loved that my work was liked on Facebook. It was thrilling to experience the engagement of others and have my adventurous spirit admired and my determination to reach Santiago followed with sincere support and encouragement. But it wasn't enough. I needed more, so much more.

Being liked on Facebook became a beacon of something unexpected on that open road—a beacon I looked to for comfort, shining bright in affirmation that I was still connected and plugged in to another being, heart-to-heart, soul-to-soul, and not alone. We have this amazing ability to create our moment-to-moment experiences in life from where our well-being springs deep inside of us—the ability to know we truly belong. It was in that simple click of a Like button that I knew why my name had been whispered.

This was exactly where I was supposed to be, taking my place in the world, sharing my voice, connecting heart-to-heart with others, and understanding that I was not alone. This experience was necessary for me to walk away from who I did not want to be, and necessary for me to walk my way back to me.

FIERCE LOVE

WINIFRED BURNET-SMITH

IT WOULD be fair to say that from the moment I met Yaron, he plunged me into chaos. Bursting my heart open and causing me to question everything, he entered my life like a tornado, wreaking havoc and turning my world upside down. I had never experienced anything like it. It was like my life had been turned from black-and-white into colour.

The excitement flowing through my body was electric, and despite all the challenges that came with him, nothing had ever felt so right.

At the time, we were both in relationships, each one of us dealing with the amount of pain that we'd inflicted on our partners. We hadn't stopped loving them, but there was just no contest. The strength of attraction that manifested between us was a force that neither of us would deny. It was dark and ugly and painful, but at no point did I ever doubt that I was doing the right thing.

After a few months of loved-filled haze, hours of Skype, unbearable longing, and heart-wrenching delays, he finally got his visa and arrived in London so we could start our new life together.

I met him at the train station. He felt different though—colder. I can see it now but didn't then. I was in a bubble of love, and no one, not even him, could burst it. This was the climax. This was the moment that I'd been waiting on for months. But he wasn't playing along. The light had gone out from his eyes. There was a wall between us, and I couldn't quite touch him. He was far from being happy, but I ignored it. We found the perfect flat. He wasn't happy. We moved in. He wasn't happy. We bought furniture. He wasn't happy. I still ignored it.

Then the bombshell dropped. It had all been too much, too fast, and he couldn't cope. Yaron was plunged into depression. He told me he didn't love me anymore. Everything he felt for me had gone. I could see the pain in him while he was telling me all this, but I was still crushed. It hurt so badly. My body felt like it was underwater. There was pressure everywhere, and it was as if I was moving in slow motion. He was painfully honest, telling me that he couldn't even stand the way that I smelt.

For some reason, I stuck around. I couldn't bring myself to leave. I loved him and hated him at the same time, yet I barely knew him. I felt responsible for turning his life upside down and making him move to London. I tried to come up with solutions. I tried desperately to help. I just wanted to fix him.

He couldn't sleep one night and made love to me. I felt a glimmer of hope until he told me he did it out of pity. By that point, I felt so broken that his words barely even registered. I'd never seen someone cry so much in my life. He had told me he'd suffered from depression. But depression was something I'd never experienced, never seen, and never touched.

I was grieving for the most precious few months of my life. How could I have been so wrong? Was I stupid?

I abused my body and wanted to hurt myself because I didn't think I could trust me anymore. I was barely eating or sleeping, and I was so desperate for this all to end. I wanted rest in my head. Yes, I wanted him back, but I didn't want this broken mess I shared a bed with.

I hit him. I hurt him. I screamed at him. I didn't get it. A few weeks prior, he was professing his love for me, and now he can't even bear to be next to me? It didn't make any sense. Was he playing some sick joke?

Every day, I told myself I was going to leave the flat, but I always went back. We slept in the same bed with this huge icy divide. It was so painful, but I couldn't leave. I still loved him. I wanted to help him find his way back, but it felt impossible. There was an impenetrable wall around him, and nothing I did or said made a blind bit of difference. I had never been so sad in all my life, and I was so tired.

He went away for a few days, and when he returned, he was a bit lighter. I didn't dare to hope. I told myself I didn't want him anymore. I couldn't bear to hand my heart over again, and I didn't trust him. We actually managed to have a conversation without him crying. And he even started to laugh again.

We packed up the flat that we'd moved into just the month before. We were breaking up as it was the only logical thing to do after all the hurt. Little by little, he was coming back though. The warmth returned. The walls started to come down. We didn't exactly know how to deal with all the things that had been said. We couldn't take any of it back. Still, we grew closer, and then we moved out.

He went away again. But this time, when he returned, he was back— he was really back. I surrendered all the pain and the hurt that I'd been holding on to and opened my heart up again. There was no choice or even any doubt that I would. This time, love's grip on us was a thousand times more potent. We'd overcome a battle of epic proportions. And we'd emerged raw, bruised, humbled, and filled with a new-found respect for each other.

We weren't disillusioned or stupid; the connection that we had felt was real. The depression had come and blown everything apart. It had made me doubt my sanity, making me question if I could ever trust myself again. The sheer relief that I still could was enormous.

Seven years and two kids later, we're still navigating this life together. Yaron manages to turn my world upside down on a daily basis. His limitless source of energy is exhilarating and sometimes exhausting, but I really wouldn't have it any other way.

We still have our ecstatic highs and our epic lows. It takes a real conscious effort to keep things alive and flowing, but that one episode was the only time when I ever felt his love for me falter.

It wasn't a promising start, but the smartest thing I ever did was to stick around in those darkest of moments, because this kind and beautiful man still manages to flood my world with vibrant colour.

WHEN DEPRESSION WINS

YARON ENGLER

THE MOMENT I arrived at the airport in Tel Aviv, suddenly, without any warning, I was hit by a huge wave of doubt. It was overwhelming. After spending such a beautiful time being in love with Wins and with life, I suddenly felt greyness, fear, anxiety, and loss. I tried to push those feelings away, but they were stronger than any of my pushes. Even stronger was the thought that those feelings were wrong. I felt weak. I felt like a hypocrite. I couldn't understand how suddenly, out of nowhere, those massive cracks began to appear in the wall of certainty that I had about this big change I was about to make.

The dark feelings stayed with me all the way to London. It felt like my body went according to plan, while my heart was in the middle of an emergency landing, trying to figure out a decent place to land, survive, get answers, and understand what the fuck was going on.

The plane and my body landed in London, and I was supposed to be happy. I was supposed to be excited to finally arrive at this moment where I would start my new life in London with Wins. But my heart was still lost in the air, searching for a place to land between the heavy clouds of confusion. I arrived at the train station and saw Wins, who looked happy and excited. I was still desperately searching for my heart.

In the following days, we lived all the clichés of beginning a new life together—finding a house, decorating it, getting furniture, and making the place feel like home. Wins looked happy and excited. But for me, deep inside, without her knowing, every step forward felt like drowning my soul in a thick liquid of dark grey confusion. I hated the situation. Hated myself. Hated Wins.

I started to realize that this woman—who so beautifully cracked all the problems in my life just a few weeks before—suddenly felt like a burden. I didn't like anything that she did or wanted. It pissed me off to see those little white hearts that she put in every corner of the flat. I hated the food that she wanted to eat. I hated the smells that she put in the rooms. I even hated her smell. I was fully absorbed in rejection, and I couldn't understand what was going on. With every moment that passed, it was harder for me to hide the storm I was carrying inside me. After a few days, Wins asked me what was going on.

I don't remember a lot of what happened in those days, but I do remember the strong pain I felt when I needed to express my feelings. It was extremely painful, yet at the same time, I felt nothing. And I didn't care about anything. Everything felt grey. Nothing had meaning. Life? What was the point of that? They call it depression.

Wins was trying to figure out what to do with the weird situation that she had fallen into. She was angry and confused. For me, none of it was new. It was far from being the first time that I had given a big welcoming hug to my depression. I knew the pain. I knew the numbness. I knew the feeling of how absolutely nothing makes sense. I knew the feeling of being hurt, and I knew the feeling of hurting others. I was familiar with the thoughts of death and the invitations they brought in those moments. The feelings of fear, anger, shame, anxiety, and frustration were all good old friends as well.

One day, Wins said that her friend told her to be more understanding because the way I was acting was not my fault. I was depressed. That gave both of us hope, and we started to have a bit more of a conversation going on. My ego loved the "It's not my fault" idea. The feeling of being a victim suited me much better than trying to handle what was going on or facing the pain that I was causing Wins and myself. Things got better for just a very short period of time, but it was clear that things couldn't continue the way they were. Wins started to spend more time with her friends away from home, and I was all alone. I hated the feeling of hurting her; but I hated the feeling of being lost, confused, and stupid even more. It was all about me. We broke up.

Just a few weeks before the breakup, I had made some of the biggest decisions of my life. And although those decisions were very hard, challenging, and painful, they felt right. I had left a country, a girlfriend I had been with for five years, a company I was codirecting, and some very good friends. There were many reasons to make those changes, but the one that was by far the strongest and the most beautiful was Wins. She was strong. She was confident, and she gave me simplicity. Back then, that was like finding water in the desert. I loved it. I loved her. But somehow it all ended when I arrived that day at the airport.

I don't know what it was exactly that made me move from full love to full rejection. Maybe it was the need to spend some time in grief for everything I had left behind and the people I had hurt. Maybe it was the time that my body and mind needed in order to digest the shift from one life to another. What I do know is that somehow, very naturally, things got back to normal. I found a nice flat that felt perfect for me. I had a lot of free time, and I spent most of it in a spiritual practice that taught me a lot about my relationship with depression.

I learned that my depression was a choice. A bad choice. I understood that I no longer needed to give a big hug to those thick grey emotions. Instead, I could observe and laugh at them. I learned that when they don't get the big hug, they go away much faster.

It's been seven years since then, and for all those years, my depression and I have walked our separate ways. I have learned to love again, and I have been living with a woman whom I love deeply. I love her strength, her clarity, and her calmness. I love the way she decorates our home and the smells she puts in the house. I love making love to her, and I love her smell. This woman is a very strong light in my life and in the life of our two children.

The name of this woman is Wins.

A REFLECTION OF SELF-LOVE

ANONYMOUS

IN 2007, my relationship with my brother changed forever. For reasons that I won't get into here, I decided to publicly disclose some information about him—a decision that rocked the foundations of our relationship and eventually led to a ten-year estrangement between us. The "who did what?" details of that history aren't relevant, but that event and the years since set the stage for the incredible insights I've gained about myself.

Brother of mine, thank you for intentionally and unintentionally teaching me who I am and who I'm not. Thank you for your patience and always demonstrating love towards me even when we were out of contact. And thank you for being the person that you are and for not being who I thought you should be. While I don't know what our relationship will become in the future, I send you my blessings, knowing with gratitude that we are each other's teachers.

On a beautiful, sunny winter's day not long ago, I sat by my dining room window, watching London's red double-decker buses pass by and reflecting on my ten-year estranged relationship with my brother. My feelings towards him were old and familiar, but something felt different on this particular day. I'd always known I needed to dig deep and discover what was at the root of these feelings, and I'd tried to do so a few times before. But this time, I both felt and thought, *Today will be different. Something is going to shift. I am ready.*

This skeleton had suffocated in the closet long enough. The time had come to give it some air, to face it head-on, and to be with it. It was time.

I tuned into my heart, wondering with anticipation what I would discover there. I knew my heart was about to go through something. A voice in my head disagreed, saying, *Jacqueline, don't go there. It's not worth it. You'll get hurt again. Don't do this to yourself.* But I chose then and there to turn the volume down in my head and to listen to my heart. I placed my right hand on my heart, reconnecting to my heartbeat.

Gently closing my eyes, I turned my attention to my breathing. Once I felt connected to the conscious, loving breath that was flowing through my body, I began my exploration within. As I observed, a loving light travelled from the crown of my head through my throat and to my heart. When the light touched my heart, I felt an expansion, and what I saw there made me pause. I saw a large section of my heart turn bright red, with vibrations of love rippling out. Feeling this warmth and love in my heart, I continued to explore. I noticed a small section of my heart that was . . . hard. It was tough, appeared to be a dark colour, and looked protected. Intrigued, I decided to be with what I saw rather than step over it.

What I found in this part of my heart was pain, anger, disappointment, shame, criticism, and disgust. My heart began to beat faster, and my breathing became deeper and deeper. I was about to enter a realm I had never explored—a realm that would transform how I saw myself.

I suddenly felt overwhelmed, as if I was going to vomit. My stomach was tight and tense.

"Be with it, Jacqueline, just be with it . . ." said my heart. Tears rolled down my face, and my breath deepened even more. I felt all those years of anger, pain, disappointment, shame, and disgust about to be purged. I leaned forward to let it all out. And at one point, I thought that I was going too deep until a little voice said to me, "Jacqueline, you need to do this. You need to go through this. This will set you free."

And then out of nowhere, it hit me. Over the past ten years, I had pointed so many accusatory fingers at my brother. I had made him wrong in so many ways, continually adding to a long list of criticisms. I'd felt angry about who he was, disgusted by his behaviour, and ashamed to call him family. Now from out of left field, I saw with instant clarity that all these feelings towards my brother were actually feelings I had towards *myself*.

Stunned by this truth, I surrendered. I surrendered to face who I am and let go of who I'd thought I was. I allowed for a few more deep breaths, eyes closed.

The purging process that ensued included looking deeply at the disgust, shame, stupidity, incompetence, foolishness, anger, and disappointment I felt for myself. As I faced each of these self-judgements, I felt an ache inside my heart—an ache I knew I was experiencing for the first time. I put my hand on my chest, crouching down to hold myself up while I caught my breath. I thought, *Oh my goodness, what have I just discovered? How could I have had such strong, negative, toxic feelings towards myself and towards another family member? How is this possible?*

With these questions swirling around in my head, I continued reconnecting to my heart. And slowly, I felt it soften. That hardened piece of my heart, darkened and protected for so long, softened with light and love. At that very moment, three police cars whisked past the window, lights flashing and sirens screaming. I took it as a sign to pay attention to what I was about to discover.

Finally, it dawned on me that what I saw in my brother was a reflection of me. I repeated it to myself so that it was crystal clear. *What I see in my brother is a reflection of me.* And I also saw that this realization, this truth, was his *gift* to me. In receiving my judgements, he allowed me to see the judgements I placed on myself. In receiving my negative feelings, he allowed me to see the negative feelings I had inside myself. In awe, I wondered how in the heck all this happened (and why it had taken me over ten years to figure it out).

Here are the judgements I've carried around for ten years, seemingly for my brother, but really for myself:

- I often felt disgusted with myself.
- I often felt ashamed of who I was or who I thought I was meant to be.
- I believed I was stupid.
- I believed I was incompetent.
- I was disappointed with the person I had turned out to be.
- I felt I'd let myself down and had caused myself much pain as a result.

It was time to let it all go—all the shame, the anger, the judgements about being stupid and incompetent. It was time to let my brother be himself and to accept him for who he was and the path he was on. It was time to choose self-love, peace, and acceptance. It was time. It was *time!*

I looked within again. And this time, I found a new level of love, acceptance, and peace of mind there. When I opened my eyes, it felt like I was seeing the world through a new lens tinted with love, peace, and acceptance. I saw love for me, peace within me, and acceptance of me. And I also saw the love in others, the peace in others, and acceptance of others for who they are.

I thought about my brother, and my heart was full of unconditional love—a joyful, peaceful, and accepting love. I sent him loving light and knew in that moment that I needed to reach out to him. I wrote him a card, thanking him for who he was, thanking him for his patience, and thanking him for the lessons he had taught me about love. I sent him an email message, asking to connect via phone, and he accepted immediately.

While the ways this experience has transformed me (and continues to transform me) are many and far-reaching, there are two insights in particular I gained that I will treasure forever. The first insight: What I see in others—the good and the not so good reflects who I am. And the second insight: We are all each other's teachers.

SEEKING FOR THE ONE

LAUREN LOVE

EVER SINCE I can remember, I have been on a search to find my prince charming. I have felt an inner ache, deep inside me, for a connection so beautiful and so strong it would melt away all that was not love. My life never seemed complete, and I always had this sense that something was missing.

In my mid-twenties, I ended up being single for over three years. This felt quite disorientating, and I would say to my mum, "I just want to love and be loved." I longed for the intensity of true love, and was waiting for the day I would find the relationship that my heart most yearned for.

It was a Sunday afternoon in spring, and I had arranged to meet a friend in Primrose Hill for a Oneness Jam, a beautiful community event where friends would gather together in the park to celebrate life through music. The sun was shining, and there was a sense of freshness in the air. As I ventured along Camden Street, I felt excitement brewing and was loving this newfound sense of joy bubbling from within me.

Strolling through the park, I saw families playing joyfully with their children and couples lying on the grass in each other's arms. A group of teenagers crossed my path, and one of them dropped a baseball glove. When I ran up to them and handed over the glove, we exchanged warm smiles. And in that moment, my heart felt truly nourished. That day was magical, and I remember having the thought, *I'm so glad that I am here. Connecting with people really is the heart's best medicine.*

As I reached Primrose Hill, I stopped and glanced around full circle, soaking in my surroundings and basking in the sun's rays. By the time I got near the top of the hill, I was a little flustered. My heart was pounding, and I was eager to meet my friends. Then I looked up, and there in front of me, walking down the hill, was the beaming, sparkly face of a beautiful friend. She was with a guy I hadn't met before, though he seemed very familiar.

My heart jumped at the sight of this man, and I had a very strange sense of this being a significant meeting. We all hugged goodbye, and I continued walking towards my friends. They were gathered at the top of the hill, where I could hear steady drumbeats and the uplifting sounds of laughter.

The next day, I was still thinking about this mysterious man. Something seemed to be nudging me towards him, but I had no contact details and couldn't recall his name. So I went onto my friend's Facebook page, the sparkly one who was with him at the top of the hill. When I clicked on her page, it showed the icons of several of her friends' profile pictures. Out of hundreds of friends, there were nine pictures in front of me—one of them being an illustration of the Hand of Fatima, an ancient protection symbol.

My heart skipped a beat. I wasn't sure why, but I couldn't stop smiling. My anticipation, excitement, and intuition urged me to click on the Fatima profile. Immediately, I started looking through the photos. I stopped in my tracks. It was him! It was the guy from the top of the hill. What were the chances?

I had to add this guy as a friend, and he messaged me straight away. He told me that he had been mesmerized by my eyes and that my voice put him under a spell, and he would love for us to meet up. Usually, I would be put off by this kind of message, yet my heart was doing somersaults. There was no denying that we had to meet. Something about him felt so familiar, and I was intrigued to find out more. We agreed to meet in a café and music venue in Camden.

As I arrived, he was eating a delicious, raw chocolate cake. I stood smiling as I watched him, noticing that I felt so much love for this man that I didn't even know. Immersed in deep conversation, I felt that nothing else existed. It was as if there was no separation between me and him. The kunzite crystal pendant that I was wearing around my neck was on fire, and I could feel the heat buzzing against my chest. Kunzite crystal is aligned with the higher heart chakra, the energy center of divine love. I definitely felt like I had been carried into the blissfulness of divine love.

The weekend after our first meeting, he was away for a plant medicine ceremony while I was house-sitting at a friend's. I loved staying at her place as her house was so beautiful and decadent. As I lay in her boudoir bedroom, he came into my awareness, and I was struck by the deepest love that I have ever experienced. It felt overwhelming as it almost seemed as though my heart was too small to contain the immensity of this love.

We met later that week and he shared his experience of the ceremony, telling me that I appeared to him and was there with him during his journey. He had felt the connection too. My mind couldn't even begin to comprehend what was happening, yet I knew that something very special was unfolding between us.

A couple of weeks later, we were in the most intense relationship of my life. It felt like a fairy tale, and I loved the spontaneity of it all. His daughter was visiting the UK, and I was nervous about meeting her, mainly because of the large age gap between her dad and me. The three of us spent the next few weeks together as a little family, and his daughter and I bonded like friends and long-lost sisters.

After a whirlwind summer romance, I moved to Scotland for a new job. We spoke for hours every day and missed each other like crazy. Inevitably, he made the decision to leave London and move to Scotland to be with me.

At first, it was like a dream. We had our cozy space and were completely immersed in our bubble of love. Yet very soon, my old patterns of relating made an appearance, and I began to feel frustrated and doubtful. We experienced immense clashes, and it got to the point that we couldn't bear to be around each other. Every little thing was bothering me, and I felt trapped, terrified of committing to a future together, and unsure if we had rushed into our relationship. It all fell apart, and he moved back to London.

I was left wondering what on earth had happened. The relationship had developed so quickly, and then it had all come crumbling down. The period after our separation was equally as intense. Despite us being apart, there was something that kept drawing us back together —a bond so deep it could only be understood by the heart.

It took time alone, and sometimes being in the depths of despair and deep loneliness, to find out who I truly was and what it was that I was actually seeking. I woke up to the realisation that successful relationships are always an inner job, yet for my entire life, I had been searching outside of myself for the perfect man to complete me. I came to understand that unless I was in alignment with myself and in a state of self-love, it was unlikely that I would meet a partner who embodied the love that I was seeking. It wasn't anyone else's job to complete me or make me whole.

MY MIND'S IN PAIN

JEFFREY DALLET

I WAS seventeen years old when I was first diagnosed with obsessive-compulsive disorder. Looking back, it had been there my whole life, going back to experiences I'd had as early as twelve years old. I just hadn't known what it was or how much it affected me.

Now when people hear the term "OCD," they usually chuckle a bit and dismiss it as some funny quirk they saw in some TV or movie character. I'm looking at you Jack Nicholson in *As Good As It Gets* or the TV show *Monk*. Visions of switching lights off and on, placing pancakes in a certain order on a plate, or the washing of hands five times after touching a door knob dance through people's heads. And they all seem to get a good chortle out of the goofy, innocuous tic. For me, OCD is a crippling, fear-based torture device that has often rendered me helpless.

It was 1993. I stood there in front of my alarm clock, wanting to set the alarm. The red digital clock read 7:03 p.m. The time 7:03 p.m. was okay because the numbers on the digital clock added up to ten. Ten was okay because I had gotten tenth place in a cross-country meet a couple of weeks earlier, which was pretty good for my skinny ninety-pound frame. However, that thought passed. And suddenly, ten was dangerous because adding up the two digits in ten would equal to one. One is no good because some tool named Tre was going out with a girl I was madly in love with, and the name Tre is one syllable. And the clock says 7:03, which equals to ten and which equals to one, so that will not work.

So I'm going to wait until the clock turns to 7:04. The time 7:04 was not too bad because those digits add up to eleven, which added together would equal to two, and two is a safe number. Wait, the name Korey has two syllables in it, and Korey is an unfunny blowhard in my high school, who is kind of a wet blanket. And I want to be a funny guy, who people enjoy being around, so I can't leave the clock on the number 2. I'll wait for 7:05. Wait, 7:05 adds up to twelve, whose two digits added up would equal to three. I'm screwed because this guy Kris Rogers, who is really slow on the cross-country team, has three syllables in his name, and I don't want to be slow on the cross-country team. So I'll wait for 7:06. My mind screw goes on for hours, ticking along with every minute, making me afraid to leave the clock and get into bed.

OCD feels irrational and ridiculous. But the fear behind these seemingly harmless thoughts comes with the force of a thousand tidal waves. The fear is paralyzing, leaving me laying on the floor clutching the clock until at least 1:00 a.m. every night, until sheer fatigue sets in. Mentally spent, I finally doze off, only to wake up and repeat the same routine to get up off the floor while looking at the clock's numbers.

In the summer of 1994, I was involved in a rollover car accident on Interstate 82 in Southeastern Washington state. Our 1979 Buick Regal rolled three times and came to rest in the median between the eastbound and westbound lanes. I was the driver, and the cause was fatigue. I had tried to count every mile marker we passed. I had to count them all or my mother would not live to see fifty.

We were outside a town called Prosser in Washington. And my friend, who was riding in the car with me, was sent to the hospital.

He hadn't been wearing his seat belt. By the grace of the good Lord, my friend was okay, save some large cuts on his back. I am convinced that boat of a car saved our lives. To think we were mocking the dated brown behemoth just hours before our crash. That potential brush with death created an immediate clarity and release from the bonds of the OCD raking my mind across the coals. I was so grateful that my friend and I were okay and that we had survived what could have been a devastating crash.

The next year at school, my mind was clear, and I was ready to make up for all the lost time the countless paralyzing hours of OCD fears had stolen from me. Heck, I even got to go out with a girl who I'd been keen on for two years. Nothing worked out between us, but I'm proud to say that at Homecoming 1994, she was my date. And while on our date, my mind wasn't taking on a life of its own. Of course, the usual nerves of being around someone I liked and my obsessive nature (the OCD never really goes away) took its toll on our relationship or lack of relationship.

As I said, the OCD never goes away. It can manifest itself in a lot of different ways and has throughout the course of my life. But for that last year of high school, I enjoyed myself more than I had at any time up to that point in my life.

Medicines have helped, but it's the realization of what the disease is and how it can present itself in many forms that can inhibit the enjoyment of what life is supposed to be. Understanding where it comes from and that it is not my fault has relieved many of the tensions and crippling issues my mind had dealt with in my teen years. I realize I'm not the worst-case scenario, and each of us has their own demons to deal with and face. And though the OCD is a fear-based, need-for-control illness, I've regained my sense of self and am able to operate in a constructive, effective manner. I am able to sit back and realize that there are quite a few things, in fact many things, I have no control over.

JOURNEY OF OVERCOMING

AMITE DUNCAN, PHD

SO THE beach is kind of my thing. It's *that* place of clarity for me, where I am in awe of God's brilliance and creative abilities. The beach is the place that ministers to my soul and my intellect and brings me to a place of peace. When I am there, my shoes have to come off immediately—no flip-flops for me! My feet need to enjoy the warm texture of the sand and the movement of the cool water.

I wanted to watch the sunrise and sunset over the ocean. There is just nothing else like the breeze on the beach. It forces you to open your arms wide and stand against it. *Oh, oh, oh,* and the sound of the waves. Who would have ever thought to create such a thing as the ocean with all its turbulence and might? Yet it makes sounds that are gentle enough to lull a person into peace.

Recently, I had been getting to know myself better. I had been sorting out what I really wanted in life versus what my life had become. When you have a caregiver personality, it is easy to get lost in the lives of others and forget about your own hopes and dreams and what is good or right for yourself.

During this process, I discovered that I hate living in the city. So why was I continuing to live where I didn't want to be? The city is not the place where I thrive. So why was I continuing to stay in a place where I didn't thrive? I guess I was just living in the city because . . . well, just because.

With some searching, I came to the conclusion that I needed more control over my life. Everything in my life, for quite some time, seemed to be about someone else's needs or opinions. My actions were telling my inner self that what I really wanted or needed was not important. But I knew I needed to overcome my fear, stare down the naysayers, and just go for it. I needed to stop letting things get in my way. My new way of living was going to be rooted in overcoming.

I had a beach town in mind—just this place I saw on a map. I had investigated it online months before, but I hadn't yet checked it out because . . . well, money, time, friends, family, and fear. I told myself, *Maybe one day, when the time is right.* I tried to shut down my desire to live near the beach, but it was still buried inside me, whimpering. I missed it; I needed it. I absolutely had to go no matter what. I had to do it now.

The questions, doubts, and fears were still in my mind, saying, Is this okay? Can I really do this? But my heart was saying, *"So what? So what if I don't have money for gas? So what if I don't know where I'll stay or how I'll eat?"* I packed some snacks that a friend had given me, along with some clothes and my favorite blanket. I simply refused to look in my wallet to even know how bad my money situation was. I had a tank full of gas in my Honda and decided that even if I were to get stuck on the highway, I was prepared to just view it as another adventure. So off I went, set on following the desires of my heart.

I left my friend's house, where I had been staying. She was fighting cancer, despite the extremely dim report the medical world had given her. I was fighting alongside her, helping where I could. The situation hadn't left me much time to go out and make money, but I live by faith.

My trip began with a visit to my husband, who was in prison. That was almost a six-hour drive from where I was living, and I wasn't really sure I would make it there. I prayed, "God, you are either going to have to increase the money in my wallet or the gas in my car," and off I went.

I did my usual routine, just as I had been doing approximately every other weekend. I put the car on cruise, enjoyed the clouds in the sky, talked to God, and sang. At some point during my drive, my youngest son sent me a text, saying, "We should talk soon."

I thought, *Okay*. And I gave him a call. This was the son that I had to kick out of my house when he was seventeen (but that's another story). He'd grown up a bit since then, and actually wanted to hear some wisdom from his mother. Miracle! The timing of the call was perfect because I was getting tired of driving, and I needed someone to keep me awake. We talked for a few hours, just having a fun conversation. Not only did he keep me awake, but he also kept me laughing. At one point, he asked where I was going. I said, "I am on a faith journey to go visit your stepdad."

"Mom, you are a maverick," was his response. "Let me wire you some money." I was shocked. Nope, I did *not* see that coming. By the time I arrived at my usual spot for a fill-up, he had sent me thirty dollars.

At this point, I decided to check my wallet. I had set out with only twelve dollars. That would have barely been enough money to visit my husband. With my son's gift, I knew I could make it to visit my husband and maybe make it back to where I had been living. But all the way to the beach? The doubts began to nag me. *Should I really press on to my sanctuary? Is that the wise thing to do? Am I just being foolish? Maybe I should just count my blessings and not push my luck any further?* Still, my spirit cried out to go. I wanted . . . I needed the beach.

My visit with my husband was one of those moments that needed to happen. He was surprised to see me, but he had been praying I would come. He had things to discuss with me, and we needed that important intimate time. Our visit was a brief two hours, but it was sweet. I left feeling as though I had made the right decision to get on the road.

At this point, I began to think that maybe listening to my own voice was okay. *Maybe it is okay to go for what I really want in life. Maybe the other people that I'm so concerned about will be okay. Maybe it's okay for me to not always feel responsible for everyone else at the expense of my own desires.*

Back in the car, I had to decide whether or not to continue on the path toward my goal. "Drive toward home or the beach?" My choice? Go visit my son.

My son lived four hours away in the general direction of my destination. I wanted to see him, and he wanted me to see his new home. On the road again, it dawned on me that nothing happens by coincidence. If I had not made the choice to listen to my heart, I would have missed out on being blessed and being a blessing.

When I arrived, we had great mother-and-son moments. I learned that it was wonderful to have my child take me out to dinner while having fun sharing a beer and taking selfies together. His generosity only increased after dinner when he said, "Mom, I want to buy you an outfit." Wow!

"Nope, just give me the cash," I said. Sixty dollars was just enough money to get me to my goal and back. Yes, yes, yes!

I made it. The beach didn't have my favorite small white sand or the bluest of water, but my feet got to enjoy both the sand and the warm water. I stood against the wind with my arms open wide and got my moments of meditation and clarity. I took the time to ponder and make some decisions. I got to carve out what I wanted my future to look like and reflect on how reaching a goal wasn't necessarily more important than the journey to get to the goal. I got to feel okay with doing something just for myself, and it made me feel valuable.

I enjoyed a great Fourth of July fireworks show as a bonus that evening. Fireworks were also one of my favorite things, so watching fireworks on the beach was absolute perfection. It was one of those times in life where you just appreciate life itself and decide that even in funky or dismal circumstances, you can make something beautiful happen.

I was determined to watch the sunrise the next morning, so I slept in my car near the beach. It wasn't my favorite part of the adventure, but watching the sunrise was definitely worth it. The night in the car was quickly forgotten as I let the waves sing me a lullaby while I took a morning nap in the sand.

I spent my afternoon connecting with interesting people and staking out the possibility of living where I was most content. The new connections were wonderful and quenched whatever embers of fear that I might have still had in my mind. This was going to be my next home. I was very aware that I could thrive in this place.

Finally, I hit the road, satisfied. I was not only satisfied that I had conquered my doubts and fears, but also, I was satisfied with the blessings I had encountered along the way. I still had a friend suffering with cancer to go back to, a husband in prison, and little to no money. However, my inner peace was triumphing over my current circumstances. I was ready for the next phase of my life—when I would move to the beach. I am confident that I will make it happen and that there will be great surprises along the way.

This story is dedicated to Tino Milner

Amite's son, Tino, lost his life in May, 2017, shortly after she had written her story for Thresholds. As can be seen from her story, Tino was a loving son—a young man who wanted to give back.

I was fortunate to have known Tino. He and my daughter, Christina, spent a few years together on the same hip hop dance team, sharing several emotional first-place wins at the World's competition at Disney in Florida. We were a dance family and when Tino died, we all felt like the heartbeat of our family was gone.

When I first thought about writing this dedication, I knew that I wanted to share how Tino was always smiling—how he lifted up those around him with his joyful presence. He had an incredible positive energy that brought life to any room he stepped in to.

But I also wanted to share some words about Tino from the perspective of someone who danced with him, someone who considered him his best friend. So I asked his friend, Enom, to describe him. In an email, Enom wrote, "He had a smile that could make you laugh and it was the first thing you noticed about him. And, he would always go out of his way to make sure your day was better."

Yes, Tino was that guy who lit up a room with his joy. He was that guy who sought others out to make sure they were okay—to make sure they felt like someone cared. Tino was also that guy who was always front and center for every dance performance with his team because of both his talent, and his ability to connect with the audience through his amazing sense of humor. He was confident in front of a crowd and audiences loved him.

When describing Tino's passion as an artist, Enom wrote, "His work ethic matched his love for dance. His heart was for kids and teaching dance to kids gave him the most irreplaceable smile ever! He left a legacy that will continue to grow."

Tino's last dance role with his team was that of Muhammad Ali. It was a role he easily embraced. On his Instagram, you'll see a quote by Muhammad Ali that Tino shared—words he lived by:

> Impossible is just a big word thrown around by small men who find it easier to live in the world they've been given than to explore the power they have to change it. Impossible is not a fact. It's an opinion. Impossible is not a declaration. It's a dare. Impossible is potential. Impossible is temporary. Impossible is nothing.

Your beautiful light will be missed, Tino.

Love,

Robin

AUTHORS

Kristina Amelong
"Rafael"
(OptimalHealthNetwork. com, 7BillionTribe. com)

Wendy Anthony
"Nonnegotiable"

Esther Austin
"Crossing Bridges, Creating Rainbows"
(EstherAustinGlobal.com)

Jeanine Becker
"No White Knight Needed" (JeanineBecker.com)

Jazzmyn Blu
"The Unlikely Birthday Gift" (JazzmynBlu.wordpress.com)

Steve Bollock
"A Sea of Anxiety" (BuddhaDogPhotos.com)

Lena Broussard
"Forgiveness Overdue"

Winifred Burnet-Smith
"Fierce Love"

Jane Bytheway
"One Powerful Decision Changed Everything" (JaneBytheway.com)

Ana Caragea
"A Loud Wake-Up Call" (StrategicDiscovery. coach)

Richie Castro
"Tea with Ms. Sophia" (HistoryHunter.org)

Deb Celec
"Epiphany on Epiphany" (Dejac7@gmail.com)

Khalil Coffeld
"Fatherless Child" (KhalilCoffield.com)

Jessy Conflon
"My Ride Home" (JessyConnflon8.wixsite.com/jessyconflon)

Angela Criscuoli
"Full Circle" (RippleEffectNutrition.com)

Anne Ferrier Crook
"Birth as I Know It" (IntegrativeRadiance.com)

Jeffrey Dallet
"My Mind's in Pain" (JeffreyDallet.com)

Russell Davis
"Vegetables, a Rabbit, and Me" (Russell-Davis. co.uk)

Dilshad Dayani
"The Balcony Girl" (DrDilshad.com and TheWWGC.org)

Laura Dewey
"The Walk" (theselfleadershiplab.com)

Jo Dirnbauer
"Freedom" (jdirnbauer@verizon.net)

Lacey Dowling
"The Fight of My Life"

Amite Duncan, PhD
"Journey of Overcoming"

Heather Duke
"Magic Tree"

Yaron Engler
"When Depression Wins" (YaronEngler.com)

Mai Fawaz
"The Revolution Within Me" (MaiFawaz.com)

Brad Finkeldei
"Tiny Bits of Courage" (BradFinkeldei.com, theherostraining.com)

Lorraine Flaherty
"The Pit" (InnerJourneys.co.uk)

Stacy Lynn Floyd "The Prosecco Moment"
(stacylynnfloyd@hotmail.com)

Cindy Frey
"Overcoming Shyness"

Chris Gardener
"Beautiful Death" (StrategicMentors.co.uk)

Karen Gedissman
"Shedding My Skin" (AboutKarenG.com)

Kirsty Hanly
"Awakening to the Angel Within"
(KirstyHanly.co.uk, InspiringLivesCoaching.com)

Jeff Harmon
"Redefining Pride" (BrillianceWithinCoaching.com)

Jo Hodson
"Glimpses of Genius" (IncludingCake.com, WholePlus.com)

Hope Hughes
"Through the Valley" (TheCheerfulChair.com)

Maureen Huntley
"The Dream of Dreams" (MaureenHuntley.com)

Alfred Jacobs
"Blood Moon" (AlfredJacobs.com)

Lucile Knight
"9:23" (LucileKnight.com)

Crickett Koch
"Dutchican"

Lauren Love
"Seeking for *the One*" (www. laurenlove.co.uk)

Leah Lund
"The Grandma Sitter" (OneWholeHealth.com)

Mandy Marshall
"Walking My Way Back to Me" (Coral-Creatives.com)

Natasha McCreesh
"Gran" (TheJoyBringer.com)

Jacob Melaard
"Limitless Opportunity in the Land Opportunity"
(TheFeelGoodGuy.com)

Lauren Polly
"Me, You, and My Diagnosis" (laurenpolly.com)

Rick Miller
"Fifty-Three Feet Down, and It's Dark!"
(Learn-Live-Lead.com)

John P. Morgan
"The First Escape" (JPMorganJr.com)

Dan Mosely
"Pushing the Edge"

Scott Murphy
"The Naked Truth" (EscapesYoga.com)

Desmond Neysmith
"Mother Africa"

Sam Obernik
"Here Is the News" (ThirdMile.co)

John Oda
"The Pond of Freedom"

Hugh Osborne "Finding the Real Dragon"
(AddictionHypnotherapy. com, HughOsborne.net)

Sue Revell
"I Had to Be Me" (MagentaChange.com)

Sabrina Santos
"When I Stopped Living for Tomorrow"
(heartevolution foundation.Org, ThePowerWithinUs.co.uk)

Tessa Shaffer
"Support from the Universe" (TessaShaffer.com)

Liz Scott
"You Are Either Pregnant or You're Not" (CoachingConnect.co.uk)

Ann Skinner
"How Changing One Word Changed Everything"
(TheHeartWorker.com)

Neil Skinner
"Running Free"

Eric Sprinkle
"Moving Past Death"
(Adventure Experience. net)

Ayn Cates Sullivan, PhD
"Mending Broken Hearts"
(AynCatesSullivan.com, InfiniteLightPublishing.com)

Leigh Tilley
"From One Life into Another"
(LeighTilleyLifeCoach.com)

Matthew Thomas
"Every Day We Ran"
(matthewthomas.totalmastery@gmail.com)

Trevor Thomas
"The Road to Acceptance"
(StepintoYourBigness.com)

Karen vanBarneveld-Price "Children Raising Children"
(HeavenlyYoga.com, KarenvanPrice.com)

Mike Weeks "Freedom Royale"
(IMikeWeeks.com and UntrainYourBrain.com)

Alexandra Wenman
"Spread Your Wings" (AlexandraWenman.com)

Tray Witherspoon
"Just Like My Dad"

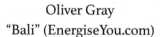

Oliver Gray
"Bali" (EnergiseYou.com)

~

Anonymous
"A Reflection of Self-Love"

~

Anonymous
"Fear, Guilt, and Love"

Elizabeth West
"The Affair"

COMPILERS

ROBIN VON SCHWARZ

Robin Von Schwarz has a passion for supporting moms who are navigating their teen's mental health, specifically in the areas of anxiety, depression, and OCD. She has a background in holistic health practices and neuro-nutrition. She is a high school educator, a mom of four grown children and a grandmother of three.

For more information go to: healthybrainnews.com.

SIMON CROWE

Simon Crowe runs a specialist coaching and consultancy practice which focuses on transformational leadership and empowerment. He has lived and travelled around the world creating partnerships with influential artists, leaders, entrepreneurs, and humanitarians, developing and delivering inspiring projects that positively impact the world. Find out more at simoncrowe.com.

Made in the USA
Columbia, SC
30 March 2018